GLIMPSES OF AUTHORS

Caroline Ticknor

GLIMPSES OF AUTHORS

BY

CAROLINE TICKNOR

WITH ILLUSTRATIONS

BOSTON AND NEW YORK
HOUGHTON MIFFLIN COMPANY
The Riverside Press Cambridge
1922

The Riverside Press
CAMBRIDGE · MASSACHUSETTS
PRINTED IN THE U.S.A.

TO THE
MEMORY OF MY FATHER
BENJAMIN HOLT TICKNOR

   . . . On me
Frown not, old ghosts, if I be one of those
Who make you utter things you did not say,
And mould you all awry and mar your work;
For whatsoever knows us truly knows
That none can truly write his single day,
And none can write it for him upon earth.

TENNYSON

CONTENTS

ILLUSTRATIONS

GLIMPSES OF AUTHORS

GLIMPSES OF AUTHORS

. .
.

CHAPTER I

DICKENS IN BOSTON

THE man behind the book. He is a never-failing
source of interest; and the more we love the book, the
more do we desire to know him. This is no undue
curiosity; it is the normal human craving to search
beneath the surface for the real motive-power that
makes alive the printed page.

A book is not just paper, text, and binding; a book
is something with a heart and a soul, and we know
that the spirit reflected there is not bound up between
the covers, but emanates from its creator. He it is
who addresses us, and if he cheers, inspires, or soothes
us, he soon becomes our friend. And which of us is
quite content to know a friend merely on paper?

With such a thought in mind it is my purpose to
present some glimpses of men and women behind
those books with which the household of a publisher
has been associated for three generations. As I look
back, a long procession of writers passes before my
mental vision; as they dawned on my youthful sight,
or as they were described to me by those that knew
them before I came upon the scene. The interesting
procession moves on, stretching from early days down
to the present time, and as it marches past, I will

endeavor to throw upon the screen some of the figures that are most clearly outlined.

The home of my grandfather, William D. Ticknor, close to the shores of Jamaica Pond, where my childhood was spent, had, since the eighteen-forties, welcomed the authors from far and near, whose personal association with their Boston publisher was a peculiarly warm one. They were his friends rather than his investments, and many of the friendships cemented in those early days have remained knit together through two succeeding generations and are still carrying on.

Among the figures that present themselves, that of Charles Dickens stands preëminent as a magnetic personality who vividly impressed himself on all who knew him, and I early became familiar with the story of his Boston experiences, and of his coming to our home. This was in 1868, four years after the death of my grandfather, so that it was my uncle, Howard Malcom Ticknor, who formed one of the trio (with James T. Fields and James R. Osgood) who arranged for his entertainment in the city, and for the famous Readings. Dickens had with reluctance accepted the urgent invitation of his American publishers to undertake a lecture tour, having determined years before, following the tempest aroused by his "American Notes," never again to set foot on these shores. But time, and the urgent demands of publishers and public, had overruled his previous objections, and feeling that his health was somewhat precarious, he was anxious to earn sufficient money to provide

Charles Dickens

New York, Twenty First April, 1868.

generously for his family, so he set sail in the month of November, 1867, upon the Cuba, bound for Halifax and Boston.

And to meet this incoming steamer, upon an icy morning, the above-mentioned trio steamed down the harbor aboard the U. S. customs boat, the Hamblin, purposing to take Dickens promptly ashore, thereby avoiding the ordeal of encountering the crowd assembling to greet him at East Boston. Besides the publishers the little steamer carried Mr. George Dolby, Dickens's business manager, who had been two months in the country making plans for his Chief, and who had brought over with him the manuscript of Dickens's "Holiday Romance," soon to be issued by the Boston house.

The hours passed, the Cuba failed to appear, and the small company aboard the tug were cold and weary of being tossed about in a rough sea; it was therefore suggested that they go ashore at Hull, where at the signal station they might discover if the ship had yet been sighted. This they did, and on struggling up the steep incline gained but the satisfaction of encountering a group of half-frozen press representatives who had been detailed to report the arrival of the ship. After a fruitless search for a warm shelter, the party from the tug decided to embark once more, having in pity bestowed upon the congealing reporters two bottles of champagne, which had been brought in order that the health of Dickens might be drunk on his arrival.

When they were once more aboard the tug, it was suggested that they steam toward the Java, which lay at anchor near by, whose captain was well known to the group. This proved a happy thought, for they were welcomed cordially aboard, and sat down to a steaming supper provided by their friend the captain; this repast they were doing justice to when the man-on-the-lookout reported, "Cuba in sight." A blithe announcement for which they had waited anxiously since morning, and which at last came at a moment when they would gladly have postponed it longer. A rush was made to board the tug, which cast off quickly and steamed toward the incoming liner, whose captain, for some unknown reason, failed to regard its frantic signals. The little Hamblin shrieked and puffed and followed in the wake of the liner, its passengers fearing that they had come upon a hopeless quest. But fortune, in the guise of a mud-bank, favored the tug, and into this the Cuba ploughed, and stuck there, to remain for several hours.

Then it was that the friends of Dickens came joyfully alongside, to find the novelist peering over the rail ready to greet them cheerily. He was promptly transferred, and carried to Long Wharf, at which place a conveyance had been stationed for hours ready to take him to the Parker House, where an ovation awaited him.

The voyage had been a rough one, and Dickens was weary and inclined to be somewhat depressed at first. Supper was served him in his private sitting-room, and he was annoyed by the waiters who persisted in leaving the door ajar, thereby enabling the promenaders in the corridor to peep at him while he was eating. He had been much exasperated during the whole of his first trip to America by an obtrusive curiosity which he greatly resented, and now on his second arrival the vision of citizens of Boston peering in through the door, to watch him eat, caused him to declare that he was sorry he had not adhered to his purpose "never to visit America again," and he exclaimed: "These people have not in the least changed during the last twenty-five years; they are doing exactly what they were doing then." But this depression soon vanished in the face of the good news about his Readings, which was immediately presented to him. (A brief report of this had already been forwarded to him by the pilot boat, twenty miles out from land.)

Before me as I write is a blue ticket bearing the words: "Good For This Evening Only, Mr. Charles Dickens's Reading, Tremont Temple, Boston. Reserved seat No. 1378."

As I regard it, I can but wonder if this alone remains of all the tickets sold for those famous Readings in the city of Boston. Two little holes have been punched in the pasteboard, which make it evident that its possessor (doubtless my father) had by special request retained it as a souvenir when passing through the gate. As I inspect this pasteboard relic, it recalls the story of the marvelous success achieved by Dickens on the platform.

Never before in Boston had any such excitement been evoked by a ticket sale as that which prevailed upon a bitterly cold day when Ticknor & Fields opened their doors at 9 A.M. to admit the first of those that had stood many hours in line in order to secure seats for the opening night. The line extended up and down Hamilton Place, and then stretched its "slow length" on Tremont Street for an extraordinary distance, including representatives from every walk in life, a truly democratic concourse. The crowd, as described by those present, was a remarkably good-humored one, stamping its feet, exchanging jokes, and bursting into song to pass away the time before the doors were opened. The sidewalk humorists did their best to keep up the spirits of the crowd, and there were other spirits that circulated throughout the waiting line which helped to banish the effect of the biting wind. At intervals the crowd sang popular selections, such as, "The Ivy Green," and "John Brown's Body," responding with enthusiasm to the suggestion of "marching on."

As the result of having taken too much of something to keep out the cold, one gentleman in a conspicuous position broke forth into a loud and eloquent address, and in the course of his remarks was seen to wave his arms toward Park Street Church, exclaiming: "Gen'lemen, there are but three men who have stamped themselves upon the civilization of the nineteenth century! Those men are Charles Shakespeare, William Dickens, and myself! Let any one deny it who dares!"

At this point the hand of the law was laid upon the shoulder of the orator, who was unceremoniously removed from his place in the line to a retired position.

The excitement attendant upon the sale of tickets for the opening course of Readings was duplicated at the second, and throughout the country, from first to last, there was no falling off in the tremendous demand for opportunities to hear the novelist, whose personal popularity was never equaled by that of any other writer.

During this second visit to America, Dickens suffered from a severe form of influenza, resulting from the exposure to great cold and many snow-storms; he was, moreover, tormented with sleepless-ness, and also at times with a painful lameness in one foot. These ailments made it on many occasions almost impossible for him to fill his numerous engage-ments; yet his indomitable spirit rose superior to his suffering, and he would rise from a couch where he had been resting in almost complete exhaustion, go upon the stage with a voice seemingly too husky to be heard, and when once behind his speaker's desk, his powerful will would assert itself, his voice would clear, and he would prove master of the situation.

Before the announcement of the Readings in Boston, it was discovered that "pirates" had en-gaged shorthand writers to attend the Course and take the text down with a view to reproduction and sale. On learning this, the Boston publishers promptly anticipated such a proceeding by at once issuing the Readings (taken from Mr. Dickens's own reading books) in small volumes and selling them at such price as made it impossible for "pirates" to make anything out of their publication.

Dickens's autograph was in such great demand that correspondence in this field became a heavy burden to his manager, who was forced to send out a printed slip announcing that "compliance with such a request was not reasonably possible." Dickens was the recipient of an enormous mass of letters, none of which he would open except those coming from Europe, or addressed in the well-known handwriting of special friends.

Among certain reminders of this famous visitor may be mentioned some souvenirs of the "International Walking Match," which has been often referred to. A framed copy of Dickens's humorous description of the affair hangs upon the wall near by, recalling the story of this event, and the banquet which followed, at which each guest received a similar printed and signed token of the author's originality. This international contest was the result of Dickens's enthusiasm as a pedestrian, and was carefully planned by him in every detail. It was a match between Mr. Osgood, representing America, and Mr. Dolby, upholding the glory of Great Britain; the former being designated by Dickens as the "Boston Bantam," and the latter, as the "Man of Ross," while Dickens appointed Fields and himself to act as umpires. Fields figured as "Massachusetts Jemmy" in Dickens's amusing account, in which he called himself the "Gad's Hill Gasper," because of his "surprising performances upon that truly national instrument, the American Catarrh."

Some days before this match occurred, Dickens took Mr. Fields over the twelve-mile course at such a pace that he was well-nigh exhausted and found it necessary to stop for a short breathing-space at Newton, the turning-point. There a search for refreshments at the roadside store brought forth only some uninviting oranges, which were, however, eagerly seized upon to quench the thirst of the panting pedestrians, who ate them seated upon the steps outside the shop.

The day appointed for the match was February 29th, and in the teeth of a bitterly cold blast the two contestants walked to Newton, over the Mill Dam Road; the "Boston Bantam" rounded the stake first, and after keeping the lead, came in seven minutes ahead of his British opponent, who afterwards declared that Osgood's ability to hold out to the end was owing to the stimulating refreshment tendered him at intervals by a lady who followed the race in her carriage. This lady replied to Dolby's protest by assuring him that had *he* been ahead, she would have done the same by *him;* which naïve confession called forth forgiveness from the defeated Englishman, who had since his arrival in America been schooled in the field of amiable endurance.

Between endeavoring to carry out his Chief's instructions, and his desire to conciliate the American public, he had a truly hard part to perform. Dickens insisted that all tickets should be kept from speculators (a task that proved impossible) and Dolby in his attempts to compass this result had many sad experiences, was hated, insulted, and reproached by the press; if things went wrong, he was the one to blame, while if they went well, no one thanked him; and he was quite accustomed to serving as a butt for any joke or pleasantry that might arise. On one occasion a printer's error in one of his advertisements gave Dickens great satisfaction. The printer had transposed the words "minutes" and "hours," and had in consequence issued the announcement: "The Reading will be comprised within two minutes, and the audience are earnestly requested to be seated ten hours before its commencement"; a happening which Dolby was never allowed to hear the last of.

Among the Readings planned was one at Worcester; this took place at the City Hall, in the basement of which a poultry show was just then being held.

As a result, Dickens was forced to read to the accompaniment of a continual crowing by a choice breed of roosters that mistook the illumination of many gas-jets for the bright morning sun. This barnyard chorus greatly annoyed the harassed reader, who was unusually sensitive to discordant sounds, although it was to all appearances unnoted by the audience, so rapt were they in the performance.

Dickens's dramatic rendering of his themes at times greatly exhausted his vitality; especially did his tremendous interpretation of the murder scene in "Oliver Twist," with "Nancy" and "Bill" Sikes, have an injurious effect upon him. This scene was constantly demanded by his English audiences during the last year of his Readings, and he insisted upon complying with this demand in spite of earnest protests from doctors and managers.

The dinner which Dickens gave in Boston, to celebrate the "walking match," was a brilliant success. Sixteen covers were laid and the host had himself superintended the extensive floral decorations which covered the table, and had provided a bouquet, or a boutonnière, for every guest. The company included Mr. and Mrs. Fields, Mr. and Mrs. Charles

Eliot Norton, Professor and Mrs. James Russell
Lowell, Dr. and Mrs. Oliver Wendell Holmes, Mr.
and Mrs. Thomas Bailey Aldrich, Mr. and Mrs.
Howard Malcom Ticknor, Henry W. Longfellow
and Miss Longfellow, and Mr. Schlesinger.

Those that were present have described the dinner
as one of never-ceasing wit and merriment, in which
the master of the feast led every sally, exhibiting the
highest spirits, despite the recent defeat sustained
by his nation's representative. Upon the outcome
of this match he had some time before put up a
wager with my aunt, Mrs. Howard Ticknor. He had
wagered two pairs of gloves that his man would be
winner, and of this bet, paid promptly, one unworn
pair remains to testify to the triumph of "Boston's
Bantam." At the banquet in question, my aunt was
seated opposite Mr. Dickens, and beside Mr. Fields.
The latter, in describing the rapid pace of Mr. Dolby,
declared that "he flashed by like a *meteor*," at which
she exclaimed: "But he could n't *com-et!*" and then
paused in confusion, fearing that Fields would not
approve of her indulgence in this the "lowest form
of wit." Dickens, however, enjoyed the pun, and later
wrote the punster some delightful notes, being also
much pleased with a small parting token which she
sent in memory of their wager; this was a charm in
the form of a tiny pair of gold gloves, which he wore
on his watch-chain when he departed. This chain of
Dickens's had evoked many comments from those
that claimed he wore "not one, but two"; the truth
being that he wore but one, which was of double
length. With the gold gloves went a brief message

assuring Dickens that it was not a "*gage de guerre*," but a "*gage d'amitié*." To which he sent reply:

DEAR MRS. TICKNOR,

The *gage d'amitié*, duly taken up, hangs at my watch-chain. Accept my best thanks for the pretty little token, and for your charming note: and believe that I should have been, even though I had not been thus bound to be,

Faithfully yours ever
CHARLES DICKENS

Dickens's signature remains unique among those of our famous writers, being perhaps the most hard to decipher, as well as the most decorative. It was reproduced upon the covers of one set of books, by Ticknor & Fields; this set being known as the "Snarleow" edition, because of the resemblance of the signature to such a word. Dickens wrote always with a quill pen, and in blue ink. He chose the latter because of his dislike of blotting-paper, having discovered that an especial make of blue ink dried instantly; his use of this in his work for the press was followed by others in England, and thus originated the "blue-ink journalism." A lead pencil was another pet aversion of the novelist's, and he was almost never known to use one, even his briefest memoranda being invariably jotted down in ink.

A souvenir of the great novelist of an unusual kind is perhaps worthy of description. This was a brown-paper reproduction of the writer's footprint, not on the sands of time (where it is firmly planted), but on

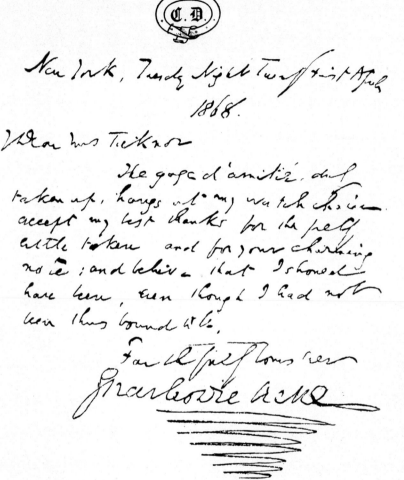

New York, Tuesday Night Twenty first April
1868.

My Dear Mrs Tichnor

    The gage d'amitié, duly
taken up, hangs at my watch chain.
Accept my best thanks for the pretty
little token and for your charming
note; and believe that I should
have been, even though I had not
been thus bound to be,

    Faithfully yours ever
    Charles Dickens

the gravel path that led to our front door. It was secured by a shy relative, who greatly admired the novelist, but was too timid to appear when he was at the house, only emerging from her seclusion in time to snatch his footprint. Recent rains had left the front path in a muddy condition, and as Dickens walked away, his feet sank deeply into the soft gravel. Following his departure, the shy relative dashed out with shears and paper, and skillfully secured a perfect impression of the author's foot: a "Dickens print" which is undoubtedly without a duplicate in any collection of Dickens memorabilia.

Dickens was never too busy with his own concerns to expend time and sympathy on behalf of his suffering fellows, and during his stay in Boston he visited the Blind Asylum, being always particularly touched by persons bearing this form of affliction. There he was impressed with the limited area of literature placed at the disposal of the blind, asserting that "the New Testament and Dr. Watts's hymns" were "apt to be the only books given them to while away the hours of darkness." Therefore before departure he left instructions to have the "Old Curiosity Shop" reproduced in raised letters for the use of each blind asylum in the United States. After his return to England this plan was carried out and the gift properly distributed.

Dolby's devotion to his Chief was absolutely untiring, and he labored under a great strain of anxiety during the whole American tour, fearing lest Dickens should break down under the effort to fulfill his lecture programme. At the close of the enterprise accounts revealed the fact that the returns were **far** in excess of what had been expected. Of the eighty Readings originally planned, seventy-six were given, and the receipts were $228,000, from which heavy expenses had to be deducted. The largest return for any lecture was that received in Boston for the farewell Reading, which brought in $3456.

Although he was showered with invitations during his Boston stay, Dickens's health forbade his attendance of all but a limited number of social functions, and he accepted few dinner invitations beyond those tendered by his publishers, and by Professor Longfellow, whose friendship dated back to his first visit to America. During this early trip, in 1842, a banquet was given him by the young men of Boston at Papanti's Hall, with President Quincy of Harvard presiding. And upon this occasion one of the evening's toasts was: "Dickens, a great name, it has not for centuries been used without the *article* before it." Time has assuredly restored the *article*, which is to-day inseparable from the name of the novelist, who remains, with none to dispute his title, *the Dickens*.

This writer's final message, delivered upon the eve of his departure from New York, in April, 1868, cannot be too often recalled to mind. Like all men of clear vision, he realized the necessity of strengthening the ties that bind together the two great English-speaking nations, and he declared:

"Points of difference there have been, points of difference there are, points of difference there probably always will be, between the two great peoples.

But broadcast in England is sown the sentiment that those two peoples are essentially one, and that it rests with them jointly to uphold the great Anglo-Saxon race. . . . I do believe that from the great majority of honest minds on both sides, there cannot be absent the conviction that it would be better for this globe to be riven by an earthquake, fired by a comet, overrun by an iceberg, and abandoned to the Arctic fox or bear, than that it should present the spectacle of those two great nations, each one of which has, in its own way and hour, striven so hard and so successfully for freedom, ever again being arrayed the one against the other."

CHAPTER II

THE DICKENS FAMILY IN LONDON

THE recollections of Charles Dickens, during his stay in Boston, as gleaned from an earlier generation, were supplemented by my own acquaintance with the Dickens family, when, many years later, I visited in London the household of the novelist's son, Henry Fielding Dickens.

Those that are interested in seeking out the many spots identified with the life of Charles Dickens find with surprise how few are left of his early haunts and abiding-places. From Furnival's Inn, Holborn, where the writer spent the first years of his married life, one may trace his various removals from one locality to another, until he settled at Gad's Hill, in 1860, after which he never again had a permanent home in the city of London. It was at Gad's Hill that Dickens died, and that place is of all others the most widely associated with his name. Yet to-day the house is no longer in the possession of the Dickens family, and the memories of the great novelist cluster about the homes of his grandchildren, and center in that of his one surviving son, Henry Fielding Dickens, K. C. This distinguished barrister had, during my stay in London, a charming home at 2 Egerton Place, S.W., and an evening spent under his hospitable roof not only enabled the visitor to enjoy a glimpse of a most united family circle, but brought one into close touch with much that was personally associated with Charles Dickens.

Upon the left as one entered was Mr. Henry Dickens's study, used also as a reception-room, where in the bay-window stood the desk at which the novelist wrote nearly all of his novels. Upon being ushered upstairs the visitor found Mrs. Dickens seated with her embroidery at the end of the long drawing-room in company with two pretty daughters. After a hearty welcome, and before offering a seat beside the fire, the hostess led the way to the balcony outside one of the long windows, where she displayed with pride the masses of bright geraniums to which she devoted much attention. (It has been frequently recorded that these flowers were the especial favorite of Charles Dickens.)

The drawing-room was spacious and admirably adapted for musical purposes, the grand piano at one end being placed on a raised platform. As we strolled about, looking at various pictures and curios, my attention was arrested by a tall silver vase that stood upon a polished table. Against one side of the vase rested a silver ladder, upon the rungs of which were inscribed the names of various members of the family, with the dates of their births and marriages. This unique gift had been designed by the children and presented to Mr. and Mrs. Henry Dickens on the occasion of their silver wedding. Up and down the ladder on either side hung tiny heart-shaped frames containing pictures of all whose names were engraved on the silver cross-bars, and as I viewed this ingenious device I was convinced that to climb one's family tree upon a silver ladder was a most pleasing method of ascent.

"We are expecting auntie to dinner," Mrs. Dickens announced, and shortly after, Miss Georgina Hogarth entered, to be enthusiastically greeted by all. She was a charming old lady, alert and youthful in her feelings and keenly interested in every movement of the day. She lived but a few doors away, and spent much of her time with the members of the Dickens family, who idolized her. As one watched her serene countenance and listened to her pleasant voice, one did not wonder that Charles Dickens found in her his "best friend." Upon a chain about her neck she wore a small gold key, which some one whispered unlocked the casket which contained the manuscript of the "Cricket on the Hearth," her dearest treasure, given her by its author.

At dinner a jolly family party assembled presided over by Mr. and Mrs. Dickens, who were enthusiastically alive to all the interests of the younger people. They were closely in touch with musical and dramatic doings, and were entertaining a young prima-donna, just back from Paris, who had that afternoon given a song recital in Westminster Abbey, which I attended. I still recall her silvery tones as she sang Gounod's "Ave Maria," while Sir Frederick Bridge at the organ accompanied the singer, giving us afterwards several magnificent selections. We were just a small handful of invited guests in sole possession of the huge edifice for one enchanting hour, while the sun's dying rays stole in through the great windows illuminating the singer with a golden touch.

Dinner being ended, the hostess suggested that all adjourn for coffee to the "Dickens Room" downstairs. This was the favorite family rendezvous; a spacious room filled with the memorabilia of Charles Dickens. The walls were completely covered with autographs, illustrations, bits of manuscript, and what was of chief interest, a large collection of portraits of the novelist, representing him at all stages of his career. Most notable among these was a fine copy of the Maclise painting, which hangs in the National Gallery, showing the author at twenty-seven years of age.

A billiard table stood in the center of the room, and Mr. Dickens and his sons indulged in this favorite game, while the ladies grouped in the cozy corners near the fireplace sipping their coffee and displaying their various pieces of fancy work. I found a seat beside Miss Hogarth, and listened to reminiscences of her late brother-in-law, of whom she loved to speak, and to her expression of interest in all pertaining to America, which she asserted she still hoped to visit some day.

In his entertaining "Life" of Dickens, Mr. Chesterton has touched with more wit than exactitude upon the incompatibility of Mr. and Mrs. Dickens, remarking flippantly that the novelist "fell in love with the three Hogarth sisters and married the wrong one." This statement is easily discredited by one who cares to verify the dates in question, as both the sisters were very young at the time of the marriage, and Georgina had only reached the age of nine.

The union of Dickens and Katherine Hogarth,

which took place in 1836, did not prove a happy one. Seven children were born to them, but as years went on, the incompatibility of tempers and temperaments made the affairs of the household more and more complicated and irritating, and in 1857 a separation was agreed upon; it being arranged that the oldest son should be established in a separate home with his mother, while the other children remained with their father; this, owing to the eccentricities of Mrs. Dickens, seemed the only possible solution of the domestic problem. It was stated that all the children wished to remain with the father, and that all adored "Aunt Georgina."

Dickens's devotion to the memory of his wife's younger sister, Mary Hogarth, who died in 1837, powerfully influenced his entire career; he mourned her as sincerely thirty years after her passing as at the first when he penned her epitaph for the stone in Kensal Green which read: "Young, beautiful, and good, God in his mercy numbered her among His angels at the early age of seventeen."

Dickens believed that her spirit was constantly near, and watching over him; he saw her in number-less vivid dreams, and it was asserted by his biographer that she was always more or less in his thoughts. On the sixth anniversary of her death he declared that he had made her his "ideal of moral excellence." And the year before his death this same influence was as powerfully felt by him as ever, and he wrote: "She is so much in my thoughts at all times, especially when I am successful and have greatly prospered in anything, that the recollection of her is an essential part of my being, and is as inseparable from my existence as the beating of my heart."

The oft-reiterated question, "And who was Dora?" has during the last few years been conclusively answered by the publication of a privately printed edition of Dickens's letters to Maria Beadnell. Biographers of Dickens have generally asserted that "Dora" was Katherine Hogarth, but this recent disclosure proved that she was none other than Maria Beadnell, who later became Mrs. Louis Winter.

Dickens made the acquaintance of the Beadnell family when he was but eighteen, and for the next three years worshiped at the shrine of Maria, who was one of three sisters. The young journalist was handsome and talented, and Maria, two years his senior, flirted with him desperately. But Dickens was poor, a young reporter without apparent prospects, whom Maria's family did not regard as eligible; therefore the parental verdict went strongly against this ardent youth, and Maria, who had previously encouraged her suitor, suddenly discarded him with a coldness and unconcern upon which his frantic appeals made no impression. Dickens made a last appeal, Maria vouchsafed no answer, and Dickens went away a changed being; his pride stung to the quick, he turned with tenfold ambition to his work, in order to demonstrate that the lover spurned was the equal of any man in London.

Two years later, Dickens married Katherine Hogarth, but nevertheless his first attachment had been very strong, as is proven by the fact that it was the vision of his first love which took possession of his fancy when, seventeen years after his parting with Maria, he sat down to pen the pages of "David Copperfield" and to recall his youthful ecstasy. Doubtless the idealized memory of his first love would have been always cherished by Dickens had not the object of his adoration appeared in the flesh to exorcise it. In 1855 this lady wrote him recalling their early friendship, congratulating him upon his great success, and voicing a desire to renew their association. Her communication touched a responsive chord and several letters passed between them, in which the novelist expressed great warmth of feeling.

Had the stout, middle-aged, and still very sentimental Mrs. Winter allowed herself to continue a lovely memory, some miles from London, "Dora" she would have remained forever, not only on the printed page, but also in the heart of her one-time adorer; but after opening a correspondence to which he responded with cordiality, she appointed a meeting, desiring once more to try her fascinations upon her former lover, now become famous.

They met, and instantly was shattered the illusion which for a quarter of a century had rested upon a secure foundation. And from the shock of this meeting Dickens turned to the production of "Little Dorrit," where in the guise of "Flora" the writer pictures the transformed "Dora" as she appeared when her former lover met her again after many years.

He writes in "Little Dorrit": "Flora, always tall,

had grown to be very broad too, and short of breath; but that was not much. Flora, whom he had left a lily, had become a peony; but that was not much. Flora, who had seemed enchanting in all that she had said and thought, was diffuse and silly. *That was much.* Flora, who had been spoiled and artless long ago, was determined to be spoiled and artless now. That was a fatal blow."

From this "blow" the early friendship, temporarily revived, never rallied, and after this disillusionment Dickens avoided all further meetings with his first love, refusing ever to set eyes upon her again.

The "Dickens Room" was truly an interesting study in Dickensiana. I strolled about it with members of the family studying the many portraits on the walls and pausing before a painting of Gad's Hill, which held so many dear associations for the family. Among the many objects of interest, I viewed the framed pages from the copy-book in which the writer taught his son Henry shorthand; a small leather bag presented to Dickens by the Count D'Orsay, which was his constant companion on many travels; and in one corner hung a framed description of the "International Walking Match," previously described, which I was told was highly prized by Dickens, who had looked back with especial interest upon this Boston episode.

A sequel to my first delightful evening with the Dickens family followed a few days later when I accepted an invitation to dine with them at Earl's Court, the favorite recreation ground in London at that time. They explained with enthusiasm that dinner in the outdoor restaurant during the warm June weather was very entertaining, and bade me meet them at a certain entrance upon an evening specified.

When at the appointed time I reached the wicket gate, I saw the smiling face of Mr. Henry Dickens gazing over the turnstile. He guided me to a seat under a tree where one or two members of the party were already assembled, and I soon found that this united family experienced some difficulty in getting together at any given time and spot. To our first group others were added gradually; first came a son, and then a daughter, and then arrived Aunt Georgina duly escorted by a devoted grand-niece. Lastly came Mrs. Dickens, and then we all adjourned to a table upon the broad veranda.

This table, engaged beforehand, was situated upon an outer corner where it commanded a pleasing view of the surrounding grounds; it was an admirable point-of-vantage to be enjoyed on a warm evening, but fate had willed it that this evening should be devoid of warmth. From the moment of my arrival the mercury fell rapidly; the wind sprang up and blew with chilling blast, which made all summer clothing inadequate. I noted with amusement that Mrs. Dickens, who left home later than the rest, was comfortably wrapped in a sealskin coat which all the others envied silently as they filed into various seats about the table spread on the veranda.

It proved to be the coldest dinner-party that I had ever experienced, in so far as atmospheric conditions were concerned, but it was not lacking in cheer and merriment that warmed the heart. The dinner courses came very slowly, and we drew our wraps about us and tried to banish frosty thoughts; the men tucked newspapers across their shirt-fronts, and I stole anxious glances over the table at Aunt Georgina, who, I felt sure, must be acquiring pneumonia upon this chilly night. I felt myself a culprit for having brought upon the Dickens family this icy dinner-party, which I feared might prove fatal in its effects.

When it was ended, we all rose with alacrity, being prepared to explore the grounds and to participate in the amusements.

As I look back upon that evening, it still presents itself as a mad whirl of lights, noise, and confusion. We darted back and forth, and lost each other continually; I was conveyed to see some novel electrical display, then to test some nerve-racking mechanical appliance; there was a dreadful boat that plunged into a subterranean cavern and emerged on the other side after a perilous passage; there was a strange room where one received electric shocks through the soles of one's shoes, when walking on the floor; and there were everywhere countless devices for getting money, and giving people painful and terrifying pleasure. I found myself at last by the border of the lagoon down which came splashing the frail craft in which heroic merrymakers were rapidly "shooting the shutes." As I shuddered at the reckless descent, I heard a cry of joy go up from members of the Dickens family: "This is the thing that we like best! You must come with us!"

I pleaded that I did not care to plunge into this seething maelstrom, and begged to be let off, but it was with great difficulty that I escaped sharing this climax to an evening's entertainment. Mr. and Mrs. Dickens "loved it"; so did the sons and daughters, and they regarded me with curious and pitying glances as one devoid of spirit. But I remained unmoved, although informed that I was "showing the white feather" and injuring the national reputation. They left me feeling much disgraced, and sped away to the top of the shute, where they embarked with joy upon the wild descent. Meanwhile, I found a seat beside Aunt Georgina upon a bench, where we conversed in peace and pleasantness, watching the members of the Dickens family shoot madly past in their joyous abandonment. When at last they returned, moist and exultant, I had discovered a subtle means of winning back my national reputation. I found a penny-in-the-slot machine that was displaying a miniature horse-race. There were two tiny handles to be turned, which made two little horses race rapidly across a certain space. I ascertained that I could make those handles revolve with great rapidity, and so I challenged the members of the company in turn, and won from each a race and penny, which proved a simple method of restoring the international balance.

The hectic evening ended in a whirl of disappearing members of the Dickens family; some vanished in four-wheelers, some went away in cabs, others walked off, and I was finally borne homewards in a cab, weary, and worried lest Aunt Georgina should not survive the strenuous entertainment, and found myself deposited at my door by the agreeable fiancé of one of the pretty Dickens daughters. As I looked back upon the merry party, I could not but reflect that the dramatic pen of Dickens himself should have done justice to the affair. (And after all, Aunt Georgina was none the worse for her night's revel.)

On the wall of the "Dickens Room," beside the mantel, I saw the author's last note written to his son Henry, on June 8, 1870, the day before his death. This and the final writing that he did on "Edwin Drood" were his last work, as he suffered a shock of apoplexy that night.

Upon the day in question he had seemed in good spirits at luncheon, had smoked a cigar in his favorite conservatory, and before dinner had written some letters, but when he was seated at table, Miss Hogarth, who was alone with him, noted that a striking change had come over his face. To her anxious inquiries he acknowledged that he felt very ill, but he refused to have her send for a doctor. As his speech was growing incoherent, she begged him to "go and lie down," and as he rose to follow this suggestion he murmured: "Yes, on the ground." These were his last words, as he fell to the floor after taking a few steps. From this time he remained unconscious until his death, which occurred twenty-four hours later. This was just five years from the day when he nearly lost his life in a terrible railroad accident, from the shock of which he never wholly recovered.

The morning which brought the last letter to Henry Dickens brought also a telegram announcing his father's sudden illness, and to the son hastening to his bedside his death came as a terrible shock.

In the will of Charles Dickens, completed only a week before his death, the following words were penned:

"I direct that my name be inscribed in plain English letters on my tomb. I conjure my friends on no account to make me the subject of any monument, memorial, or testimonial whatever. I rest my claim to the remembrance of my country on my published works, and to the remembrance of my friends in their experience of me in addition thereto."

He lies in the Poet's Corner in Westminster Abbey, surrounded by men of genius, but in accordance with his own wish his best monument has been that accorded him by millions of appreciative readers, while the claim upon the remembrance of his friends and those nearest to him has strengthened rather than weakened with the accumulation of years. As I wandered about the "Dickens Room," which seemed pervaded by the strong personality of the departed, and listened to the expressions of love and enthusiasm kindled by the great writer's memory, I realized how much alive Charles Dickens is to-day, not only in the world of letters, but in the homes of those who loved him best.

Since my last visit to London there have been breaks in the happy family circle that welcomed me so warmly. Miss Hogarth passed away in April, 1917, at the age of ninety; she had survived her famous brother-in-law some thirty-seven years, and to the end remained the idol of his children and grandchildren. During the thirteen years which followed Dickens's separation from his wife, she presided over his household, ministering untiringly to the wants of all. Miss Hogarth lived to see the youngest of her beloved grand-nephews give his life in the World War, when heavy clouds descended upon the happy and united household.

The gallant conduct of the grandsons of Charles Dickens should not be overlooked by those that are reckoning that writer's contribution to his country. Major Cedric Dickens, the youngest grandson, who was killed upon the western front towards the end of 1916, had been a choir-boy at Brompton Oratory at the opening of the war, and did such energetic recruiting that nearly all of his companions in the choir of this famous church joined the army with him.

Philip Dickens, the older brother, known to his friends as "Pip," was wounded in action, and only awaited recovery to again hasten to the front. And another brother served all through the Dardanelles campaign, and later, in the intelligence department of the admiralty.

In answer to a letter of sympathy which I sent to Mr. Henry Dickens in 1916, the bereaved father wrote of the loss of his youngest son:

"He died a splendid death, and so far as the dear boy is concerned, there is no need for pity. He died the death which he would have wished; but to us who mourn the loss, this gives only a poor degree of consolation. It cannot eliminate the feeling that one of our loved ones has gone from us. My wounded son is better and is not likely to return to the front for some

weeks. When he does, our feeling of constant appre-
hension will return." Mr. Dickens closed with the
words: "But we in this country have steeled ourselves to bear whatever fate may thrust upon us."

Surely the author of the "Christmas Carol," which
has done more than any other work of fiction to
spread the doctrine of "Peace on Earth, good will
towards men," is still contributing to the welfare of
his country, not only through his works, but through
the legacy of noble manhood which he has bequeathed his nation.

CHAPTER III

HAWTHORNE AND HIS FRIEND

FROM his home in Jamaica Plain, my grandfather, William D. Ticknor, had gone out for the last time, in March, 1864, to accompany his friend Nathaniel Hawthorne upon a southern trip, which it was hoped would benefit the latter's health. Hawthorne was failing, and it had been suggested that a journey to a milder clime might prove the one thing needful; therefore, his publisher, on whom he had for years depended for all manner of kindly offices, consented to take charge of the invalid, little dreaming that it would be his own last journey.

The story of this friendship has been already chronicled,[1] but a brief outline of it can hardly be omitted here without leaving these literary memories quite incomplete.

The journey above referred to was not the first that had been taken by Hawthorne and his publisher, for the novelist and dreamer shrank from the management of small details, and had on numerous occasions turned to the sturdy companionship of his friend when he desired to take some trip. If he had planned to go to Washington, he dreaded it until Ticknor had promised to accompany him, and when President Pierce appointed him to the Liverpool consulship, he would not embark unless his publisher

[1] See *Hawthorne and His Publisher.*

would consent to go with him and start him upon the new enterprise.

So it was that in 1853 Ticknor sailed with the Hawthornes for England, and saw them satisfactorily settled in their new home. Taking leave of his friends he crossed the Channel in season to witness the brilliant military fête in Paris held in honor of Napoleon III; visited De Quincey in Scotland; and returned for a last stay with Hawthorne, who accompanied him on a pleasure trip to Chester before he sailed for Boston. This excursion, which was later described in Hawthorne's Journal, was greatly enjoyed by the two; all the members of the Hawthorne family were to have accompanied them, but owing to the threatening weather, they remained at home, the children being mollified by the prospect of gifts to be purchased in the old town. And the following day found little Julian parading round the garden blowing a new trumpet, and dragging behind him a wooden cannon straight from Chester.

Soon after this excursion the friends parted, and on October 8, 1853, Hawthorne's pen was following the traveler homewards:

"While I write you this, you are tossing in mid-ocean; but I hope it will find you safely ensconced in your Paradise at the Old Corner. We all miss you very much. . . ."

This letter marked the opening of a trans-Atlantic correspondence with his publisher which Hawthorne kept up during his entire stay abroad. His letters, of which over one hundred and fifty have been preserved, are full of characteristic reflections, com-

Concord, Oct 11ᵗ 1861

Dear Fields,

Mrs Hawthorne has was
in reading to send to England a
certain trunk, of which the Ticks
& you a long time ago will you
see that it is shipped aboard some
steamer, to sail soon. Mrs Hawthorne thinks it best not to send
the key, but to allow the lock to
be forced by the custom House
examiner & the trunk is to be carried to the Wildings, who, I suppose will take charge of it after
it arrives in Liverpool.

Truly Yours,
Nath¹ Hawthorne

P.P. Mrs H wishes the trunk
to go by one of the Cunard steamers
for Liverpool, or one of the screw
steamers, if less expensive

ments, and observations. In them the writer depicts many incidents connected with his diplomatic life, and in these spontaneous communications reveals himself with a freedom from all restraint not to be found elsewhere in his letters and journals.

One of the most amusing literary episodes which took place during his consulship was the sponsoring of Delia Bacon's volume, "The Shakespeare Problem," the first production ever put forth to exploit the Baconian theory. Hawthorne theoretically objected to women writers, declaring in a mood of extreme cynicism that he considered "all ink-stained women detestable." Yet upon very slight acquaintance with the author of this work, and without being in sympathy with her Baconian belief, he deliberately proceeded to finance the publication of her book, an expense he could ill afford, because he sympathized with the discouraged writer and thought her book had literary merit.

Thus in the kindness of his heart did Hawthorne launch the Bacon-Shakespeare controversy, losing money in his venture, and winning slight gratitude from the eccentric author who had produced it, and who was highly indignant with him when it went to press because he failed to furnish for the book the precise introduction which she demanded.

When the volume finally appeared, Hawthorne regretted that he had not wielded the blue pencil in connection with the Baconian theory, and he wrote to his Boston publisher:

"Matters look dark, as regards Miss Bacon's book. I shall certainly not 'save my Bacon' there. It was absurd in me to let her publish such a heavy volume;

and in fact, I never thought of authorizing the publication of such an immense mass, which is enough to swamp a ship of the line. However, this shall be the last of my benevolent follies, and I never will be kind to anybody again as long as I live."

In spite of this protest, Hawthorne continued to help those that were constantly appealing to him for financial aid, many of whom proved even less appreciative than the luckless Delia, who never forgave him his refusal to state that he believed in her Baconian theory; this lady only survived the publication of her work two years, being at the last quite mentally unbalanced.

Hawthorne's trials in furnishing funds tor the return passages of irresponsible fellow-countrymen were many and varied. He sympathized with their tales of woe and generally aided the applicants, who sometimes returned the loans, but very frequently failed to do so. Hawthorne was prone to leave to his publisher the pleasant task of communicating with the relatives of the impecunious ones whose sense of honor did not impel them to refund a loan without a delicate reminder when once they were safely within the borders of the homeland, and it will never be known how many of the consul's "deserving cases" realized his expectations.

Hawthorne's sojourn in Italy, which followed his diplomatic service in England, is interestingly described in letters to his publisher written during this period, when he was busied with the production of the "Marble Faun"; in one of these he says:

"We are now in the height of the Carnival, and the

young people find it great fun. To say the truth, so do I; but I suppose I should have enjoyed it better at twenty. The Prince of Wales is here, and seems to take vast delight in pelting and being pelted, along the Corso. The poor fellow will not have many such merry times, in his future life."

In regard to his home-coming he continues:

"I should be very reluctant to leave Concord, or to live anywhere else than by my own hillside; that one spot (always excepting the 'Old Corner') is the only locality that attaches me to my native land. I am tied to it by one of my heartstrings, all the rest of which have long ago broken loose.

"I told you in my last, that I had written a Romance. It still requires a good deal of revision, trimming off of exuberances, and filling up vacant spaces; but I think it will be all right in a month or two after I arrive. I shall do my best upon it, you may be sure; for I feel that I shall come before the public, after so long an interval, with all the uncertainties of a new author. If I were only rich enough, I do not believe I should ever publish another book, though I might continue to write them for my own occupation and amusement. But with a wing of a house to build, and my girls to educate, and Julian to send to Cambridge, I see little prospect of the 'dolce far niente,' as long as there shall be any faculty left in me. I have another Romance ready to be written, as soon as this one is off the stocks."

Hawthorne had from earliest days delved into the mediæval history of Italy, and he arrived there prepared to appreciate to the utmost what that poetic

and artistic land had to offer, and to weave it into
his forthcoming romance. Certain vivid impressions
received soon after his arrival began to form a nucleus
for his plot. One morning he chanced to enter a
church where a Capuchin monk was lying dead, whose
strange appearance stirred his imagination; and later,
when he visited the Capitol, he was greatly charmed
by the Faun of Praxiteles, and at once began to
develop the train of thought which it suggested. He
wrote in this connection:

"This famous race of fauns was the most delightful
of all that antiquity imagined. It seems to me that a
story with all sorts of fun and pathos in it might be
contrived on the idea of the species having become
intermingled with the human race; a family with the
faun blood in them having prolonged itself from the
classic era till our own days. The tail might have
disappeared, by dint of constant intermarriage with
ordinary mortals; but the pretty hairy ears should
occasionally reappear in members of the family; and
the moral instincts and intellectual characteristics
of the faun might be picturesquely brought out."

The idea of making the Faun the center of his story
gradually grew and developed into the longest and
most elaborate of his works! He said of its length,
that he had not the heart to cancel his many descriptions of Roman and Florentine scenes which it had
given him so much pleasure to pen.

Relinquishing his plan for an immediate return to
America, Hawthorne remained another year abroad
in order to finish his book in England and so secure
the British copyright. When the work neared com-

pletion, considerable discussion arose in regard to its title. The author wished to call it "The Marble Faun," or else "Saint Hilda's Shrine," while Mr. Fields preferred "The Romance of Monte Beni," and Smith and Elder, the London publishers, insisted upon naming it "The Transformation," under which title it finally appeared in London.

While finishing this book the author spent some time at Whitby, where the ruined abbey, built by Saint Hilda, undoubtedly suggested the name which he used in his romance. From Whitby he went to Redcar, and then to Leamington, where in November, 1859, he put the final touches to this work, experiencing his usual dissatisfaction with his finished product; of which his wife wrote at this time:

"My husband has just finished his book, 'The Romance of Monte Beni,' . . . As usual, he thinks the book good for nothing, and based upon a very foolish idea which nobody will like or accept. But I am used to such opinions, and understand why he feels oppressed with disgust of what has so long occupied him. The true judgment of the work was his first idea of it, when it seemed to him worth the doing. He has regularly despised each one of his books immediately upon finishing it. . . . Mr. Hawthorne has no idea of portraying me as Hilda. Whatever resemblance one sees is accidental."

The warm reception which the book received did much to cheer the author, and a month before his return to America he wrote expressing his satisfaction with the result, but at the same time suggesting that his work was of little consequence as compared with the great prize-fight then taking place. He wrote:

"I am glad that the romance has gone off so well. Here, it may also be called a successful affair; Smith and Elder having got out the third edition, and perhaps more by this time; for the good opinion of the "Times" has great weight with John Bull.

"Just now, however, the English public cares very little for any American except John Heenan, the prize-fighter. You cannot imagine the interest that is felt in the battle, nor their surprise at Heenan's standing up so sturdily against their champion. No moral or intellectual triumph that we could possibly win, would inspire them with half the respect, or half the mortification, that the loss of this fight would have caused them. It is, indeed, a great pity that it was left undecided; that is, provided (as there were ten chances to one), the event had turned out favorably for our side."

Although "The Transformation" was received with great eagerness by the British public, some disappointment prevailed because of its vague conclusion, and in consequence, the author, in half-ironic mood, penned the brief chapter which is now appended to the book.

June, 1860, found Hawthorne at home again and settled at the Wayside in Concord, where the remainder of his life was passed. And after his return, as before his departure, his various little journeys were made in the company of his publisher; the former often insisting that his identity should be concealed on the hotel registers under the incognito of a "friend."

The frequent references which Hawthorne makes

to the "Old Corner" recall the fact that this was a
place which he loved to frequent. In the small
counting-room was "Hawthorne's chair," in a secluded nook; there he was wont to sit dreaming in
the shadow, while the senior partner was busy at his
desk close by. Across the office, in the opposite
corner, was the little green-curtained sanctum of
Mr. Fields, where the sociable spirits invariably
gathered, but in the counting-room, which was ele-
vated two or three steps above the level of the store,
was a secluded point-of-vantage. There Hawthorne
would take up his position where he could see and
yet be out of sight, and in this chair, for many years
it was his custom to ensconce himself, whenever he
visited the "Corner"; he often spent whole hours
there resting his head upon his hand apparently in
happy sympathy with his environment. And those
that looked in at the counting-room recalled the
picture as truly characteristic of the two friends; one
in the light, brimful of stirring activity, the other
watching in the shadow.

In 1862 Hawthorne and Ticknor made a memorable trip to Washington, investigating war conditions,
and enjoying an interview with Lincoln. On their
return the former produced an article for the "Atlantic Monthly" entitled "Chiefly About War Matters,"
in which he embodied a striking description of the
President. This seemed to Mr. Fields too frankly
realistic to suit the pages of the magazine just at that
time; he therefore cut out a large portion of it which
was not printed until nine years later, when it appeared in his reminiscences.

The interview with Lincoln was an exceedingly amusing one, for it was found that to accomplish it speedily, the friends must join a delegation which had been dispatched from a Massachusetts whip-factory, to bestow upon the President a splendid whip, with golden ferules and a carved ivory handle. In the rear of this delegation went Hawthorne and Ticknor, accompanied by their friend Major Ben: Perley Poore.

The whip was impressively presented, and its bearer in a set speech suggested that it was "emblematic," and that the President would doubtless recognize the fact; the spokesman discreetly suggesting the thought that such an instrument might be effectively used on the rebels. Hawthorne has entertainingly described this episode, and the great tact with which Lincoln handled, not only the whip, but the accompanying suggestion, which he waved gracefully aside, assuring the spokesman that he accepted the gift as an emblem of peace and not of punishment. He held aloft the "emblematic" whip in great good-humor as if he were touching up a pair of fine horses, and thus dismissed the delegation in the best of spirits.

This visit to Washington had proved so beneficial to Hawthorne's health that it was vainly hoped another journey South might be productive of a similar result, and when in the spring of 1864, the writer's family began to despair of his recovery, it was suggested that his publisher should once more accompany him upon a trip.

The travelers set out upon March 28th, planning

to journey southward by degrees, breaking the trip at several places where they might find a milder climate. But from the beginning they were pursued by storms and hurricanes, and the tempestuous elements kept them imprisoned, first in New York, and then in Philadelphia, where they remained at the Continental Hotel awaiting pleasant weather before continuing southward.

From there, Ticknor wrote Mrs. Hawthorne, on April 7th, that they had seen the first ray of sunshine since their departure, despite which fact Hawthorne seemed gaining steadily; he also stated that they had taken a drive to Fairmount Park that afternoon, with friends. He did not state, however, that on this drive, which proved a very bleak one, he had taken off his overcoat and wrapped it about Hawthorne, fearing that he might be chilled, and had himself added to a cold from which he had been suffering.

Following this letter came the news that Ticknor had been stricken with congestion of the lungs; and upon April 10th he passed away at the Continental Hotel, leaving his companion stunned by this calamity. In all his life Hawthorne had never stood beside a death-bed, and now to witness the sudden departure of his friend was to him a staggering blow from which he proved powerless to rally.

On his return to Concord, a few days later, he seemed completely broken, and quite unable to throw off the deep depression that had settled upon him. The image of death that he had witnessed would not be banished; he dwelt upon the tragic happening, and would reiterate that he, and not Ticknor, should have died.

After a month it was decided that Hawthorne must not remain in Concord, where he was brooding upon the loss of his friend and living over again those last painful hours. It was therefore arranged that he should once more try a change of scene, although he was almost too feeble to undertake the journey.

As has been frequently recorded, Hawthorne and Franklin Pierce set out for the White Mountains about the middle of May. When they reached Plymouth, New Hampshire, they put up at the Pemigewasset House, where Hawthorne retired early and fell asleep. His friend looked in upon him from time to time, and found him resting comfortably. Returning again, however, soon after midnight, he noticed that the sleeper had ceased to breathe. In answer to his often expressed wish, Hawthorne had taken his departure in his sleep.

And so in a month's time the invalid followed his vigorous companion whose death-bed he had guarded, and who had given his life in a vain effort to win back his friend to health. And on the home from which the active man, of only fifty-three years, had gone forth never to return, the shadows rested heavily; as they did on the group at the "Old Corner," from which the corner-stone had been suddenly uprooted. There, William D. Ticknor's sons, and his partner, James T. Fields, continued to carry on the traditions of the publishing house he had established; and in the home at Jamaica Plain members of the literary fraternity still found a welcome awaiting them.

CHAPTER IV

THE POET LONGFELLOW

THE figure of the poet Longfellow, with his beautiful white hair and beard, and his illuminating smile, forms one of my earliest recollections. His verses were among the first I ever learned, and it was an event of great importance when I was taken to his home with several other children, and was allowed to wander through the various rooms, viewing the "old clock on the stairs," and seeing the treasures that had been once the property of other famous men. There was the scrap-basket that had belonged to Thomas Moore, the inkstand that once was Coleridge's, and on a certain table was something very terrible! Fragments of a great poet's coffin, in a glass box. A statuette of this same poet, whose name was Dante, looked down at us from a bracket upon the wall, and by the fireplace was a chair given to the poet by the children of Cambridge, who loved him dearly, even as he loved them.

I know that on the day in question Longfellow met us at the gate, and "jumped us down" from the vehicle in which we had arrived, and later, when we had wandered through the house, and had recited some of his poems (especially acquired for the occasion), we were all led into the dining-room, where light refreshments had been ordered.

I recall vaguely that the refreshments were not

ready, and that the poet was troubled by the delay; also that I stood near him at the time and had some conversation with him, but what I said had faded from my memory until it was recalled by an aunt, who had accompanied me, and who asserted that I remarked: "We don't mind, Mr. Longfellow, for we remember you have told us 'to learn to labor and to wait.'"

My early admiration for this poet was always coupled with deep sympathy, for no more tragic story had been recounted to my childish ears than that of the terrible death of Mrs. Longfellow. I had been told how on a July day she was happily sitting in the library with her two little girls, who had just had their curls cut off; she was engaged in sealing up these curls in two little packages to keep, when her light muslin dress caught fire and in a moment she was all ablaze. I knew that Mr. Longfellow was himself severely burned in trying to extinguish the flames, and that his lovely wife died the next day, and was buried upon her wedding anniversary, with a wreath of orange blossoms upon her head.

The memory of this tragedy darkened the poet's life, but he hid it in his heart, and never let it cloud the joys of others. In one of his early letters he had written, "With me all deep feelings are silent ones," and no word of his sorrow found expression in his verse, except in that one exquisite sonnet, discovered in his portfolio and published after his death, entitled "The Cross of Snow." This bore the date July 10, 1879, which was the eighteenth anniversary of Mrs. Longfellow's death.

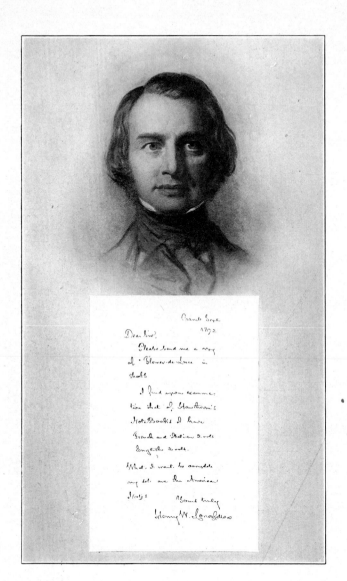

From this sorrow Longfellow turned to the translation of Dante, feeling the need of some absorbing task to occupy his thoughts, and for a time he translated a canto each day, although the work was not completed until five years later.

Near me as I write hangs an autograph letter, written by Longfellow (then twenty-two years old) in 1829, when he was in Vienna. It is illustrated by pencil sketches of bits of armor, and of a mediæval castle; that in which "Richard of the Lion-Heart" was once imprisoned. The writer describes his visit to the ruins of this castle at Greifenstein, and his ascent along the winding pathway that leads up to it, then he continues: "Upon the angle of the rock on which the castle stands is the impression of a human hand. This, according to tradition, gave rise to the name. *Greifen* answers to our *grip;* and *stein* to *stone.* Every knight, when he entered and gave his right hand to his host, laid his left hand on the stone (as guard against a treacherous blow); so, in the process of time, the stone was worn away, and the impression of a hand remains."

It is an interesting suggestion, this hand-print on the rock, symbolic of the "glad hand" perpetuated in stone. A symbol also of special inspiration for a writer, who may perchance with a light touch engrave a lasting record. One may, in passing, question whether the memory of the hand-print on the stone flashed through the poet's mind when he penned the oft-quoted line, "footprints on the sands of time." An echo of this line came back to Longfellow, seventeen years after it was written, when a letter from

Lady Byron stated that a dying soldier on the field before Sebastopol was heard repeating it.

In concluding the above-mentioned letter, Longfellow wrote:

"I have before me a copy of a song made by Richard during his confinement, which I picked up in France among some old troubadour poetry of the twelfth century. It is in the dialect of Provence. He begins by lamenting his sad fate, and says that his friends should blush to leave him 'nearly two years in chains':

> 'Let them know, my noble barons,
> English, Normans, and Gascons,
> That never so poor a yeoman had I
> That I would not have bought his liberty.
> I may not reproach their noble line,
> But chains and a dungeon still are mine!'

"He then calls upon his fellow troubadours, for Richard himself was a troubadour, and tells them to name him in their songs. . . . It is, throughout, very simple and beautiful, the most so of any troubadour poetry I have read. I would translate the whole for you; but what I have already written is so lame and inexpressive that I desist."

This letter was written about six months before Longfellow's return to America to take up a professorship at Bowdoin College, where he had graduated in 1825. This position he occupied for five years, and at the end of this time he was offered the Smith Professorship of Modern Languages at Harvard University, where he succeeded George Ticknor, in 1836.

Among Longfellow's classmates at Bowdoin was Nathaniel Hawthorne, and though the two saw little of each other during their college days, their early association was later renewed, and soon strengthened into a lasting friendship. In 1837 Hawthorne sent Longfellow a copy of his "Twice-Told Tales," at the same time praising the other's volume "Outre Mer," and congratulating him upon his literary success. This called forth Longfellow's warm appreciation of his classmate's work, and he wrote a complimentary notice of it for the "North American Review," in which he said: "This book, though in prose, is written nevertheless by a poet. . . .These flowers and green leaves of poetry have not the dust of the highway upon them. They have been gathered fresh from the secret places of a peaceful and gentle heart. Another characteristic is the exceeding beauty of his style."

Hawthorne's early letters to Longfellow do much to discredit his subsequent insistence that he disliked poetry, and was himself no poet; and such exclamations of his as: "What a terrible thing is poesy! Thank Heaven I am a humble proser."

He wrote to his classmate in 1839: "I read your poems over and over again and continue to read them all my leisure hours, and they grow upon me at every perusal." He reviewed the other's poems with keen appreciation, and asserted in another letter, "I do not claim to be a poet, and yet I cannot but feel that some of the sacredness of that character adheres to me and ought to be respected in me unless I slip out of its immunities."

Longfellow regarded "Evangeline" as a gift from

Hawthorne, who had presented him with the plot on
one occasion when they were dining together. The
story had first been recounted to Hawthorne by his
friend the Reverend H. L. Conolly, who had urged
him to make use of it. Longfellow was much touched
by the recital of the story, and said to Hawthorne:
"If you really do not want this incident for a tale,
let me have it for a poem." To which suggestion the
other willingly consented.

Out of this grew "Evangeline," the heroine of which
was first called "Gabrielle." The poem was finished
on Longfellow's fortieth birthday, February 27, 1847,
and was published the following autumn. A week
after its appearance, the author declared: "I have
received greater and warmer commendation than on
any previous book." And at the end of six months,
he wrote: "Ticknor prints the sixth thousand of
'Evangeline,' making one thousand a month since its
publication."

Hawthorne, then busy with his work in the Salem
Custom House, wrote an appreciative notice of this
poem, after expressing to the author his pleasure in
its beauty, and Longfellow responded: "I thank you
for resigning to me that Legend of Acady. This
success I owe entirely to you for being willing to
forego the pleasure of writing a prose tale, which
many people would have taken for poetry, that I
might write a poem which many people take for
prose."

The introduction of water into Boston at about
this time (October, 1848), was the occasion of an
extensive celebration; a great procession took place,

and Longfellow was asked to write an ode for the affair. This honor he declined, and the ode was prepared by Lowell, while Longfellow penned for his own amusement the following epigram, suggested by the controversy which had arisen regarding the sanitary danger of lead pipes, and also expressive of his own distaste for producing poems of occasion.

> Cochituate water, it is said,
> Tho' introduced in pipes of lead,
> Will not prove deleterious;
> But if the stream of Helicon
> Thro' leaden pipes be made to run,
> The effect is very serious.

At this period Longfellow describes a call at the "Old Corner":

"Go to town. At Ticknor's I find Park Benjamin sitting on a three-legged stool and discoursing oracular speech as from a tripod. He is going to make lecturing his profession. There sat Benjamin discoursing loudly and having for his auditors on this occasion Felton, Perley Poore, the editor, Giovanni Thompson, the artist, Captain Sumner and myself; and hovering far and near was Fields, laughing and dispatching parcels."

This little group, described as listening to the eloquence of Park Benjamin, was characteristic of the many gatherings that took place at this literary "Corner." There great men of the bar, pulpit, and university exchanged their notions of science, ethics, history, poetry, or politics. Rufus Choate stopped to explain some bit of his own writing, which no one could decipher; Dr. Holmes told of his medical classes; Thackeray there recounted his American experiences; while among other literary habitués were Starr King, Whittier, Emerson, and Mrs. Stowe; to this group were added many favorites of the stage, including Kellogg, Cary, Murdock, Forrest, Davenport, and Ole Bull.

The publication of "Hiawatha," seven years after the appearance of "Evangeline," proved another milestone in the history of its author's poetic successes. On the day of its appearance, November 10, 1855, four thousand out of the five of the first edition printed were sold, and a new edition of three thousand ordered. The demand for this poem continued to increase, and over fifty thousand copies were sold in the four years following its publication. It was also read to delighted audiences in many places, and scenes from it were presented at various theaters. "Grace Darling" read it to crowded houses in Philadelphia, and Mrs. Barrow, at the Boston Theater, delivered "Hiawatha's Wooing" in costume after the play.

In addition to the widespread praise which this poem evoked came also a blast of ridicule, and among the unfriendly critics, the "Boston Daily Traveller" was numbered. Soon after the appearance of the poem it printed the following: "We cannot but express our regret that our own pet national poet should not have selected as the theme of his muse something higher and better than the silly legends of the savage aborigines. His poem does not awaken one sympathetic throb; it does not teach a single truth; and, rendered into prose, Hiawatha would be a mass of the most childish nonsense that ever dropped from human pen. In verse it contains nothing so precious as the golden time which would be lost in the reading of it."

The result of this bit of appreciation was a brief note from Messrs. Ticknor and Fields withdrawing their advertisements from the "Traveller," and asking to have the paper stopped. The "Traveller" responded by printing a copy of the publishers' note, and charging them with trying to influence the press, by making their advertising patronage depend upon favorable opinions of new books. This created a considerable stir and newspapers from coast to coast were soon engaged in a general "Hiawatha" controversy, which included criticisms concerning the sources from which the theme was drawn, and the poet was accused of imitating the "Kalevala" in measure and material. During this petty storm the author remained calm and untroubled, but it is said that Mr. Fields was much annoyed, and one day hurried to Cambridge in a state of great excitement, the morning's mail having brought an unusually large batch of letters containing attacks that seemed to him of a damaging character. Bursting into the poet's study, he exclaimed: "These atrocious libels must be stopped!" Longfellow glanced over the papers, and then said quietly: "By the way, Fields, how is 'Hiawatha' selling?"

"Wonderfully!" replied the excited publisher; "none of your books has ever had such a sale!"

"Then," said the poet calmly, "I think we had better let these people go on advertising it."

Echoes of Longfellow's popularity in England were wafted back in Hawthorne's letters to his publisher written during his consulship, and he wrote Ticknor, in January, 1856:

"It gives me pleasure to hear of the great success of 'Hiawatha.' On this side of the water, too, it is received with greater favor, I think, than any of Longfellow's former works, and has gained him admirers among some who have hitherto stood aloof. Nevertheless, the following lines have been sent me:

Hiawatha! Hiawatha!
Sweet Trochaic milk and water!
Milk and water Mississippi
Flowing o'er a bed of sugar!
Through three hundred Ticknor pages,
With a murmur and a ripple,
Flowing, flowing, ever flowing
Damn the river! damn the poet!

"Everybody seems to be seized with an irresistible impulse to write verses in this new measure. I have received a lampoon on myself (in manuscript) of as much as a hundred 'Hiawatha' lines, some of them very laughable. I would send you a copy, but have already transmitted the verses to Mrs. Hawthorne."

And a few months later Hawthorne wrote to Longfellow: "I have been in all sorts of parties within the last few weeks, and in every single one of them your name was spoken with the highest interest and admiration. Your fame is in its fullest blow; the flower cannot open wider. If there is any bliss at all in literary reputation, you ought to feel it at this moment. I am not quite sure that it is a very enjoyable draught; but if you drink it at all, it is best to take it hot and sweet, and spiced to the utmost. So, do come to England this summer."

"The Courtship of Miles Standish" met with an even greater public response, when it appeared in 1858, three years after "Hiawatha," and on October 7th, Longfellow wrote: "Fields comes out to make a new proposition about 'Miles Standish.' They have printed ten thousand copies, and want to print ten thousand more without delay."

Two days later he made the following note: " 'The Courtship of Miles Standish' published. At noon Ticknor told me he had sold five thousand in Boston, besides the orders from a distance. He had printed ten thousand, and has another ten thousand in the press. Met George Vandenhoff, who reads the poem in public to-night."

And again he wrote, on October 23rd: "Between these two Saturdays 'Miles Standish' has marched steadily on. Another five thousand are in press; in all, an army of twenty-five thousand in one week. Fields tells me that in London ten thousand were sold the first day."

In honor of this success, the poet gave a small dinner to Messrs. Ticknor and Fields, upon the evening of November 6th. Among the guests were Edwin P. Whipple and the Reverend Starr King.

Hawthorne's suggestion that his friend come again to England was one that Longfellow was unable to carry out for some years, but when, in 1868, he made his last trip to Europe, he spent some time in London, where he was the recipient of the highest honors. He was flooded with cards, invitations, and letters; he breakfasted with Gladstone, Sir Henry Holland, and the Duke of Argyll; had a special audience with the Queen at her request; was given the degree of Doctor of Laws at Cambridge, and before crossing to the Continent spent a couple of delightful days with Tennyson. The autumn of 1869 found him at home again, and in writing his publishers on receipt of some of their new publications at Christmas-time he exclaimed:

"A merry Christmas!

"What dusky splendors of song there are in King Alfred's new volume! His 'Holy Grail' and Lowell's 'Cathedral' are enough for a holiday, and make this one notable. With such 'good works' you can go forward to meet the New Year with a conscience void of reproach."

A last fleeting picture of Longfellow is one which presents him standing near a doorway about to take his departure. Beside him is my father, who steps forward prepared to assist him with his overcoat, but as he is about to do so, Longfellow draws back, and says reprovingly: "Never do that. A young man does not need it, and an old man does not want it." A bit of excellent advice which those that heard it never forgot.

In discussing the commercial aspect of poetry it may be of interest to state that for his single poems Longfellow received payments ranging from the sum of one dollar, paid for his college verses in 1825, up to three thousand dollars, paid by Mr. Bonner of the "New York Ledger" for the "Hanging of the Crane," in 1873. Beginning with his early poems, for which he received a couple of dollars, his work steadily increased in monetary value. "The Village Blacksmith" brought him but fifteen dollars in 1841; three years later, he was receiving at least fifty dollars for each poem, and after 1850 he was paid one hundred or one hundred and fifty dollars. The Harpers paid him one thousand dollars for "Kéramos," and also for "Morituri Salutamus." The latter poem was written in 1875, for the fiftieth anniversary of the poet's class at Bowdoin College. At this time thirteen members of the class were living, and of these, twelve were present, upon whose ears the title, "We who are about to die, salute you," must have fallen with impressive solemnity.

A few days before Longfellow sailed for Europe on his last trip abroad, a parting dinner was given him at the home of Mr. Fields. Greene, Holmes, Agassiz, Dana, Lowell, Norton, and Whipple were present, and during the evening Holmes read a poem which he had written, bidding the traveler *bon voyage*, and expressing the admiration and affection which he cherished for his friend. These sentiments were evinced on many occasions, and his response upon the receipt of the "Life of Longfellow," sent him by the publisher, in 1886, four years after the poet's death, voices his lasting appreciation and sincere feeling. Holmes wrote of this work:

"Every page of it has interest for me. . . . It is a record of a very lovely life; one that shed benign influences all around it, whether he was present as a companion or reflected in his books. I am glad that the story was traced by the hand of a brother, and that he was allowed to reveal so much of himself in his own letters and journals. Wherever English is read, and beyond that limit wherever the name of Longfellow is heard, the book will be warmly welcomed."

CHAPTER V

SOME EARLY PICTURES

My early association with authors as household companions convinced me that, although they much resembled other visitors in many ways, they possessed certain characteristics quite their own. As a whole they were less observant of practical details and more intent on mental processes; they needed much prompting and supervision regarding dinner-hours and the keeping of engagements; they did not notice clothes except as an artistic adjunct, nor did they generally exhibit much taste in the selection of their own personal adornment. In this respect I noted that authors might be divided into two classes, those that were not successful enough to wear expensive clothes, and those that were so eminently successful that they wore anything they chose, because it did not matter. (This early classification is doubtless obsolete to-day, when authors are so much more men-of-action, and men-of-the-world, than they were "once upon a time.")

In regard to their attitude toward the table, authors again resolved themselves into two classes, those that had sensitive digestions and could partake only of certain viands, and those that paid but slight attention to what they were consuming, being so much absorbed in conversation and the discussion of pet themes as to be almost wholly unconscious of what they ate. I have seen many choice and dainty dishes wasted upon a literary craftsman for whom they had been carefully prepared, and who partook of them with an indifference that might have been bestowed upon baked beans or oat-meal porridge. Between these two extremes were varying types, as in the field of clothes, where certain writers were marked by excellence of style. In Edmund Clarence Stedman one found the most exacting standard of dress always adhered to, and Thomas Bailey Aldrich belonged in this same category, which formed a striking contrast to that in which "Mark Twain" and Walt Whitman figured preëminently. Aldrich was a gracious and charming visitor, responsive, tactful, and quick to take a cue; with a wit always flashing and instantaneous. I can recall a trifling incident which occurred at the breakfast-table when he was passed a dish of omelette in which the cook had accidentally left a silver fork. As Aldrich came upon the fork in trying to help himself, he announced lightly, before his hostess could offer an apology: "I have enjoyed many delicious omelettes, but not until to-day have I been served with *omelette à la fourchette*."

Elihu Vedder was a powerful personality, whose very presence seemed to shake the household's calm to its foundations. His big frame and commanding voice, as well as his decisive ways, awed all about him to meek submission. He loved to shock the ultra-conventional, and told with glee how he had been oppressed with too much ceremony at the home of Alma Tadema, in London, where he had been a recent guest. Being convinced that Tadema needed a bit of shocking, he said that, on the morning after his arrival, he took great pleasure in crossing the hall to where his host was in the process of preparation for breakfast, and calling out in a loud tone: "Oh, I say, Tadema, where do you keep the scissors you trim your cuffs with?" This seemed to Vedder a beneficial lesson, of the kind calculated to draw his host from the demoralizing path of conventionality which he was treading.

Vedder was one who spoke the truth spontaneously and loudly, and I remember his sweeping humiliation of my aunt, who had mildly suggested that he write something in her autograph album, which contained many famous signatures. "Madam," he thundered, "I never write in autograph books!" After her prompt and crestfallen withdrawal, my sister and I, willing to try our fortunes in the same quest, and impervious to snubs, ran for our modest autograph books, which we thrust upon him; to be rewarded for our impudence by each receiving a decorative signature, beneath a graceful flourish in the form of a palette, executed, no doubt, in order to get rid of us. These we showed to our discomfited aunt with an exultant glee.

Our daring was doubtless inspired by the remembrance of a story which Vedder had recounted of discipline in his own family. He had said that his little daughter was prone to disobey his orders, but, as he told a friend on one occasion, he always *would be obeyed*. The friend remarked admiringly upon his characteristic firmness, which Vedder strove to illustrate. He saw his little daughter in the garden, and called to her to "come." She made no move to do so. He called again, and she paid no attention. After repeated efforts, all equally unavailing, he issued the command: "Well, you stay where you are; I *will be* obeyed." The memory of this capitulation to one of our contemporaries nerved us to follow up our aunt's discomfiture with a victorious attack. We had learned something of the powerful man's vulnerable spots.

The custom of placing shoes outside of doors at night was always one which interested my childish mind. Not having reached a point when I could gauge men by their heads, I focused attention upon their heels. A man's shoes always told one a great deal about the man, and I studied length, breadth, and thickness, as well as quality of make, with the eye of an expert. Every night the shoes of the male portion of our household were carried to the barn, where they were polished by the coachman and brought back in good season to be distributed. I still remember a tragic morning when a distinguished guest, who was leaving at an early hour, to address some special meeting, found that his shoes displayed a dull and dauby surface. Inquiries proved that a new man had polished all the shoes with harness-grease; a dire calamity, which made them persistently retain the beautiful dull surface, desirable for harnesses, but far from satisfactory upon the shoes of a prominent lecturer.

Edwin Lasseter Bynner was so frequent a visitor

at our home as to seem almost a member of the family. His literary gift, which flourished for only a few years, would doubtless have brought him into much greater prominence had he lived longer. As it was, he produced a number of delightful books; "Patty's Perversities"; "Penelope's Suitors"; "The Tritons"; and "The Begum's Daughter"; while his best-known historical novel, "Agnes Surriage," will doubtless remain the classic of Marblehead. This novel owed its origin to the careful historical research which Bynner carried on in the preparation of a chapter for "The Memorial History of Boston," relating to the Provincial period. The facts connected with the romance of Sir Harry Frankland and the Marblehead beauty were included in Bynner's story of the time which was the product of the most careful and painstaking research. At the conclusion of Bynner's work, it was found necessary to curtail his contribution somewhat, and on his expressing regret in this connection, he was asked why he did not embody his work in a novel of Marblehead, thus using the romantic story he had so carefully verified. This suggestion he carried out, and the historical accuracy of the work may be traced to his previous share in the production of "The Memorial History of Boston." (In his poem of "Agnes," Dr. Holmes has also used the story of the Marblehead maid.)

Bynner was always a host in himself; the soul of every company, full of gay stories and able to entertain a roomful. Every dinner at which he was a guest was an assured success, and his great versatility made him a source of never-ending surprise to those that did not know the extent of his talents.

Nora Perry spent many weeks at the home of her publisher; she was a vivid and intense personality, absolutely frank and uncompromising, loyal to her friends, sharp and satiric toward her enemies. She was not personally beautiful, but was very proud of her wealth of reddish-golden hair, which as a child I was privileged to see brushed out, and hanging far below her waist. Golden hair figures in many of her poems, and she dwells in her verses upon abundant locks, invariably including them in her descriptions of feminine charms, while that most popular of her poetic productions, with which she first captured her public, opens with the stanza:

> "Tying her bonnet under her chin
> She tied her raven ringlets in,
> But not alone in that silken snare
> Did she tie her lovely floating hair,
> For tying her bonnet under her chin
> She tied a young man's heart within."

In the field of schoolgirl literature, one in which few writers have made good, Miss Perry's stories have rarely been equaled. To know her was to appreciate her sterling qualities, to realize how hard she worked, and to discover how high an ideal she followed. She used to express emphatically her disapproval of many of her friends who persisted in working in the slums, instead of seeking out those needing help in higher walks of life, where so often people were too proud to acknowledge their needs and

sufferings. She always claimed that we can best help
those nearest us, because we understand them. Miss
Perry was quick to discover talent in young writers,
and frequently suggested to her publisher some clever
literary aspirant. She was a devoted friend to Mrs.
Rose Terry Cooke, a writer of charming verse, and
also of stories of New England life, quite the equal
of those produced by Miss Wilkins; only, Mrs.
Cooke's stories came a bit too soon for the wave of
interest in the theme on which Miss Wilkins rode to
success, and she struggled with ill-health and adversity to the end, realizing very little from her admirable work.

Nora Perry belonged to the literary circle in Providence, Rhode Island, which centered about Sarah
Helen Whitman (once betrothed to Poe), and to
which John Hay brought his early literary enthusiasms. She was one of his warm friends and he sent
her his youthful poems to criticize. After her death
it was my privilege to write a little appreciation of
her, and among the boxes of letters and clippings
which were sent me by Miss Perry's relatives I
found a little packet tied with blue ribbon, containing John Hay's early letters,[1] written after he had left
Brown University and was still clinging to his poetic
aspirations, while trying to adapt himself to an un-
sympathetic environment in the West. These proved
to be almost the only early letters of the writer that
had been preserved, and they were by this lucky
chance rescued from oblivion. In one of these communications, dated March 4, 1860, Hay makes a

[1] See *A Poet in Exile.*

prophecy regarding the life ahead of him, which he believes will be short, and completely uneventful. So striking is the contrast between this and the entry in his journal two weeks before his death, June 14, 1905, that it seems only fitting that the two statements should now be brought together:

Hay wrote in 1860: "It is my duty, and in truth it is my ultimate intention to qualify myself for a Western Lawyer, *et præterea nihil*, 'only that and nothing more.' Along the path of my future life, short tho' it be, my vision runs unchecked. No devious ways. No glimpses of sudden splendor striking athwart. No mysteries. No deep shadows, save those in my own soul, for I expect prosperity, speaking after the manner of men. No intense lights but at the end. So my life lies. A straight path — on both sides quiet labor, at the end, Death and Rest. Yet though I know all this, though I feel that Illinois and Rhode Island are entirely antipathetic — though I am aware that thy people are not my people, nor thy God my God, I cannot shut my friends out of my memory or annihilate the pleasant past."

And forty-five years later, the dying man summed up his career in the words:[1] "I have lived to be old, something I never expected in my youth. . . . I have had success beyond all the dreams of my boyhood. My name is printed in the journals of the world without descriptive qualification, which may, I suppose, be called fame. By mere length of service I shall occupy a modest place in the history of my time. If I were to live several years more I should

[1] See *A Poet in Exile*.

probably add nothing to my existing reputation; while I could not reasonably expect any further enjoyment of life, such as falls to the lot of old men in sound health. I know death is the common lot, and what is universal ought not to be deemed a misfortune; and yet — instead of confronting it with dignity and philosophy, I cling instinctively to life, as eagerly as if I had not had my chance at happiness and gained nearly all the great prizes."

How true to all human experience are these contrasting points of view! In John Hay's letters to his friend in Providence, the college youth expresses indifference to life, and a grim satisfaction in his belief that he would not live long; and at the end, the old man, ill and spent, pens his reluctance to relinquish an existence which holds for him small comfort.

Nora Perry numbered among her intimate friends Whittier, Wendell Phillips (about whom she wrote one of her finest poems), and George William Curtis. Her friendship with Whittier was a particularly warm one, for she possessed his love and confidence to a rare degree. The serious poet exchanged jests with her, told her stories and delighted in the gay, audacious speeches which she only would have dared to venture; and with Wendell Phillips, she enjoyed the same spontaneity of intercourse and frank goodfellowship.

Another visitor, who was at the time producing a long list of novels, was Edgar Fawcett. He was large and impressive, with courtly manners and an air of underlying tragedy about him, produced no doubt by his belief that literary critics were nearly all intent upon slighting, maligning, or persecuting him. Before his death, which occurred in London, in 1904, he had published some twenty novels and several volumes of verse, yet he brooded continually upon the thought that fortune had passed him by, and success mocked at his turbulent muse.

The visit, that I recall with great distinctness, took place at the time when he had completed a poetic drama, which was to make its début in Boston, and in which George Riddle was slated for the leading part. The author of this play had high hopes for its appreciative reception by a Boston audience, and on the opening night sat with the family of his publisher in a stage-box, ready to answer promptly any insistent calls for "author" which might arise.

A few choice literary friends were asked to meet the author at dinner before the opening performance, and I was allowed to be present on this occasion, and was accorded the privilege of painting appropriate dinner-cards to grace the table. What the cards lacked in beauty or artistic merit, they made up in a diversity of humorous inscriptions, chosen from a recent book of Mr. Fawcett's, entitled "Social Silhouettes." From this assortment of clever satires I chose a title for each guest, and as I now look back upon the various selections, I am convinced that they were more clever than polite. These titles included: "The Lady Who Hates to be Forgotten"; "The Young Man Who Imagines"; "An Anglo-Maniac with Brains"; "The Destroyer of Firesides"; "The Young Lady Who Tries too Hard"; and other

equally suggestive titles, of which the least desirable
were meted out to members of my family. However
much these various designations might have offended
the sensibilities of other guests, they pleased the
guest-of-honor, upon whose card were beautifully
inscribed in gold, or copper paint, the words: "The
Gentleman who Succeeds." I recall that this delicate
compliment proved very gratifying to the author,
who told the youthful decorator of dinner-cards to
let him know when next she visited New York; a
dazzling suggestion that filled her with just pride.

The dinner went off satisfactorily, but not as much
could truthfully be said of the ensuing performance
for which the playwright had cherished such great
expectations. The jovial state of mind that characterized the author and his friends in the stage-
boxes at rise of curtain, gradually evaporated as the
evening advanced; it was an evening of increasing
chagrin and disappointment, to be succeeded the
following morning by damning criticisms from the
press, which Fawcett felt as usual was a vicious
enemy lying in wait to slander him.

Had Riddle been a greater actor, or Fawcett a
greater dramatist, the opening night, at least, might
have been less disheartening. But such was not the
case; Riddle was a delightful reader, and Fawcett a
writer of excellent dramatic verse, but theirs was not
a combination calculated to fill a Boston theater
many nights when the play was a gloomy tragedy
without one gleam of lightness to lessen its funereal
atmosphere.

How its creator could have imagined that it might

win a warm reception from the general public is difficult to understand, yet he had written to his publisher a couple of months before with much assurance: "George Riddle opens in a play of mine at the Hollis Street Theater on Easter Monday. I shall drop 'down' to Boston then D. V. . . . I hope Boston is not so hatefully cold and disagreeable just now as New York."

Boston unfortunately proved itself as chilly as the unappreciative Metropolis, and even the friendly atmosphere which emanated from Fawcett's numerous friends, who filled the front seats of the theater upon the opening night, failed to affect the verdict of the house which was quite unmistakable. And it is certain that this performance must ever remain in the minds of those that attended it as a most melancholy experience.

The tragedy had for its theme the story of two devoted brothers who fall in love with the same girl, and on a certain day, while they are visiting a lonely cave, one of them (the girl's favorite) enters the gloomy opening, and suddenly, a great loose boulder rolls from its place and blocks up the cave's mouth! The other brother, allowing his passion for the girl to blot out filial affection, turns away from the fatal spot leaving his rival to his fate, and turning a deaf ear to the resounding cries of "Help! Help! Help!" which echo from the rocky depths.

All further details of the plot have vanished from my memory, but I recall the gaunt and rather stooping figure of George Riddle, in a semi-Greek costume which did not become him, struggling with horrible remorse through several acts, and ever haunted by the dreadful cry: "Help! Help!" Throughout the play these words were constantly reiterated, to torture Riddle and the audience, although, like other ghostly messages, they were unnoted by the other actors on the stage, who went about their gloomy business unconscious of the cry. Hollow and harrowing, the words, "Help! Help!" continued to sound upon the air, while everybody shuddered at visions of the tortured brother trapped to his death by the great boulder.

As the successive cries for "help" continued to ring out, the strain upon the audience became too great to be endured, and all at once that fatal sense of the ridiculous, which is so close to the sublime, assumed control. Alas, for dramatist and actor, when at the sound of those reiterated utterances, "Help! Help!" the house began to smile. The memory of that evening of ghostly gloom and of hysterical and fitful giggles is mingled with a recollection of the sense of relief which followed the final falling of the curtain. I know not if there arose any calls for "author," but if there were any, they must have been too feeble to reach the injured dignity of the grieved dramatist, who saw his Boston audience slip away in ominous silence. The reassuring friends who grouped about him, insisting that the piece was a "remarkable success," could not conceal the harsh and obvious truth; the play was a dead failure! The morning papers finished the crushing blow, and Fawcett turned his back on Boston, thenceforth to him a place teeming with low-brow prejudice.

Alas, for the choice of a motto for this writer's dinner-card! The *gentleman did not succeed*, nor did the drama upon which he had pinned such high hopes.

Fawcett's career was not an enviable one owing to his own temperament; the fault was in himself, or in his stars, who shall say which? At all events, he was at odds with nearly every one, and had a wealth of grievances, while everything seemed to go wrong with him. He possessed something akin to the dramatic and tragic qualities that characterized that other *Edgar*, and like Poe, gloried in his misery in verse, and suffered in amazingly expressive prose.

In dealing with his publishers, he was a voluminous correspondent, and must have often tried their patience by his lengthy discussion of every detail, and his many protests concerning unjust criticisms. One may learn from his letters that Stoddard had for years endeavored to persecute him upon the printed page; that Miss Jeanette Gilder was his arch-enemy, and that a dozen other critics were hounding him from motives of dislike or envy.

The following quotation from a letter written during the publication of a little book of poems, entitled "Song and Story," presents a very enlightening sample of what the poet is apt to look for in the production of a tiny book of verse, which from the start the publisher well knows will be an absolute financial loss to him, not because it is an inferior kind of work, but because time has proved that poetry, barring a few exceptional cases, does not pay for publication. Such little books are patiently accepted as a recognized financial loss, pocketed with the view of binding more closely to the publisher some future novel, or prose production, that is likely to have a wide appeal.

Of his forthcoming volume Fawcett wrote:

"Yours of the 2nd instant received. I hope I shall like one size larger type, but I fear that I shall have to beg you to make it even larger than that. My former book, 'Fantasy and Passion,' never pleased me in that respect. I have the most sincere dislike of books printed in anything but bold, large type, and especially books of poems; and I also have a conviction that this outward feature of poetry has a great effect upon its success. Nor does this dislike seem to me wholly unreasonable, on one account. I think the people who start a book of poems are almost invariably the students, thinkers, readers. And these have an ample percentage of weak (or not wholly strong) eyes. My own sight is good, and yet a sonnet, or lyric, in big type always arrests it quicker than one in fine. To my thinking it gives verse a new robust dignity. I fancy that if I had seen 'Home, Sweet Home,' or even 'Beautiful Snow' printed thus, I should feel for both those maudlin achievements a certain inalienable respect.

"Do you know Rossetti's 'Ballads and Sonnets,' by Roberts Brothers, dated 1881? I have that book on my table now, as I write. Its type seems just the desirable thing. If possible, I wish you would glance at it.

"If silver tarnishes too rapidly, do not let us have it for the cover of 'Song and Story.' What, then do you say to violet linen (plain, glazed linen) and gold?

Better, perhaps, than the design I proposed would be a large golden lute, representing song, flung in the heart of a copse of tall *fleur-de-lys?* What we call flag-flowers here, these representing *Story*, you know, through their royal and historic symbolism. Or do you like better the idea of the lute lying under three or four massive pine-trees in gold? That would suggest, especially, the leading poem of the book, 'Alan Eliot,' where the pine-engirded homestead by the sea is especially dwelt upon. I like the uncut leaves of Maurice Thompson's poems, and the paper of that book greatly pleases me, except that I would like it a little thicker, with a little more body."

Thirty years ago Fawcett was a celebrity, and one of the best-known literary figures in New York, and to the end of his life he remained distinctly a novelist of that city, which he had studied so faithfully to depict, even though he spent his last years in England. His familiarity with the fashionable side of the metropolis provided admirable equipment for his pictures of life among the rich, but he worked conscientiously to familiarize himself with all phases of the city's life. Those that explored the out-of-the-way places often found him studying such localities, following some squalid funeral, strolling through the poorer districts, or at times seated on a bench in Stuyvesant Square with tablet and pencil in hand, a dignified and ponderous figure, pausing now and then to make pictures for the children who flocked about him, unconscious of his social importance, a fact which he could never quite forget.

Among bits of manuscript in his writing I find the

following lines which were penned after a long evening spent with a company of fellow-writers; these he read aloud with intense satisfaction to a friend who dropped in upon him the following day, and aroused him from a prolonged morning nap. After remarking to his visitor: "Those fellows stayed late last night!" he proceeded with delight to read aloud the following tribute to his arch-enemy the critic, whose frailties had no doubt been the subject of the previous evening's debate:

A NEWSPAPER CRITIC

For blood, an adder's gall;
For brain, a gnat's weak hate;
For heart, a pebble small;
For soul, a "whiskey straight."

For conscience, pelf and hire;
For pride, a donkey's tether;
For ink, the gutter's mire;
For pen, a goose's feather.

—E. F.

CHAPTER VI

MEMORIES OF WHITTIER

THE problem of the poet, who was also an abolition-ist, was one of serious moment in Whittier's early days, and it is hard for the present generation to realize the intensity of feeling that was arrayed against the writers who had espoused that cause. Not only were their writings tabooed, but their persons were attacked in public. In 1835 Whittier, in company with George Thompson, was mobbed and pelted with stones and rotten eggs at Concord, New Hampshire; and in 1838 the former was even more violently assailed in Philadelphia, where he was editing an anti-slavery journal, the "Pennsylvania Freeman," which had its office in Pennsylvania Hall. A mob attacked and burned the building, and Whit-tier, in order to save his property, disguised himself with a wig and long white overcoat, and, joining the crowd that was sacking his office, rescued many of his own papers.

That the animosity he had aroused might be sometime visited upon him was long feared by mem-bers of his family, who were cautious about the open-ing of packages sent him. After the close of the Civil War a small but heavy box arrived by express from Chattanooga, and when the cover was removed, an array of iron points appeared, which filled the poet's niece with alarm.

Oak Knoll
Danvers
11th Mo. 20 1883
Dear Friend
By all means
add my name. I
would be very sorry
not to join in welcoming
up the gifted Southern
writer to New England,
where his genius is
fully appreciated.
Truly thine
John G. Whittier

"Don't touch it!" she cried; "it is some dreadful explosive thing these Southerners have sent to kill you!"

It was decided to bury the dangerous machine in the garden; from which premature burial-place it was, however, resurrected after the receipt of a letter from a friend, who stated that he was sending a paper-weight, modeled from Northern and Southern minié-bullets, picked up on the battle-field of Lookout Mountain. Following its disinterment the paper-weight occupied a place of honor upon the poet's desk, and after his death it was given to Henry O. Houghton, who was then publishing his works.

Some idea of the violence of the antagonism which Whittier's early anti-slavery articles awakened may be gleaned from such incidents as the arrest of a physician in Washington for the misdemeanor of lending a copy of his pamphlet, "Justice and Expediency." In 1834 this occurred, and the physician afterwards died from the effects of his incarceration.

Loyalty to his faith, his country, and to his friends was one of Whittier's ruling characteristics, and if, as Spenser has asserted, "thankfulness is the tune of the angels," he was one who deserved a leading part in the angelic chorus, for gratitude was a distinguishing trait with him.

An example of his appreciation is spread out before me in a letter written to the son of his early publisher, forty-three years after the publication of his poems, "Lays of my Home" (issued in 1843). At that time the imprint on the title-page meant much to one whose work as an ardent abolitionist had brought him into popular disfavor, and in recalling this the poet wrote in 1886, in response to an inquiry regarding the future publication of his Biography:

"I have intrusted the care of my Biography to my friend S. T. Pickard, Esq., of Portland, and have requested him to make your house the publishers of the same. I do this because I have a grateful remembrance of the favor done me by the old firm of Ticknor and Fields, in publishing my poems at a time when as an abolitionist my name was 'cast out as evil.' Mr. Pickard will give you assurance that he will faithfully regard my request.[1]

"Yours truly
"JOHN G. WHITTIER."

While touching upon Whittier's appreciation of past favors, it is worth mentioning that Tennyson should be included in the chorus of "thankful" ones, for after forty-seven years he too voiced his gratitude in a communication sent to the son of his early publisher. In this he recalled the fact that the first check (wholly unsolicited) ever paid by an American firm to an English author was received by him in 1842 from the Boston house, which began and maintained the practice of paying for works of writers across seas, although they were entirely unprotected by any international copyright.

Thus it was that after nearly half a century the *Poet Laureate of England*, and the one who has been called the *Poet Laureate of New England*, exhibited the same rare trait.

[1] When the Biography was finally published, Houghton, Mifflin & Co. had succeeded to the publication of Whittier's works.

Forty-three years before the date of the letter quoted above, Whittier had written to his publisher concerning his volume "Lays of my Home": "In regard to the matter of publication I know little or nothing about it. I shall leave it altogether to you, thinking that if the work meets with a ready sale, you will do me justice, as I shall, I am free to confess, like to realize something from it."

And in this hope he was not disappointed, for this proved to be the first book from the sale of which the author received any remuneration, all previous work having been of limited circulation, or put forth for "the cause." Indeed, up to the year 1847, Whittier's labors upon the various papers he had edited had been frequently suspended on account of the delicacy of his health, and from none of them had he received a salary of more than five hundred dollars a year; yet on this amount, supplemented by small sums received for his services as secretary of anti-slavery societies, he had been able to support himself and those dependent upon him.

The memory of those early days was evidently strong within him when he referred to that period, more than forty years later. He did not regard with favor the thought that the story of his life was being called for, but fearing that, in the absence of correct data, a biography full of inaccuracies might be given to the public, he assisted Mr. Pickard by many suggestions, and authorized the collection of material which he used. From the first, he desired if possible to secure the services of some well-known literary friend to father this editorial work, and in the following letter he discusses the matter more fully: "I have not yet decided as to the writer of the biography. Whoever may be fixed upon I shall expect your house to publish it. . . . I must consult Mr. Pickard, Ed. Portland Transcript, and my niece his wife, before deciding upon the biographer, and shall turn over to him what I have of letters and papers for him and his wife to look over and select what seems to them proper to be placed in the hands of the writer.

"As I think I told thee I destroyed the great mass of my letters from correspondents up to 1860. Since then I have saved a large portion of them. My own letters are widely scattered and are generally brief, referring to matters of immediate intent. I shall give a clew to those of different character, which may be of more general interest, and which indicate my views on matters of importance.

"If Professor Thayer is not inclined to accept the proposal (if it is made to him) I am thinking of Mr. Scudder. I should name Mr. Whipple if I thought he would, or could, do the work, but his age and health seem to make it questionable. Otherwise I should not hesitate to ask him, as one of my old acquaintances and friends, and as an exceptionally able writer.

"I had intended to ask James T. Fields to say what is needed to be said of me, in case of his surviving me. He knew everything about me, and could have had access to all that is required for a full biography.

"I must beg thee to keep this whole matter to thyself. I do not wish to see it paraded in the ever-prying newspapers. Be especially careful of giving it any publicity while I am living to see it tossed from paper to paper by unscrupulous hands."

Again Whittier writes in this connection, showing his characteristic loyalty, which had caused him to sacrifice a desired biographer:

"I have placed the matter we have been talking of in the hands of Mr. Pickard. . . . I have hoped that Mr. Howells would do the work with Mr. Pickard's aid, but his engagement with the Harpers makes it impossible. If the Harpers were to be the publishers, they might consent to it. I told him that it must be published by your house, and that seemed to settle the matter so far as Howells is concerned. I am very sorry. Mr. Pickard will have my letters, etc., and look over and arrange them, and unless I find some one who seems more suitable and interested in the thing, he will prepare the biography. He is a good writer, and will do it well, I think, but I shall try to see Mr. Howells, and see if he cannot in some way arrange matters with the Harpers, and be able to give his name and experience to the biography; at any rate, whoever is the author your house will be the publisher."

When the "Atlantic Monthly" started in 1857, it proved of material value to Whittier, who was then struggling to maintain himself, his mother and sister. At this time editors and publishers in general were not hospitable to free thought, and were shy of writers like Whittier, Lowell, Emerson, and Mrs. Stowe, who were determined to speak their minds. Many of Whittier's literary friends had other sources

of income outside of their writing, but he, not accepting calls to the lecture platform, had no resource but
his small salary as corresponding editor of the "National Era" except the occasional sale of a poem and
the royalty on his books, which did not then amount
to much. It was not strange that at this period his
finances were at their lowest ebb and he narrowly
escaped having to mortgage the homestead. However, his contributions to the "Atlantic" brought him
a better return than those to any other periodical had
done, and from this time, the sale of his books steadily
increased, though it was not until 1866, after the
publication of "Snow-Bound," that his straitened
condition was permanently relieved.

To the second number of the "Atlantic," Whittier
contributed "Skipper Ireson's Ride," writing to its
editor, Mr. Lowell: "Will it do? Look at it, and use
the freedom of an old friend towards it and its author.
The incident occurred sometime in the last century.
The refrain is the actual song of the women on this
march. To relish it, one must understand the peculiar tone and dialect of the ancient Marbleheaders."

Mr. Lowell replied that he liked the ballad and
would insert it in the next number, but suggested
that he would like to print it in such a way as to give
more fully the Marblehead dialect; to which the
writer consented. He had first heard the story from
a schoolmate at the Academy in 1828, and for thirty
years the theme had remained in his memory.

Mr. Lowell's great kindness of heart in some instances interfered with his success as an editor. He
would at times accept manuscripts that were not up

to his standard because the writer was poor or very sensitive. Once a schoolgirl from Maine sent him a poem which he thought excellent, all but the final stanza. Rather than reject the verses and disappoint the young author, Lowell rewrote the final verse; and so the poem as it appeared, signed by another's name, contained one stanza by James Russell Lowell.

My uncle, Howard M. Ticknor, who at this period acted as an assistant-editor of the "Atlantic," had many amusing bits to tell about the earliest contributors and some of their peculiarities. Mrs. Stowe's manuscripts required special editing, as she regarded spelling and punctuation as something quite outside the author's field, to be supplied by editor and printer; beside her faults in spelling, her constant repetition of some word which pleased her fancy, and which she would persist in using over and over again, caused the editor to rack his brains for synonyms; to which the writer made no objection when she perceived the changes. Her amiable acceptance of suggestions and emendations contrasted with the attitude of other members of the Beecher family, who were very positive in their methods. After having written repeatedly to Henry Ward Beecher in regard to some contributions for the "Atlantic," and receiving no reply, the assistant-editor chanced to meet the clergyman and charged him jokingly with having used the return postage-stamps for some other purpose than that intended. To this Beecher replied that his "wife captured all the stamps," and as for himself, he was "too lazy in summer, and too busy in winter to answer letters." Following this, the editor proceeded to write him in October, and was rewarded by a prompt reply. It was said of Edward Beecher that he was always in a great hurry, but never failed to be both faithful and punctilious in the discharge of his religious duties, and he was known to rush into the house at family-prayer-time, shouting: "All down on your knees; let us pray; I've just seven minutes to catch the Hartford train!"

A characteristic bit of Whittier's wit and courtesy peeps from the pages of a little autograph book, which bears the signatures of nearly all of the writers who frequented the Old Corner Bookstore, and was originally the property of a bright young woman who was for years identified with the publishing-house. Some of the playful lines inserted there by well-known authors are worthy of quotation, as are the lines of Whittier, who wrote:

> Ah, ladies! you love to levy a tax
> On my poor little paper-parcel of fame,
> Yet strange it seems that among you all
> No one was willing to take my name,
> To write and re-write, till the angels pity her,
> The weariful words,
> > Thine truly,
> > WHITTIER.

John G. Saxe had written:

> My autograph? 'Tis pleasant to reflect,
> (Although the thought may cost a single sigh)
> That which a banker might with scorn reject,
> Should have a value in a lady's eye!

In the round, clear hand of Wendell Phillips, are penned the words:

> Peace if possible, Justice at any rate.

While on one page is inscribed:

My dry old pen, alas! no moisture yields,
And so I only write, yours, J. T. FIELDS.

And on the next page follow the lines:

The force of "natur" will no farther go,
And so I sign myself, yours, H. B. STOWE.

Aldrich's decorative handwriting follows that of Mrs. Stowe, and on Christmas, 1872, he writes:

"God bless us every one!" says Tiny Tim:
I can't do better than re-echo him.
T. B. ALDRICH.

And two years later, Bayard Taylor inscribes just underneath these lines:

I'm quite content, to-day or any day,
To stand below my old friend, T. B. A.

Mrs. A. D. T. Whitney adds on the next leaf:

The best things have been said before;
Why should I make a couplet more?
Or measure quick and clever strokes
With such a crowd of "Real Folks"?

Almost every one of the hundred pages in the little book bears an autograph familiar in the world of letters, and on the final one a bit of masculine humor is succeeded by a playful feminine response:

A woman shall not have the last word,
SAMUEL A. DRAKE.

But to me it has just occurred,
This last line to take,—

writes Lucy Larcom, at the very foot of the final leaf, making it quite impossible for any one to rob her of the feminine prerogative.

Lucy Larcom was a lifelong friend of Whittier's, who first knew her when she was employed in the mills of Lowell, and was beginning her literary career; he assisted and encouraged her, and she soon became the dearest friend of his sister Elizabeth, and a welcome visitor at their home. When that sister passed away, it was Miss Larcom who did the most to comfort the sorrowing brother, by procuring an admirable portrait of her friend; this and the picture of his mother were looked upon by Whittier as his dearest possessions. In 1875 Miss Larcom assisted Whittier in compiling "Songs of Three Centuries," a collection in which it was decided to include no warlike poems, but after some hesitation Whittier concluded to make an exception in favor of Mrs. Howe's "Battle Hymn." They had also jointly edited a collection of poems called, "Child Life," some three years earlier.

The Quaker poet, despite the unusual beauty of his eyes, was color-blind, and liked to amuse his hearers by telling them how on one occasion he went shopping by himself and bought a carpet which he thought to be a quiet combination of browns and grays, but which, on its arrival at Amesbury, horrified his household guardian by its loud pattern of red roses on a field of cabbage-green.

Whittier was a great admirer of Dickens, and when in 1867 the latter came to lecture in this country, the poet wrote to his publishers to secure a seat for him. But after that was done he could not make up his mind to undertake the trip, and wrote asking that the ticket be given to "gladden the heart of some poor wretch who dangled and shivered all in vain in the long queue the other morning." Whittier concluded, "I dreamed last night that I saw him surrounded by a mob of ladies, each with her scissors snipping at his hair, and he seemed in a fair way to be 'shaven and shorn,' like the Priest in 'The House that Jack Built.'"

Some years ago, I discussed with his biographer the subject of Whittier's various friendships with women, and Mr. Pickard asserted: "Whittier was a great admirer of the ladies, and on one or two occasions came very near to the verge of matrimony." Whereupon he recounted various anecdotes connected with those that had charmed the poet's fancy or touched his heart.

In his boyish days Whittier saw a great deal of his second cousin, Mary Emerson Smith, when visiting at his grandmother's home, and she undoubtedly was very dear to him. His poem "Memories" (1841) refers to her, and several lines in it are the same as those in "Moll Pitcher" published nine years earlier. She was also referred to in "My Playmate," and years after, the poet gave this the place of honor in his collected poems. She married Judge Thomas, but their friendship always remained strong and true.

A match with this cousin would have been marrying "out of the Society," and the same objection was potent in the case of Whittier's early sweetheart, Evelina Bray, of Marblehead, who has been often referred to; she was a classmate at the Academy, in 1827, when he was nineteen and she but seventeen.

Both his family and hers were opposed to the match, and Whittier commemorated their last afternoon spent together on the rocks overlooking the harbor, in his poem, "A Sea Dream." After this parting they did not meet for fifty years. Then on one occasion they sat side by side in a Philadelphia church; but Whittier went away without recognizing his early flame, and she was too shy to make herself known to him. She married an Englishman named Downey, and after his death occasionally corresponded with Whittier, who induced her, when she was seventy-three, to come to a reunion of his schoolmates. At this time she gave him a miniature of herself as a girl, which he greatly treasured.

Whittier's biographer recounted the story of another early flame, who had married and gone away to live, but who returned after some years of widowhood. Some correspondence had undoubtedly passed between them, and the poet had made up his mind to ask the lady to marry him. On a certain day he dressed himself in his best and drove off full of joyful expectancy. But on meeting the lady, after years of separation, a wave of disillusionment evidently swept over him. What took place his biographer never knew, but he was aware that Whittier quietly returned from his day's excursion, apparently content to remain in single blessedness.

Undoubtedly the fact that his fancy had from the first strayed outside the Society of Friends had much to do with his remaining single. As he wrote upon one occasion: "The care of an aged mother, and the duty towards a sister in delicate health for many

years, must be my excuse for living the lonely life
that has called out thy pity. It is some poor consolation to think that, after all, it might have been a good
deal worse."

And who shall say that the vision of the widow,
whom he did not marry, might not have flashed into
his mind as he penned those closing words; thus
supplementing his own oft-quoted line:

"The saddest are these, it might have been,"

by the addition of a word, perchance culled from his
own experience, suggesting that there is consolation
in the thought that it "might have been *worse*."

A few years before Mr. Pickard's death, he welcomed to the Whittier home at Amesbury an association of nearly a hundred New England writers,
several of whom could then be numbered among
Whittier's contemporaries. A special car brought
down from Boston this literary delegation, which
was met at the station at Newburyport by such a
unique collection of equipages as has seldom been
rivaled. Pickard had made arrangements with the
local livery-stables for enough vehicles to transport
to Amesbury this literary cavalcade. The order was
a large one, and it had drawn heavily upon the re-
sources of the old town. But still it had been filled,
and when the delegation alighted upon the platform
at Newburyport, drivers innumerable were beckoning
"this way." Drawn up beside the station was every
species of conveyance, from Holmes's "One Hoss
Shay" to the shiny and elegant barouche, in which
rode Julia Ward Howe and Thomas Wentworth

Higginson, leading the way. Behind them came poets, novelists, short-story writers, and the producers of popular juveniles.

Such a procession as slowly and impressively wound through the streets of Newburyport would have delighted the pen of any writer, but those in the parade failed at the time to comprehend the humor of the situation. It was a hot day and the road to Amesbury was deep with dust that rose in unpleasant clouds and filled the noses and the throats of the paraders. Only the first barouche, containing Mrs. Howe and her attendant Colonel, escaped unscathed. As the procession passed through the streets the wondering inhabitants came hurrying out to see the unusual sight, and one young girl was heard to cry out breathlessly: "Oh, ma, come quick and look at them! Every one's written a book!"

After the five-mile drive over the dusty road the guests were glad to reach their destination, where they were welcomed by their host, and by Whittier's favorite cousin, Mrs. Cartland, with whom the poet spent his last days. Her gentle and winning personality seemed to recall that of her kinsman, as she stood in the hallway saying to each one: "Thee is welcome."

In the small front parlor were many things of interest; the desk at which Whittier wrote "Snow-Bound," old books and first editions, and on the walls, bits of framed manuscript, and the last poem penned by Whittier, and dedicated to Dr. Holmes.

The room most closely associated with the poet is the small study in the rear of the house, where he did the greater part of his work, and where he loved to rest quietly gazing out at the little garden at the back of the house. In Whittier's study a group of authors might have been seen that day listening intently while Mrs. Cartland recalled the tender memories of her cousin's last hours. An interesting feature of the afternoon was the presentation to Mrs. Howe of a book which she had sent to Whittier fifty-one years before. Upon a fly-leaf was an inscription in her writing, and throughout the book were many passages underlined by the recipient, who had jotted down various comments upon its pages.

Apart from its minor discomforts the day was truly memorable, for in the home of Whittier were gathered for the last time a group of his old friends who recalled many personal associations with the "Quaker poet." Every one present caught the awakened echoes of those early days when Colonel Higginson was hated as an abolitionist, when Frank Sanborn was championing John Brown, and when Mrs. Howe was writing her "Battle Hymn"; and one could not but feel that Whittier's spirit was there among the others.

When the bright summer afternoon was waning, and it was finally suggested that the poetic atmosphere must be relinquished, a voice was heard announcing that an electric-car would take back to the station any who might prefer this means of transportation. Immediately a hasty rush was made for the friendly electric, and the procession of vehicles was so reduced that the return progress of the head carriage was robbed of its impressive following.

Yet there was punishment in store for the deserters. The special car, well filled with literary passengers, was side-tracked on the way to Newburyport, and so delayed that when the Boston train steamed into the station, it was not in sight. While great consternation prevailed, and appeals to the conductor to "hold the train" filled the air, the delayed car appeared on the horizon, and many heated authors ran panting down the adjacent slope, headed by the club's secretary waving the tickets for the company which were in his possession. The sympathetic conductor was not unmoved by such a spectacle, and waited patiently until the last and stoutest author was "aboard"; then, as the train steamed out of sight, the old town, which had been deeply stirred by this unwonted excitement, resumed its usual tranquillity.

The extraordinary collection of vehicles which that day graced the streets of Amesbury recalled to mind the fact that, from the numerous carriage-makers in that vicinity, Whittier once secured aid for a pet project. Being desirous of raising money for a school for the Freedmen, he suddenly bethought him of a novel plan. He appealed to the different carriage-makers to furnish him with certain portions of a carriage; one gave the wheels, one gave the body, and so on, until all had bestowed some part. Then all the pieces were assembled and the result was sold for two hundred dollars, the exact sum which Whittier wished to raise.

The poet's seventieth birthday was widely heralded despite his protests, and a banquet was given in his honor by the "Atlantic Monthly," to which he was with the greatest difficulty persuaded to come. He finally consented to appear, and on December 17, 1877, the notable dinner took place at the Hotel Brunswick, with Mr. H. O. Houghton presiding. On his right sat Whittier, Emerson, and Longfellow, and on his left, Holmes, Howells, and Warner, and about fifty of the leading writers of the country made up the company.

Mr. Houghton opened the evening's programme with a brief history of the magazine, whose twentieth anniversary was also being celebrated, and when he introduced Whittier all the company rose and cheered; then the guest-of-honor made a few modest remarks, ending with the statement that as his voice was of a "timorous nature and rarely to be heard above the breath, Mr. Longfellow had promised to read a little bit of verse," which he had brought. Longfellow then read the "Response," written for the occasion by Whittier, after which followed poems and speeches by Holmes, Emerson, Stoddard, Howells, Norton, Warner, Higginson, and Story.

Emerson, who was then beginning to fail somewhat, selected Whittier's poem of "Ichabod" to read aloud, which choice filled Longfellow with consternation, as he regarded it as a terrible denunciation of Webster, which was quite out of place at that friendly celebration.

On this occasion, in requesting Longfellow to read his "Response" for him, Whittier said: "I shall be very much obliged to him, and hope that at his ninetieth anniversary some of the younger men will do as much for him" — a hope which was not destined to be fulfilled, as Longfellow passed away ten years before the friend whose poem he read that evening, and it was to Whittier that Aldrich, then editor of the "Atlantic Monthly," turned for a poem of appreciation after Longfellow's death in 1882. To this request Whittier responded:

"It seems as if I could never write again. A feeling of unutterable sorrow and loneliness oppresses me. I must leave to thee,[1] or Dr. Holmes, the poem for the 'Atlantic.' I have written a few verses for the next number of the 'Wide-Awake,' in reference to the celebration of Longfellow's last birthday by the children, and I do not feel that I can do any more at present, if ever. We must close our thinned ranks and stand closer together."

[1] Aldrich's last poem, published in the *Atlantic Monthly*, was written for the Longfellow Centenary.

CHAPTER VII

LEW WALLACE

THE tall, spare figure of General Lew Wallace formed one of the earliest pictures in my youthful collection. Kind, affectionate, and gentle, he was one to win the childish heart immediately, and his possession of a unique gold compass upon his watch-chain added to his attractiveness; by means of this small guide he found his way about the crooked streets of Boston, scorning to be directed by any other method. My early admiration for the compass was evidently not concealed, for, on departure, he told me that when he came again the compass should be mine. Several years passed before he made a second visit, but then, true to his promise, the little token was promptly delivered.

To listen to his discussion of the Civil War with my father, whose military title of "Captain," he always used, was an absorbing pastime, and I can well recall his terrible earnestness in setting forth his true position at the battle of Shiloh, following which he was reprimanded by Grant for a fault not his own. I have to-day the sketch which he drew of the battle-ground and its approach, for the enlightenment of his hearers. Wallace always regarded himself as the victim of unjust criticisms, which were the result of Grant's early misunderstanding of the reason for his failure to bring his forces to the front on the first day

of the battle in question, when reënforcements were
desperately needed. Although later exonerated by
Grant, and his position backed by the testimony of
his brother officers, he still felt that his military
record must continue to suffer from an unwarranted
censure.

The explanation of his tardiness was, in a nutshell,
as follows: His division was in column ready for
action, and halted, waiting for orders at the fork of
two roads, one of which led to the original right of
Grant's line, while the other came out some two miles
farther to the rear. Between the two roads was an
impassable morass and woods, rendering "cutting
across" impossible. After long and impatient waiting
an aid brought General Wallace an order "to join
the right of the line," but he was not told that the
line had been driven back two miles. The General
at once took the road leading to where he knew the
"right" had been that morning, and where he supposed it still was. He marched until overtaken by a
later dispatch, upon receipt of which he realized the
situation, and he was forced to counter-march back
to the fork, and start again upon the other road.
This delay made him too late for the day's work,
and before the exact circumstances were understood, he was censured for "non-arrival with
reënforcements."

General Wallace did not take up the pursuit of
letters until after the close of the Civil War, although
"The Fair God" had been begun in his eighteenth
year; and when only sixteen he had written a novel
entitled "The Man at Arms; a Tale of the Tenth

Century." From his youth he had been particularly interested in Mexico, and the invasion of Cortez had possessed an especial fascination for him. He had written a portion of "The Fair God" when the Mexican War broke out, at which time he laid aside his pen and his law studies, raised a company, and went to the war as a second lieutenant. At the expiration of his term of service, Wallace returned to Indianapolis, resumed the study of law, and won for himself an honorable place in that profession. During the period which intervened before the opening of the Civil War, the writing of "The Fair God" was taken up at odd moments; then came the stirring years of military action, and a long time elapsed before the completion of this book. The manuscript was finally submitted to Messrs. James R. Osgood & Co., in Boston, and was promptly accepted, being highly praised by Mr. Samuel Crocker (founder of the "Literary World"), who supplied a reader's criticism. Mr. Crocker's enthusiastic commendation contrasted strikingly with that earlier received by the author, who, some years before the book was finished, asked permission to read the opening chapters to Dr. White, of Wabash College (a lineal descendant of Peregrine White, of Mayflower fame). Dr. White listened politely to the reading and then took off his spectacles, and gravely advised Wallace to "abandon the field of authorship." "The Fair God" when published proved a distinct success, although it met with nothing like the popular response that greeted its successor "Ben Hur," which followed seven years later; yet many critics still consider that the earlier book possesses superior literary merit.

One of the General's visits to our home was made after the publication of "Ben Hur," and of exceeding interest was his account of his complete change of attitude toward the Bible, which took place during the seven years spent in its preparation. From the standpoint of an unbeliever, his scriptural studies carried him to the most fervent upholding of the Christian faith, and one who has never read his chapter on the Crucifixion has missed one of the most powerful word-pictures in literature.

In the production of his work Wallace followed the most painstaking methods, and not even the decorative handwriting of Eugene Field can equal his in beauty and precision; each punctuation mark is accurately placed, and one looks vainly for a correction or erasure. Wallace began with a first draft upon a slate, followed by penciled copies, then he revised and altered every chapter until final perfection of workmanship had been attained. "Ben Hur" was written over seven times, and was the result of the most conscientious study and research relative to its Oriental background. In view of the erroneous statement, sometimes made, that the writer derived his inspiration for this work during his sojourn as Minister to Constantinople, it is worth while to recall the fact that the book was published before its author ever set foot in Palestine.

After his return from Constantinople, Wallace used to describe his own astonishment experienced when he for the first time explored the Holy Land,

and found how marvelously accurate were his descriptions of the place. He asserted that in traveling to various points, where his imagination had been forced to supply certain details, he was fairly startled at the discovery of the actual existence of what he had thought the creation of his own fancy. He was particularly impressed by the location of an interesting old well, of which his description, purely imaginary, tallied exactly with the existing structure, and he was wont to suggest that he felt he had worked under the guidance of special inspiration.

The first edition of "Ben Hur" was dedicated: "To the Wife of My Youth"; a tender tribute to a most devoted helpmate. This, to the surprise of the author called forth a large number of inquiries from readers, who asked "if the writer had a second wife?" and wanted to know "why he had a pronounced preference for his first one?" In order to clear up this debated point, the later editions bore the supplementary clause, which in the General's decorative hand was inscribed in the early copy which he sent my father. After the words "To the Wife of My Youth," he penned the explanatory clause, "Who Still Abides with me." And this inscription will be found in all later editions of the book.

Wallace was exceedingly interested in the occult, and was convinced that the eyes of the spirit might, in this sphere, perceive far more than we are wont to believe possible, and he recounted many experiences of genuine psychological value.

On the occasion of his last visit to our home, a reception was planned in his honor, to which were bidden a number of Boston writers. The guests were asked at four o'clock, and as the General was apt to need a little prompting in regard to the fulfilment of social obligations, it was a relief when he retired to his room in ample season to prepare his toilet. It has been stated on good authority that the literary mind is not prone to consider the importance of a time schedule, and whether this is a fact or not, it certainly held good on this occasion. Promptly at half-past three, the first of several writers who wished to have a few words with the General before the others came was ushered in.

As my mother was at that moment putting the final touches to her toilet, it was my painful duty to entertain the General's friends until the time of his appearance. A hurried knock upon his door elicited the cheering news that he was not engaged in the process of dressing, but had thrown himself down for a brief nap, and was greatly surprised to learn that it was time to bestir himself. Meanwhile the fact that his room was to be used for the reception of the wraps belonging to a portion of the guests added another complicating touch to the afternoon's arrangements.

The moments crept by very slowly during my labored conversation with those impatient writers, who kept their eyes fixed on the door, awaiting the General's coming; but at last he came, and my burden of conversational responsibility was lifted, while hasty efforts above-stairs brought order out of chaos in the guest's room.

Wallace's book, "The Prince of India," gradually took shape in his thoughts during his stay in Turkey, and before he began it he made a careful study of the history of the Ottoman Empire in accordance with his usual conscientious method. Soon after his arrival in Constantinople he was presented to the Sultan in solemn audience, and at this time made a lasting impression upon the Turkish sovereign.

On the day of the presentation, in August, 1881, the General and his suite were conducted in state to the royal palace where they were to remain until the court carriages came to convey them to His Majesty's favorite residence on the summit of a hill a mile distant. After awaiting the court equipages some time, Wallace remembered that it was an arrogant custom of the Turks to humiliate a foreign envoy by keeping him waiting. Grasping the situation, he informed the imperial chamberlain that he was ready to proceed at once. The astonished official replied that he was sure the carriages were on their way, but still they did not come. Then the American Minister announced decisively: "Please say to His Excellency that I do not wish to wait."

"But they are here!" exclaimed the Turkish representative, at once leading the way into the courtyard, where the carriages were standing, and where they doubtless would have stood much longer, but for the alertness of the new Minister.

When he was finally ushered into the presence of the Sultan, all the Turkish dignitaries withdrew except the Minister of Foreign Affairs and the Grand Master of Ceremonies. These two remained to lead the General and his suite into the splendid audience chamber, where at the end of the room stood His Majesty, wearing no ornament or decoration, and dressed in European costume, save for the crimson fez upon his head. He was Abdul Hamid Khan II, the thirty-fourth saber-girded Sultan, and the twenty-first in descent from Osmun Khan, the founder of his house.

General Wallace advanced to within a few yards of the Sultan, and he and his suite made a deep obeisance to which His Imperial Majesty responded. Then the interview proceeded, the interpreter stating to his imperial master the reason of General Wallace's presence, and in turn translating into English the Sultan's replies. Toward the close of the audience, the General turned suddenly to the interpreter, with the words: "And now say to His Imperial Majesty that as representative of the American people I desire to take His Majesty's hand."

This proposition came like a clap of thunder into the royal circle. For Turks do not shake hands, nor must a Christian, even an accredited envoy, aspire to touch the royal hand. The interpreter failed to repeat the presumptuous words.

"Say it," the General insisted.

The trembling interpreter murmured the sacrilegious statement to the Minister of Foreign Affairs, who in turn remained dumb.

"What is it?" inquired the Sultan, noting that something unusual was occurring. The Foreign Minister, ready to prostrate himself with fear, conveyed the audacious request, and for a moment the Sultan himself paused in perplexity; then gradually a faint smile glimmered upon his countenance; he stepped forward and the two hands met.

This was the beginning of what developed into the heartiest appreciation by the Sultan of the American Ambassador, who had overridden sacred tradition and pressed the sovereign's hand; subsequent interviews strengthened the friendship thus begun, and while he held this post, Wallace exerted a personal influence which enabled him to guard effectually the interests of his countrymen in the Near East.

Letters to my father written during his residence in Constantinople contained vivid descriptions of his diplomatic life in the city which he pronounced "the most beautiful in the world." In that period many unique presents were sent us from the Oriental embassy; sometimes it was a wonderfully embroidered scarf bearing the Sultan's crest; sometimes a beautiful long pipe, studded with beads; or again, it was an ivory cigarette-holder accompanying a huge box of Turkish cigarettes; such tokens as His Majesty delighted to bestow upon the American Minister, who promptly refused the more valuable gifts which were frequently proffered.

In October, 1881, Wallace wrote from the U. S. Legation, enclosing a scene from his play "Commodus," in response to a suggestion that he contribute some original bit to the literary material which his Boston friend was gathering together for a little sheet to be sold for the benefit of the "Soldiers' Home Bazaar," a project then awakening widespread interest:

My dear Captain:

I was delighted to hear from you; and as to your

request to help forward your soldier scheme, I send you a scene taken from the play which I am just finishing. It happened to be the one I was trying to whip in shape to my satisfaction the instant your letter was put into my hand. If unsuitable for the purpose, don't hesitate to put it aside. My wife has concluded, as her aid, to send you a lot of Turkish daily papers — or rather the newspapers of Constantinople published in Greek, Armenian, and Turkish, all of late date. They might, she thinks, sell as curiosities at a Boston Bazaar.

I am pretty hard pushed just now for time, having a lot of official business on hand, some quite delicate, and to see the sights of this old capital. Lord, how far back I'm plunged at every step! Yesterday we rode round the old walls of Byzantium, did the Ambassadors' towers, with inscriptions back as far as 1500, lingered in front of the gate of S. Romanus, where Constantine XI fell in the last great fight with Mahmoud II, made the circuit of the great palace of Belisarius, thence on to the Sweet Waters of Europe. All now in ruins! The old walls and towers make the second thing in the world, sight of which did not disappoint me, the first being Niagara.

I must stop rigmaroling. As to a book; around that gate of S. Romanus, I may find a catastrophe to justify. Quien sabe!

Very truly your friend
LEW WALLACE

The tragedy of "Commodus" begun at this period was not completed until after the writer's return. It was founded upon the story of Maternus, an escaped slave, who at the head of a band of outlaws planned to capture Rome, and who upon his elevation to the throne was betrayed and murdered by his mistress, Marcia. This tragedy was highly praised by Lawrence Barrett, who believed that it would succeed as a great acting play, but other actors and dramatic critics failed to regard it favorably, and it was never produced upon the stage.

In December, 1881, its author wrote of it:

"I was delighted to hear you thought the scene from 'Commodus' would answer the purpose. The play, by the way, is finished. All my spare time since coming here has been put in it. The whole thing had to be recast. Once I intended it for a spectacular piece; but I saw the impossibility of mixing that element with tragedy, and in the reformation the latter feature is alone preserved.

"The character of Commodus drew on me heavily. In him I was required to delineate an Imperial madman, without conscience, and along with much childishness, doing most devilish things to make the world believe he was what he really thought himself — a god.

"On the other hand, the episode of Maternus gave me a great deal of pleasure. I think it a fairly rounded picture of a wretch who, with many noble sentiments, is going to a desperate enterprise oppressed with its uncertainty, yet inspired with the conviction that he is an instrument chosen by the gods. He may be said to be a 'crank,' like Guiteau, only, in view of the daily horrors indulged in by

Commodus, we cannot help giving him sympathy and wishing his errand well-sped.

"Now that the task is done, I am debating, while I take a rest, what to do with it, whether to send the manuscript to a publisher or to Barrett or McCullough. Not long ago you asked me to let you have my next work. You meant the next story, of course. Plays I know are not to a publisher's delight. Yet that beautiful volume, the *très-joli 'Lucile'*! If the tale there given could justify such wealth of illustration, and lavish of tree-calf and gold, why not 'Commodus' in plain clothes? So, my dear Captain, if my courage grows sufficiently, I may forward the manuscript to you for reading. If it is thought well enough, publish it; if not you can send it on the other stage — to Barrett or McCullough, as you think best. For publication, a copy will have to be specially made. In that there is more work. (I'll think about it.)

"By the way, I received the other day the copy of a note written by Sir Charles Dilke to Lord Dufferin, H. B. M. Ambassador here. . . . Verily the praise made me quite proud!"

Before quoting the appreciation to which Wallace refers, it is amusing to recall a previous letter from Sir Charles Dilke, sent to my father on receipt of a complimentary copy of "The Fair God" which had been forwarded to him with the suggestion that it was an unusual piece of work. The unresponsive note which follows was intended to show the American publisher that a wide gulf lay between Sir Charles as a person, and as one associated with the London

"Athenæum." It also illustrates how completely the book won its way in England on its own merits.

MY DEAR SIR,

My grandfather used to refuse all books, but that was in the early days of the "Athenæum," and its character now stands too well-known to make that course necessary. So I accept with pleasure the work for myself, not for the "Athenæum," and I will read it with interest.

Of course I shall not review it, and it may suffer any fate. This I need hardly tell you

Truly yours

CHARLES W. DILKE

The letter from the same writer, sent to Lord Dufferin, after he had read the book, forms an amusing contrast to his previous communication:

November 21, 1880.

MY DEAR LORD DUFFERIN,

I was very sorry to miss General Lew Wallace, and, not having his address in London, not to be able to write him. His "Fair God" is in my humble estimation the best historical novel that ever was written: better than "Romola," better than "Rienzi," better than "Old Mortality."

Yours ever sincerely

CHARLES W. DILKE

This note Lord Dufferin forwarded with the words:

My dear General Wallace,

I have the pleasure of sending you the enclosed copy of a note I have just received from Sir Charles Dilke. I congratulate you most warmly upon the pleasant terms in which it is couched.

Yours sincerely
Dufferin

And the London "Athenæum" wrote in review: "We do not hesitate to say that the 'Fair God' is one of the most powerful historical novels that we have ever read. . . . The scene where in the sunrise Montezuma reads his fate, the dance scene, and the entrance of the Spaniards to the capital, are drawn in a style of which we think few living writers are capable, and the battles are Homeric in their grandeur."

In January, 1885, General Wallace wrote from Constantinople, following the election of President Cleveland:

"I fear you are about ready to strike me from your books as incorrigible in the way of correspondence. Don't do so, I beg. If only you knew how often and how gratefully I think of you, I am sure I would have the benefit of a special exemption. For my part, Captain, I would rather be thought of many times, than written to once in a while, and then dismissed from mind.

"I had fully determined to go to Boston before sailing the last time for Constantinople. The object was solely to spend at least one day with you. Unhappily the Secretary of State took the two days I

had meted out for the visit. Is n't it possible for me
to prevail upon you to take the will for the deed?

"The election! Heaven help us, Captain! I feared
the result from the beginning. We had so many
quarrels amongst ourselves! Blaine is unquestion-
ably our greatest man; but it is a law that he who
takes vengeance must look for vengeance; and of
that he fell. And where are we who fought in the
great war? Each one of us has a little bunch of
laurels; let us not look at them again. They died
that cold November day. Another four years and
they will be dust. A little further on, and we too
will be dust. Then history, which is as the hand that
writes what it pleases. I believe in God, not history.

"But to return one moment — I have been sick,
very sick, bed-fast, then room-fast for weeks. Your
last letter was given me while I was in bed. The little
strength left me had to go to my wife and to business.
I am better now, and beginning to feel like my old self.

"You have a MS. of mine in your hand. Don't
do anything with it. When I get back to America,
I will call for it. I have written it anew; and put it
through so many changes you would not recognize
it. The Harpers have offered to publish it; but I
am afraid. In fact I grow cowardly in the matter of
publication as I grow older; and as my confidence
oozes out, I become fastidious, in so much that everything I write turns odious under my eyes. Did you
ever read my 'Battle of Donaldson' in the December
'Century?' I was under the whip, and dictated it
between speeches, for the campaign was in its hottest.
I have not seen it since publication.

"You speak very kindly of my suggestion of something of an historical or descriptive nature about the East, such as I could easily do, and ask if I would be willing to consider and perhaps take hold of it for you. My dear Captain, I would do a great deal for *you*. Maybe I cannot; wherefore I can only say, send me the suggestion, and let me look at it. I can't let the novel go entirely; yet it may not be a bad thing to mix it some. . . ."

When the coming-in of the Cleveland Administration made a new appointment probable, the Sultan anxiously inquired if it were true that General Wallace would now resign his post?

Upon his replying that such would be the case, he urged him to leave the service of his country and to take office under him, declaring that he would make him either ambassador to London, or Paris. It was with great difficulty that the General declined these urgent offers without hurting the feelings of his imperial friend.

In return for the Sultan's great kindness, General Wallace wished to leave with him some parting gift, and after discovering that His Majesty would prize a fine dog, he spent four days in London inspecting countless varieties. This city was famed as the finest dog-market in the world, and he was soon in touch with the well-known dealers who brought to the Langham Hotel numberless specimens, ranging from tiny King Charles spaniels to huge boar-hounds. Their prices ran as high as three thousand dollars, which discovery filled the would-be purchaser with consternation, for while he wished to get nothing but the best for his royal friend, there was a limit to his spending capacity.

Yet the dog he sought must answer certain requirements. He was to be both the friend and body-guard of His Imperial Majesty. He must be strong, faithful, good-natured, and courageous. The General's first choice was a St. Bernard, but he found that this species would not do for the warm climate of Constantinople. He next thought of a boar-hound, such as Bismarck had for a companion, but when he looked one in the face he shrank away; moreover, he felt sure that the Sultan would be afraid of this variety; then he examined stag-hounds, but they did not suit; and finally the choice fell on an English mastiff. The one brought him was truly magnificent, having taken first prize in the United Kingdom, but alas! the price was twenty-five hundred dollars, and the General could not consider it. Then the dealer suggested that one of the mastiff's sons, aged eight months, might be secured for a less exorbitant sum. The puppy was brought and the bargain closed.

In writing to his son in America at this time, the General described his purchase:

"A finer dog I never saw. He has a head like a lion's, a body to correspond, is quite thirty-six inches high already, and measures, from point of tail to muzzle, over six feet. His color is exactly that of a lioness. His face below the eyes is as black as ink, so is his mouth.

"A crowd gathered in the portico of the hotel to see him. One man climbed to a window on the outside and looked in, suggesting a burglar or thief.

The dog saw his head; his eyes reddened; all the hair on his back stood up straight, and I never heard a growl so *basso profundo*. It was a fine exhibition of nature. I took him at once, paid the money, and sent him express by sea to Constantinople.

"He came safely a few days after I landed, and was taken immediately to the Sultan, who had already dispatched several messengers to ask about him. He is in clover, and his master is delighted with 'Victorio.' When Mehymet, the *cavas*, took the dog to the palace, every one in the reception-room gave a glance, and then ran. 'It is a lion!' they said. At last accounts he was playing with the little princess, and, it is said, the Sultan is getting acquainted with him.

"You think the price a large one to give for a dog; and so it is. It would buy an excellent horse at home. But it was to be a present; I remembered the beautiful order offered me — the Arab horses of which the law forbids my acceptance — the jewels I may not receive. Better to forget His Imperial Majesty has asked for a dog than to bring him a second-rate animal."[1]

Just before General Wallace's departure from Constantinople the Sultan sent his parting compliments, and the Imperial Decoration of the Medjiedie, founded by the Sultan Abdul Medjid in 1852. It has five classes differing in size and value, the design in each being a silver sun of seven triple rays, with the device of the crescent and the star alternating with the rays. On a circle of red enamel in the center

[1] See Lew Wallace's *Autobiography*.

of the decoration is the legend in Turkish, whose significance is "Zeal, Honor, and Loyalty." The decoration was of the First Class, and with it was a purple velvet case which sprang open at a touch and displayed a cigarette-box about as large as a lady's card-case. This was made of pure gold and the lid was set with twenty diamonds, and in the center were the Sultan's initials, "S. H.," set in smaller diamonds.

Wallace's farewell interview was a memorable one. The Sultan shook hands with him, and after he had finished delivering his letter of recall, replied that he would accept this letter unceremoniously, to make him understand that he was to His Majesty far more than a Minister, and that since he had come to the throne, no foreigner had so won his friendship. He concluded that it was hard to part with him, and that he deeply regretted that the General would not accept his offer and remain in his service. He realized, however, that he preferred to live in his own country. Then he bade him be seated, and remarking that now that he was out of office he could accept a decoration previously refused by him, bestowed this honor upon him.

When twenty years later General Wallace lay in his casket, it was draped with the flag presented him, at the beginning of the Civil War, by his towns-women; beside him was the last sheet he had penned for his "Autobiography," and on his breast was pinned the decoration bestowed by the Sultan of Turkey. Thus the symbols of his military, literary, and diplomatic services offered a mute reminder of his manifold attributes and achievements.

CHAPTER VIII

BELLAMY AND "LOOKING BACKWARD"

I KNEW Edward Bellamy only by his picture, and by his erratic handwriting which was hard to decipher; yet, from the time of the appearance of "Looking Backward," he seemed a veritable household friend, so keen was the interest that this work evoked and so exhaustively was it discussed on every side. Had its creator lived beyond the age of forty-eight he might perhaps have produced another work as notable, although it is seldom that an author scores two such successes.

At the time of the publication of its predecessor, "Miss Ludington's Sister," my father was keenly interested in Bellamy's work, feeling sure that he possessed great imagination and originality. The latter quality is one which, while always theoretically in demand, finds itself scantily appreciated whenever it appears. Especially is the publisher's reader prone to distrust anything new and not in line with an established precedent.

That Bellamy's "Looking Backward" called forth the helpful suggestions of the "reader," who would gladly have sharpened the writer's point of view, is evident from the following communication, penned after the acceptance of the book, at which time there had been some talk of having it appear anonymously.

In October, 1887, Bellamy wrote:

"Yours at hand proposing to publish this new book. . . .

"If you tackled it, how soon could you bring it out? I am particularly desirous that it should see the light as quickly as possible. Now is the accepted time, it appears to me, for publications touching on social and industrial questions, to obtain a hearing. As to the anonymity business, I don't care about that. I think the book had better bear the author's name. The only reason wherefore I suggested anything else was that the fiction underlying the plot is rather given away by the bold confession of a nineteenth-century authority. But probably the public will not even notice so fine a point as that.

"As to the criticisms of your reader, the first point he makes is that on awakening from his trance of a century, to find himself surrounded by the marvels of the twentieth century, instead of being carried away by his surprise and curiosity, as I have represented him, the hero ought to be primarily and chiefly impressed by painful recollections of the past life, from which he finds himself so far removed. I had carefully considered this very point and am confident that I am right psychologically and that your reader, begging his pardon, is wrong.

"I believe I could convince him of it if I had a chance at him. As to the other points, that I ought to make more of the differences of speech and dress between this and the twentieth century, I see no reason, as to speech, to suppose a century will see differences developed much greater than those between the speech of Washington's contemporaries and ourselves; that is, none at all as regards the written speech, barring a few trifling mannerisms, while as to the colloquial usage, we have no means of judging.

"I admit, however, that if we are to suppose the present tendency to slovenly script and slangy conversation progresses indefinitely, I am in error not to represent our descendants as having abandoned all attempts at speech and wholly dependent on the sign language. Concerning the dress of the twentieth-century people, one guess is as good as another as to how it might differ from ours.

"It is only because I believe that as to their social and industrial usages, one guess may not be quite as good as another, that I have ventured to write about them at all.

"Excuse me for boring you with so many words concerning a book in which your interest, though kindly, can scarcely be as great as the author's. As I asked you at the outset, when can you bring the book out if you undertake it, and is it of a length, do you think, suitable to make a $1.50 publication of it?

> "Yours truly
> > "Edward Bellamy"

After reading the author's dismissal of the objections of the publisher's reader, it is of interest to turn to the opening pages of "Looking Backward," where in a footnote, Bellamy has taken pains to reply to each of the above criticisms; perhaps deciding, upon further reflection, that the average publisher's reader might also represent the standpoint of the average novel-reader. At all events, after describing the awakening of his hero, in the Boston of the year 2000, and picturing him, not at first overwhelmed by the loss of all previous associations, but alert and "in a state of feverish elation," the writer adds in his footnote:

"In accounting for this state of mind it must be remembered that except for the topic of our conversations there was in my surroundings next to nothing to suggest what had befallen me. Within a block of my old home in the old Boston, I could have found social circles vastly more foreign to me. The speech of the Bostonians of the twentieth century differs even less from that of their cultured ancestors of the nineteenth than did that of the latter from the language of Washington and Franklin, while the difference between the style of dress and furniture of the two epochs are not more marked than I have known fashion to make them in the time of one generation."

Thus did the criticism of the publisher's reader register upon the final copy.

That this book, which had been woven out of its writer's sincere desire to hasten the coming of some such industrial Utopia as he described, was bound to make an impression, Bellamy was firmly convinced, although it is doubtful if he dreamed of anything like the widespread interest which it called forth. In writing to his publisher at Christmas-time, some weeks after the previous communication, he said:

"The book 'Looking Backward' is now done so far as proof-reading is concerned. The printing has proceeded in a very leisurely way, but so long as the book could not be got out before the ruck of Christmas publications, it was doubtless best to postpone it to January, and consequently the delay has not mattered. . . .

"I am not in the main a very favorable critic of my own work, but in reading this book in proof I have been strengthened in the conviction that if pushed with the vigor which no doubt you will use, it is calculated to make an impression."

That Bellamy did not like being boomed, despite this suggestion, is evident from subsequent communications, one of which is quoted below, revealing his extreme reluctance to have his picture used for advertising purposes:

DEAR MR. TICKNOR:

I assure you that nothing but my great desire to spread this book and the ideas it suggests, induces me to submit to being boomed in any way except through, and by, the book itself. Boom me mighty gently, and as to the photograph, please let me know what you intend, if anything.

Very respectfully yours, but a little shy on this booming, I am

EDWARD BELLAMY

Just ten years from the time this note was written,

Bellamy passed away at his home in Chicopee Falls, Massachusetts. He had published a volume entitled "Equality," the year before his death, but had not in any intervening work approached the popularity evoked by "Looking Backward." This, after thirty years, is still in demand; over half a million copies of it have been sold in America, and it has been translated into several foreign languages.

When Bellamy's creation of an ideal state was criticized, on the score that he did not describe the steps by which it was attained, he replied:

"If you want to induce a bachelor to enter matrimony, you don't begin by giving him a manual of courtship and wedding etiquette; you just show him the girl and let him fall in love with her, and after that he will find a way, or make one."

Mark Twain was from the outset particularly fascinated by Bellamy's work and his industrial scheme; he induced the writer to make him a visit, and discussed with enthusiasm the labor problem, which always deeply interested him.

Bellamy had no desire for his own fame or aggrandizement, but he was all-absorbed in his vision of social reorganization. He believed, heart and soul, in the nationalization of industry, a theory which he exploited in "Looking Backward," and continued to develop in "Equality," and also by strenuous personal endeavor. In May, 1889, he spoke in Tremont Temple, Boston, on "Plutocracy or Nationalism," expressing his belief that one, or the other, must be the choice of the American people at the end of ten years' time.

And now, at the end of thirty years, with the vision of Russia's tragedy on the horizon, one may question if Bellamy's dream is any nearer realization than ever before. He has been called a prophet, and to a most surprising degree his seeming wild imaginings have, one by one, been materialized. His telephonic connection with speakers and concert-halls is to-day among our latest acquisitions; and who shall say that his "association of nations" is not almost an accomplished fact? He says of the European countries:

"The peaceful relations of these nations are assured by a loose form of federal union of world-wide extent. An international council regulates the mutual intercourse and commerce of the members of the union, and their joint policy toward the more backward races, which are gradually being educated up to civilized institutions. Complete autonomy within its own limits is enjoyed by every nation."

Bellamy had first come to be deeply impressed with the hopeless social conditions prevailing, when on one occasion he looked at his own children and reflected that he could not place them beyond the chance of want by industry, or forecast, or providence, and this he realized was true of all. He practically wore himself out thinking of and working for his solution of this problem. And he believed that some of his contemporaries would live to see his dream come true.

One of the most suggestive passages in "Looking Backward" is that which deals with the literature of the new era. When the newly awakened hero turns

to a novel, by a writer of the new epoch, he is struck
by the discovery that it offers no background of
poverty or ignorance, and he asserts:

"What most impressed me was not so much what
was in the book, as what was left out of it. The
story-writers of my day would have deemed the
making of bricks without straw a light task compared
with the construction of a romance from which
should be excluded all effects drawn from the con-
trasts of wealth and poverty, education and ignorance, coarseness and refinement, high and low, all
motives drawn from social pride and ambition, the
desire of being richer, or the fear of being poorer,
together with sordid anxieties of any sort for one's
self or others; a romance in which there should,
indeed, be love . . . but love unfretted by artificial
barriers created by differences of station or possession, owning no other law but that of the heart."

In the chapter where he deals with the attitude of
his new world toward the rising generation, he
propounds the thought nearest his own heart; that
they place the responsibility to posterity above all
else, living up to the principle expressed in his words:

"Over the unborn our power is that of God, and
our responsibility like His toward us. As we acquit
ourselves toward them, so let Him deal with us."

Howells has called attention to the fact that
Bellamy in his work kept always to the study of the
small-town people, thus representing the real American average (a tendency prevailing in recent fiction).
Howells asserts: "We are *village-people* far more than
we are *country-people*, or *city-people;* this average

whose intelligence forms the prosperity of our literature, and whose virtue forms the strength of our
nation, is the environment which Bellamy rarely
travels out of, even in his airiest romance. It is by
far the widest field in American fiction." And he
concludes: "I am sure that one cannot acquaint one's
self with his merely artistic work, and not be sensible
that in Edward Bellamy, we were rich in a romantic
imagination surpassed only by that of Hawthorne."

And in connection with this thought, it is worth
while to recall the fact that the first story of "Main
Street" was written by Nathaniel Hawthorne, for
whom this theme seemed to possess a special fascination; he saw this artery of the town not merely as it
was, but in its whole historical significance:

"In my daily walks along the principal street of
my native town, it has often occurred to me, that, if
its growth from infancy upward, and the vicissitudes
of characteristic scenes that have passed along its
thoroughfare during more than two centuries of its
existence could be presented to the eye in a shifting
panorama, it would be an exceedingly effective manner of illustrating the march of time."

After presenting such a procession winding down
Main Street, Hawthorne still feels that the story of
this thoroughfare is incomplete; he has looked *back;*
he should also like to look ahead, and he concludes:
"I should have given the crank one other turn, and
have brought out the future, showing you who shall
walk the Main Street to-morrow, and perchance
whose funeral shall pass through it. . . . The scenes
to come were far better than the past."

And it is surely a coincidence worth noting that it was Bellamy (who, Howells felt, more closely than any other, resembled in imagination the "Wizard of Concord") who took up the theme and turned his magic lantern upon the Main Street of the years "to come."

CHAPTER IX

LAFCADIO HEARN

As I open Lafcadio Hearn's first book, "Stray Leaves from Strange Literature," several closely penned letters, in purple ink, fall out from between the pages, recalling the story of the early struggles of this author to obtain a hearing for his exquisite "gems of literature." At the time of the publication of this volume, the writer was endeavoring to awaken some public appreciation of artistic translations; he urged that only an artist and an able man-of-letters could hope to reproduce the spirit and the form of foreign masterpieces, and yet few editors, or publishers, could be made to realize this fact, or its importance in the book world.

Hearn was filled with resentment at the thought that there was in America no magazine that might give the public worthy renderings of the masterpieces from other literatures, so many of which were hidden from sight. And in writing to his publisher while "Stray Leaves" was going to press, he broached this suggestion, and was surprised to find that it evoked a sympathetic response. In consequence of this, he wrote on June 25, 1884, from New Orleans:

"Your very kind letter took me by surprise. My observation about the Magazines was induced chiefly by memory of the fact that your firm had founded the two leading periodicals of this country, and the hope that a third might some day make its appearance.

"I should be very glad to obtain a hearing; but I have reason to fear that the work I offer might prove unsuitable. In the old days the 'Atlantic' used to publish delightful exotic papers such as those matchless sketches of Indian life, and those singular contributions about South American dictators and gauchos. I was in hopes that I might be able to contribute something in the same strong tone of color on Oriental subjects to some leading magazine; but the editorial policy now appears to exclude papers not of a popular character, or of *immediate* interest.

"I tried successively, 'Harper's,' the 'Century,' and finally the awful 'Atlantic,' with a paper on the 'First Muezzin,' and received only a compliment in each case on the character of the contribution, which might, or might not, have been purely formal. Not to weary you, however, with an account of my efforts, I will only state that in wishing to contribute to some magazine I desire only to follow up one artistic purpose, the popularization of the Odd and Curious and Unfamiliar. The lesser magazines have requested me to write on popular Southern topics; but I have never done so, as I wish to make each article I write one chapter of some future volume. The Legends of the Saints of Islam, the Traditions of the Poets of the Desert, the Stories of Monteyemin or the Love-martyrs of Arabia, and the very peculiar Folk-lore of the Sahara tribes — are subjects almost unrepresented in English popular reading; and I would like to obtain publicity for my studies of them.

"However, all this is perhaps premature. I would not have presumed to write about it but for your kind inquiry. If you should find the 'Stray Leaves' so well received as to justify any efforts made in my behalf, I assure you that I will do what I can to prove myself grateful. In the interim, I am quite content to await the result of our 'experiment.'"

While busied with his translations for "Stray Leaves," he wrote in reference to this same subject:

"It is unfortunately true that the translators who work for English publishers are far more competent than those who do similar work in the United States; forasmuch as trans-Atlantic firms are glad to print cheap popular translations, while only inferior American firms care to undertake them. Another obstacle to good translations in the United States is that none of the great literary periodicals will devote space to them. The English and French magazines and reviews are less conservative, and some very wonderful translations have been published by them. Artistic translations might be admirably developed in this country by the establishment of a new magazine policy."

Hearn was remarkably gifted as a linguist, no doubt because of his cosmopolitan inheritance, and the acquisition of a foreign tongue seemed but child's play to him. He was the first to render Pierre Loti's works into English, and during his stay in New Orleans he became greatly interested in the Creole life and dialect. As a result of this study he issued his second little book entitled, "Gombo Zhebes," a compilation of quaint sayings and proverbs in six different Creole dialects, translated into French and English, with notes.

The early part of Hearn's stay in New Orleans was marked by great discouragement and privation, and he hardly knew which way to direct his uncertain course. At this time he wrote to one of his few friends that he was "halfway down to Hell"; that he could carry on no kind of business, could keep no situation for any length of time, could start nothing without getting into trouble; and he concluded: "My heart always feels like a bird fluttering impatiently for the migrating season. I think I could be quite happy if I were a swallow and could have a summer nest in the ear of an Egyptian Colossus or a broken capital of the Parthenon." During these direful days it is said that he at one time became the proprietor of a five-cent eating-house; then the tide turned with the publication of his beautiful translations of Gautier, which appeared in the New Orleans "Times-Democrat," and then followed the publication of his first book, "Stray Leaves."

During Hearn's residence in New Orleans, and while he was endeavoring to win appreciation for his unique translations, he made the acquaintance of Joel Chandler Harris, who, with the keen perception of genius for its own, at once was deeply impressed by the other's work, concerning which he wrote:

"There is in New Orleans a man of letters who has already made his mark, Mr. Lafcadio Hearn, who has managed to translate the body and soul of some

of Théophile Gautier's writing into English. Indeed
I am inclined to think that Mr. Hearn has imparted
to his translations a sensitiveness, a delicacy, a
spiritual essence not to be found in the originals. A
ten minutes' talk with Mr. Hearn is among my most
vivid recollections of a brief stay in New Orleans.
He struck me as a man capable of putting versatility
to new uses. He is a specialist in almost every branch
of information. I hope to hear that he is writing a
book which shall be a translation of the mysteries of
his own mind and imagination."

In his struggle for a livelihood, Hearn was handi-
capped by several things. He had no knowledge of
practical affairs, his health was not particularly
robust, he was not personally prepossessing, nor
were his manners such as to ingratiate him with the
majority of people. Yet it is difficult to find among
modern writers another figure as unique and picturesque, and his family history was not less romantic
than his own.

He was the son of an Irish father and a Greek
mother, the former a surgeon in the English army
who married a beautiful maiden in one of the Ionian
Islands, where he chanced to be stationed. During
the wooing of his bride, the gallant young Irishman
was one night attacked by a jealous rival, who
wounded him severely so that for days Dr. Hearn
hung between life and death. Upon recovery he
married the Greek maiden, and Lafcadio was the
younger of the two sons born of this union; his name
being derived from Leucadia, the town where he
first drew breath in 1850.

Never had an author a more cosmopolitan career. His childhood and boyhood were passed in Wales, Ireland, England, and France. Then at the age of nineteen, he was sent to America to make his own way. His relatives had early intended that he should enter the priesthood, but he succeeded in convincing them that the Church was not his proper sphere.

From the East, where his occupation had been proof-reading, he drifted to Cincinnati, and there as a reporter took his first lessons in journalism. While in this locality he haunted the river-front, sitting for hours at a time absorbed in watching the negroes, and listening to snatches of their songs as they unloaded the river merchandise.

Finding the climate of Cincinnati too severe for his health, Hearn removed to New Orleans, where he remained for three years after the publication of "Stray Leaves," on which he expended most painstaking workmanship and which he felt had launched him upon a sea of literary achievement. During its proof-correction he wrote to his publisher:

"By the time you receive this I shall have sent on the last proofs, excepting perhaps a few revises I expect to glance over. I have done what I could to redeem the little book from such weaknesses as are incident to journalistic labor generally, and to improve the text wherever it could be done without causing trouble or vexatious delay. Some little changes I made will, I fancy, please you. The volume will be quite pretty typographically; and I trust you will find its contents worthy of the workmanship. . . .

"I feel more confident than before that the little

book will have a good sale. It was at first my intention to include Arabic, Chinese, and Malayan legends or fairy tales, but I found the first subject alone so rich and curious that I determined to save the material for a more serious volume; while a separate work could be devoted to the Malay and Indo-Chinese curiosities of literature. In the course of two years, if our little volume creates the interest I hope it will, perhaps I shall have something much more extraordinary to show you."

Hearn asserted that this little work was the result of his desire to share with the public his own delights in connection with strange and beautiful bits of literature, and that he hoped his popularization of such fragments would stimulate others to produce something still worthier in this field. This exalted hope may or may not have found its realization among subsequent aspiring translators, but the immediate result of Hearn's publication was to provoke a tendency on the part of other writers to steal his thunder and profit by his painstaking research and dainty fancies. Hearn was perhaps too keenly on the alert to discover such a tendency, but he promptly detected what he thought an infringement on his work, in a poem by Mr. Stoddard. And in a letter written November 25, 1884, he protests:

"In the December number of the 'Harper's Magazine,' I observe a poem by Stoddard, entitled 'The Judgment of Solomon' which is neither more nor less than an almost literal reproduction of the story in 'Stray Leaves' entitled 'Boutimar the Dove.' No credit whatever is given; yet all the similes, the de-

scriptions, the idealism are wholly mine. A glance at
Eastwick's 'Anvari Soheïli,' or at Semelet's French
translation from the Persian (page 144 in 'Notes
to Gulistan') would convince anybody that Mr.
Stoddard drew no inspiration from those sources, nor
from the original text. The poem, therefore, seems
to me a sort of infringement of copyright, which
might be pardonable were credit given, but inexcus-
able when no allusion whatever is made to the original prose of mine which inspired it. There are *no
descriptions* in the Oriental; and the similes I used
are nearly all borrowed from other sources than the
Persian, which was too extravagant in style to use."

What answer Mr. Stoddard made to this com-
plaint, which must have reached him, cannot now
be chronicled.

In 1887 Hearn's *wanderlust*, which was ever drawing him on in search of some ideal environment,
started him once more upon his quest and he took
flight to the West Indies. For two years he remained
at Martinique, obtaining there needed rest and re-
cuperation, and writing meanwhile a series of
sketches. Then, in 1890, he found himself at last in
the country of his dreams. Japan with its artistic
setting appealed to him as nothing else had done.
He found himself at home among these polite, sensitive, contented people. His line of thought responded
to their philosophy; their customs charmed him;
he learned their language, and his imagination
reveled in their fantastic folk-lore.

He had gone to Japan under contract with a New
York publishing house, accompanied by Mr. Weldon,

who was to illustrate the articles which Hearn was to produce. Hardly had the first article been written, however, when Hearn revolted at some stipulations of the publishers, and in a burst of indignation threw the contract to the winds and vanished. Soon after this he accepted the position of teacher of English in a west-coast town and retired completely from public cognizance. He lived among the Japanese, wore their garb, ate their food, and studied their language with the same faithfulness that he had previously shown in his study of other languages; and eventually he married a Japanese woman. In 1896 he was appointed to the chair of English Literature at the Imperial University of Tokio, and one learns best from the lips of appreciative Japanese scholars how thoroughly he had absorbed the spirit of Japan, its customs and literature. Subsequently he became a naturalized Japanese subject, under the name of Yakuma Koizumi, and avoided all intercourse with visitors who came to Japan, his friendly association with Edward H. House and Professor Fenollosa proving almost the only exceptions to this rule.

For a while Hearn occasionally joined the intellectual circle that met at the home of Mr. House, but after a little he withdrew even from this social intercourse, and, when questioned, explained that he enjoyed himself too much to come any more. "I get my mind off of my own work and my own life so much that I am unable to get to work again. I am discontented. And I must work now. I must write and publish what I can, for the sake of my boy."

Hearn's death occurred in October, 1904, when he was but fifty-three years old; and according to his desire, he was buried from an old Buddhist temple. His funeral procession, which wound through the streets of Tokio, was headed by bearers of white lanterns, wreaths, and great bouquets, then followed men carrying long poles from which hung streamers, and boys with little cages containing birds that were released on his grave. Following these Buddhist emblems came the portable hearse carried by six men in blue-and-white, and behind, on foot, followed the chief mourners including Hearn's older son; then in rickshas came his Japanese wife and his daughter, followed by priests carrying food for the dead, while professors and students from the University of Tokio formed the end of the procession, which wound its way to an old temple where, with chants and tinkling of a bell and the burning of incense, the ceremonies were completed. It was such a scene as Hearn himself had often described, and in which he delighted. On the day following these ceremonies his body was taken to the Zashegaya Temple, where the final cremation rites were performed and where his ashes are interred.

CHAPTER X

MARK TWAIN'S "LIFE ON THE MISSISSIPPI"

MARK TWAIN was from my earliest days a favorite in my gallery of authors. Although I seldom saw him, he was so closely identified with what he wrote that he seemed always peering out between his stories, laughing behind the "jumping frog," and casting merry glances over the shoulder of the man who "put up lightning rods." It was an epoch in my juvenile reading when I was privileged to peruse the manuscript of the "Prince and the Pauper," which was given to us little folks to read, without the writer's name affixed. We were instructed to "guess the author," and it must stand a testimony to our Yankee heritage that we guessed right.

Among this author's various books, perhaps none entered the field of letters after so many trials and tribulations as did the "Life on the Mississippi," which was many years in the making. Although its opening chapters appeared in the "Atlantic Monthly" in 1874, seven years elapsed before an anxious publisher secured its final pages, and it was not issued in book form until 1883.

This work owed its original inspiration to an amusing walking-tour, in which its author took part in 1874. At this time the fancy seized him to walk from his own city to Boston, and he persuaded his friend and pastor, the Reverend Joseph H. Twitchell,

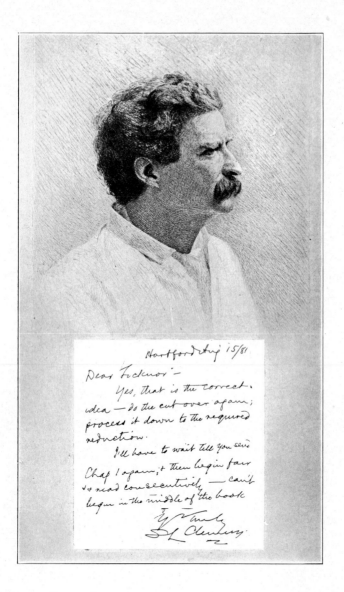

Hartford Aug 15/81

Dear Ticknor –

Yes, that is the correct
idea – do the cut over again;
process it down to the required
reduction.

I'll have to wait till you send
Chap I again; & then begin fair
& read consecutively — can't
begin in the middle of the book

Ys Truly
S L Clemens.

to accompany him. At 8 A.M., on November 12, the two pedestrians started from the East Hartford Bridge, the former carrying a luncheon basket, the latter a small bag. Despite their unostentatious method of departure, the papers soon got wind of this excursion, and its progress was watched at every point and chronicled for the edification of the public. After a march of twenty-eight miles, the travelers reached Westford, lame, but elated. Here they spent their first night (a very poor one), and on the following morning sallied forth, stiff but undaunted. The second day's accomplishment measured up but six miles, which brought them to North Ashford, where they discovered that their pedestrian enthusiasm had vanished; they therefore promptly relinquished the joys of walking for the less arduous process of railroad travel, and boarded the train for Boston, where Howells was awaiting their arrival with keen amusement.

The travelers, who appeared unabashed by this inglorious "wind-up," were immediately transported to the Howells home in Cambridge, where a warm welcome was bestowed upon them, and where the history of their adventures was freely poured into the ears of the intimate associates who gathered to greet them. A close friendship had sprung up between Clemens and Howells, dating from their first meeting in the office of the "Atlantic Monthly," in the pages of which the latter had reviewed "The Innocents Abroad," in 1869, with an appreciation that greatly pleased its author. It took Howells a little while to accustom himself to the startling figure that had dawned on his vision attired in a sealskin coat, with a tangle of red hair and a flowing red mustache, but he soon came to admire the real Mark Twain, and learned to forget the eccentric superstructure.

The walking-tour gave the Boston papers an opportunity for merry comments on this achievement, of which the instigator declared: "We made thirty-five miles in less than five days. This demonstrates that the thing can be done."

On the night following the arrival of the pedestrians, Clemens was the host at a small dinner at which he entertained Howells, Aldrich, and other special friends, who were immensely amused by the account of the Hartford-to-Boston trip. And it was as a sequel to this visit that Howells, then editing the "Atlantic," urged the sending of some contribution for the magazine. Clemens replied that he could think of nothing to contribute, and then followed this prompt refusal with a second letter, in which he reconsidered the suggestion.

In letter number two he stated that an idea had occurred to him during a walk with Twitchell, when he had started to recount some of his early experiences upon the Mississippi. To this recital his friend had listened with keen interest, assuring him that it was just the sort of material suitable for a magazine. Recalling this, Clemens suggested that he would write a series of papers upon this subject. Howells expressed his satisfaction with the idea, and the first contribution to this series shortly appeared in the pages of the "Atlantic Monthly."

Thus the first twenty chapters of the "Life on the

Mississippi" made their appearance in serial form. They were composed by their author with pleasure and enthusiasm, and the contemplation of this theme, dear to his heart, awakened in him a keen desire to go over the old ground and obtain fresh material which could be added to his preliminary work. In turn, he urged Howells, John Hay, and James R. Osgood to accompany him upon this trip, but at the time none could arrange to do so, therefore it was indefinitely postponed, and with it the completion of the book.

Seven years later the long-deferred journey was taken in company with Osgood, who had repeatedly urged Clemens to finish the book. The friends started upon their memorable expedition, taking with them Roswell Phelps, who was engaged as a stenographer to take notes.

They embarked on the steamer Gold Dust, and Clemens's plan was to travel under an assumed name; a plan soon relinquished, as he was promptly recognized by certain former associates, a circumstance graphically set forth in the book. At New Orleans the friends were met by George W. Cable and Joel Chandler Harris, with whom they spent some entertaining hours. They then arranged to take the trip up the river to Baton Rouge, and Clemens spent much of his time in the pilot-house, besides constantly taking notes in his memorandum-book. As they progressed up the river, Clemens stopped off at various places examining old landmarks, and talking with the elderly men and women, whom he had taken leave of as girls and boys. On the whole, it was a

varied and interesting journey, offering much that
was new and suggestive of modern conditions, and
also a good deal that was depressing, in view of the
vanishing of the good old times held warmly in the
affections of the past-pilot.

When at last the trip was ended, Clemens set about
carrying out his promise to complete the book, but
it did not "finish" with the ease that its author had
anticipated. The earlier enthusiasm was lacking, and
the last chapters dragged on painfully, their completion being blocked by all kinds of interruptions. The
publishers protested that the time-limit had expired,
and the author responded that he had never had such
a struggle with any previous book. When at last the
much-delayed volume was finished, in May, 1883,
a breath of relief was drawn by all concerned.

Not least among the tribulations attendant upon
its production were the author's protests regarding
the shortcomings of the illustrations, and his desire
to change them after the page-proofs had been
printed; a procedure which culminated in the tragedy
of the "cancelled cut." This picture, which originally
appeared on page 441, showed a head in profile (an
unmistakable likeness of the author) being consumed
in flames; a presage of possible future punishment
which Mrs. Clemens did not relish, and which she
insisted must be omitted. This illustration followed
the writer's reflections upon cremation, where he
remarks:

"As for me, I hope to be cremated. I made
that remark to my pastor once, who said, with
what he seemed to think was an impressive man-

ner, 'I wouldn't worry about that, if I had your chances.'

"Much he knew about it, the family all so opposed to it."

Then at the foot of the page came the "cremation cut," to which the family certainly were "opposed."

It was useless for the publishers to protest that almost the entire edition had been printed; Mrs. Clemens remained firm in her decision that her husband's profile should not be thus burned in effigy for the edification of posterity, and her husband obediently insisted that the "cut should be cut out."

This edict, which brought consternation to the publisher, proved a bonanza in the book-collector's world, for though the cut was cancelled in practically the whole edition, it was too late to prevent the escape of a few copies which had already been bound up, and had gone forth to take their places in the "smart (book) set," eagerly sought for by all collectors of Mark Twain's works.

While this especial illustration was the only one cancelled, it was not the only one which fell under the ban of the author's displeasure. Others provoked derision, and he would have banished them likewise had not his demands been quite too numerous to be complied with. Consequently the other illustrations remained unaltered, although the author's comments sent his publisher upon the proof freely voiced his disdain. These annotated pictures were, nevertheless, carefully preserved by the amused recipient. On page 301 the author protests from the pilot's point of view against the use of an electric light while "running in a fog." He writes: "Be sure to make this correction. The idea of using an electric light in a fog is a hundred times too, too. We should lose the respect of the river-men."

The next protest arises at the foot of page 356, a glance at which cannot fail to put the reader in sympathy with Mrs. Clemens. Under this cut is written: "Knock this picture out. The madam's orders are peremptory. She says the chapter is plenty dreadful enough without it. Yours, Mark." Another suggestion reads: "This house is too sound. Can't it be turned into a ruin somehow?"

Not only the illustrations, but certain anecdotes were subject to unlooked-for changes, doubtless at Mrs. Clemens's earnest solicitation. The repetition of a story told the author by Twitchell evidently caused some debate, for the latter writes the publisher: "I return herewith the proof submitted me. I do not find anything in it to correct in particular, since I gave Mr. Clemens leave to tell the story. I'm a little dubious as to the propriety of its being told, but that is none of your affair, and anyway there's no help now for it, I suppose."

A letter from Clemens, written a few days later, seemingly refers to the illustration accompanying this incident.

DEAR TICKNOR:

I telegraphed you about that scene in church, because I wanted to make sure to rectify the thing before you get to printing it. You can fill up that space with any kind of cut you please, provided it

journey down **the river, you will hunt ou**
and send it to **Adam Kruger,** care of the
which I have mentioned.   It will make a
and I shall sleep **the sounder** in my grave
I have done what I could for the son of the
to save my wife and child — albeit my hand ign
him down, whereas the impulse of my heart wou
to shield and serve him.

Dear Osgood — Knock this
picture out. The madam's
orders are peremptory. She
says the chapter is plenty dreadful
enough without it. Yrs Mark

does not refer in any way to any part of the text, and is utterly without humorous suggestion. I care nothing about what the subject of the cut is so long as it bears no hint of the text, and is not funny. A landscape is a good thing, and can be called, scene in the Adirondacks, or Palestine, or somewhere. The reader can put in such idle time as he may have in trying to arrive at the connection between the picture and the reading-matter. This will give him pleasant occupation for an idle week and will cost us nothing.

You make mention of the cuts that are already printed. Let them go. Cuts that are already printed must stay so and take their chance. We will only try to rectify those not already printed.

Yours truly
S. L. CLEMENS

That the writer was doubtful about his publisher's willingness to make all these corrections is evinced by a final note, which reads:

TICKNOR:

Make these various changes if convenient, not otherwise. It ain't any matter about the 50,000 already printed — no importance.

MARK

Sometime previous to these comments Clemens had written conveying instructions not to tamper with his punctuation, in which he declared he was an expert. He wrote:

"If the printers will only follow copy strictly, in

the matter of capitals and punctuation, my part of the proof-reading will be mere pastime. I never saw such beautiful proofs before. You will observe that in this first chapter I have not made a mark. In the other chapters I had no marks to make except in restoring my original punctuation and turning some 'tis's into 'it is'— there being a dern sight too many of the former. What I want to read proof for is for literary lapses and infelicities (those I'll mark every time); so, in these chapters where I have had to turn my whole attention to restoring my punctuation, I do not consider that I have legitimately read proof at all. I did n't know what those chapters were about when I got through with them.

"Let the printers follow my punctuation — it is the one thing I am inflexibly particular about. For corrections turning my 'sprang' into 'sprung' I am thankful; also for corrections of my grammar, for grammar is a science that was always too many for yours truly; but I like to have my punctuation respected. I learned it in a hundred printing-offices when I was a jour. printer; so it's got more real variety about it than any other accomplishment I possess, and I reverence it accordingly.

"I have n't seen any chapter 2, nor chapter 4 — nor the prefatory paragraph. But no matter; if my punctuation has been followed in them I will go bail that nobody else can find an error in them. Only, you want to be sure that they've been set up and not omitted."

And again, he writes in reference to his punctuation:

"The proof-reader has marked a hyphen. . . . No hyphen will be found in the copy. Let the copy be followed strictly, for I hate to mark up a proof. Sometimes I even spell words erroneously; but I do it purposely, and out of hatred of the dictionary, and I want the copy followed in those cases too.

"Another point for your circular — state that the book is not going to be issued 6 months, or a year, after the date promised, but *promptly and on that date*, without fail. (Many of the canvassers will believe this, but of course more of them won't.)"

An interesting reminder of the process pursued in the evolution of the "Life on the Mississippi" now remains in the library of its late publisher. It is a curious volume by Mrs. Trollope, published in 1832, from which Clemens saw fit to select numerous passages for insertion in his book. Mrs. Trollope's work is entitled "Domestic Manners of the Americans"; and at the time of its appearance it was considered highly instructive by the British public, although it provoked a storm of resentment upon this side of the water. Indeed the Preface to the American edition is devoted to reviling the author of this treatise, who had seen fit to pen such unflattering pictures of her American cousins.

In 1827 Mrs. Trollope sailed up the Mississippi, which trip she has described in great detail, introducing picturesque bits of native conversation, and interspersing throughout the book her own reflections upon America's crude and defective social customs.

When Mark Twain embarked upon the second

portion of the "Life on the Mississippi," he selected for a literary traveling companion this quaint production of the Englishwoman, following not only her journey, but her curious account throughout the book, with characteristic marginal annotations. He picked out various passages which he thought worthy of comment and quotation, and when he had finished his work, he sent the Trollope book to his publisher with instructions to use certain marked passages for copy.

But these selected passages were quite apart from his own humorous marginal comments, which ran through the book, expressive of his enjoyment of the Englishwoman's conclusions. These were penciled solely for his own edification, but one only regrets that Mrs. Trollope could not have had the privilege of perusing them.

A few examples of this marginalia may prove of interest:

In the course of her visit to New Orleans, Mrs. Trollope tells of being introduced to a certain milliner, who proves to be socially prominent; the writer says, however, that despite this fact she feels hardly justified in saying that "Milliners took the lead in the best society" in this part of the world. Clemens writes on the margin: "She is very fair and thoughtful."

Her picture of the interior of a Mississippi steamboat, on which she traveled, is very realistic; she cites the terrible condition of the carpet in the cabin, and adds: "I would infinitely prefer sharing the apartment of a party of well-conditioned pigs to being confined to its cabin." Clemens remarks: "This is the boat I saw."

His pencil follows the lady's journey, as does his subsequent account of the places visited by him as he progressed up the river.

When she quotes the retort of a Captain Hall, to the assertion that the greatest difference between England and America is, "the want of loyalty," and adds, "were the same question put to me I should answer, 'the want of refinement.'" Twain comments, "She hit it." And he pencils the exclamation: "A fair shot," when she writes: "The greatest difficulty in organizing a family establishment in Ohio is getting servants, or, as it is there called, 'getting help,' for it is more than petty treason to the republic to call a free citizen a servant."

Twain's approbation is withdrawn, however, when the lady enlarges unduly upon the impudent style of conversation indulged in by the typical maid-servant, and then announces that such conversations "were written down with all the verbal fidelity" her memory permitted. He decorates the margin with the words: "But your memory was woefully defective as to details."

Mrs. Trollope's description of Western manners during neighborly visits, reads: "If it was a female (caller) she took off her hat; if a male, he kept it on, and then, taking possession of the first chair in their way, they would retain it for an hour together without uttering a word." The commentator remarks here briefly but expressively: "Changed now."

But he responds sympathetically to the writer's

statement: "The well disposed, those whose own feelings would prevent their annoying others, will never complain of the restraint of law. All the freedom enjoyed in America beyond that enjoyed in England is enjoyed solely by the disorderly at the expense of the orderly." "True yet," writes Mark Twain in the margin.

At the end of the book his pencil notes with approval that which is doubtless the most discriminating of the Englishwoman's conclusions: "In all my travels, both among heathen and among Christians, I have never encountered any people by whom I found it so difficult to make myself understood as by the Americans."

Whatever the failure may have been on the part of the average American to comprehend Mrs. Trollope during her travels up the Mississippi, one cannot study the marginal comments made upon her volume half a century later, by one well acquainted with the subject which she chose to set forth for the instruction of her English readers, without feeling convinced that the annotator, who followed her journey in spirit and in truth, knew Mrs. Trollope far better than she knew any of his compatriots.

While the "Life on the Mississippi" was going through the press, it was decided to omit chapter forty-eight, in which the writer had drawn some rather too lively comparisons between the North and South, not essential to the interest of the book. This chapter was cancelled, and its existence forgotten until it was discovered years after, together with a number of the pages preceding it; these pages had been set aside by the publisher, who made a practice of preserving all hand-written "copy"; and were thus saved unwittingly for the purpose intended by their author. He had promised the manuscript to a leading collector, and his hand-written work was being nicely copied and the typewritten matter sent to press, up to the moment when the above-mentioned chapter was reached. Then his copyist fell ill, and for some days the author filled the gap by forwarding hand-written pages; these were set aside by his publisher, who did not dream that an eager collector was awaiting their receipt. When finally, after the author's death, the intervening pages came to light, the mystery was solved; the gap in the auto-graph manuscript after a quarter of a century, was filled at last, and the cancelled chapter "forty-eight" was also restored to its original place, where it re-mains a literary curiosity.

A truly characteristic bit of Mark Twain humor decorates the last half sheet of a letter sent by his publisher in regard to a proposed meeting between them. The latter ends his letter with the words:

God be with you, for I cannot.
Yours
B. H. TICKNOR

Twain returned the sheet, at the foot of which he had inscribed the words:

DEAR TICKNOR:
He did n't come. It has been a great disappoint-

ment to the whole family. Hereafter, appoint a
party we can depend on.

Yours   MARK

It was during the period in which the "Life on the
Mississippi" was marching toward completion that
its author delivered an after-dinner speech which
later filled him with contrition. The gathering was
one which brought together a brilliant galaxy of the
New England writers, at one of the "Atlantic
Monthly" feasts, to which Clemens was bidden to
give the principal address of the evening. In thinking
over certain humorous suggestions, he hit upon the
thought, which seemed a happy one to him, of picturing three of Boston's literary idols as being per-
sonated by three disreputable tramps. Feeling
assured that all the company would enter heartily
into his merry jest, he launched forth his description
of three "dead-beats" arriving at a California
mining-camp and imposing themselves upon the
innocent miners as respectively Ralph Waldo
Emerson, Henry Wadsworth Longfellow, and Oliver
Wendell Holmes.

Howells, on whom had devolved the responsibility
of presenting the speaker, and who had set forth in
glowing terms the treat that all anticipated, listened
with consternation while Clemens blundered on en-
larging upon the ribald and uncouth appearance of
his three hoboes, Longfellow, Emerson, and Holmes.
Meanwhile the idols of New England sat silently
regarding him, and all around the table were startled
glances and tightly compressed lips. I can recall my

father's description of the icy reception accorded this would-be humorous dissertation which so sadly missed fire. When it was ended, only one person at the table laughed, and his name has been mercifully withheld from ignominy, while the speaker stood cold and solitary amid the ruins of his jocose master-piece. The three subjects of his discourse remained mute and immovable; Longfellow sat erect eyeing the speaker with a puzzled air; Holmes, in preoc-cupation was fingering his menu, and Emerson, whose mental grasp was failing, remained oblivious of the whole occurrence.

At the close of the evening Clemens rushed back to his hotel to spend a sleepless night, leaving for Hartford on the earliest train next morning. Once there, he wrote back in contrition to each of the three "tramps," who all responded with characteristic graciousness. Longfellow freely pardoned with a gentle indulgence; Holmes understood, and begged the perpetrator never to give the matter another thought; and Emerson was merely agreeably mysti-fied. But Clemens was bitterly and lastingly sorry and mortified; he was the only one who really minded, and so deep was his contrition that he voiced his con-viction that no story by his unworthy pen should ever again disgrace the pages of the offended "Monthly." What he had done was far worse than a crime — it was a Boston blunder.

Among my mental photographs of this writer is one which stands out more clearly than all the rest. This is the picture of him as he arose to his feet at the close of the complimentary banquet tendered him by the Harpers upon his seventieth birthday, which was attended by some two hundred writers.

On this occasion it had been planned to give to each guest a plaster bust of Twain as an appropriate souvenir, and at the conclusion of the dinner came an influx of these snowy reproductions of the guest-of-honor. The waiters set them down at every plate until the dining-room seemed suddenly to have blossomed into a statuary emporium; these busts which were excellent likenesses of the author, stood about a foot high, and gave the room a most extraordinary appearance when viewed in its entirety; moreover, on account of the numberless mirrors which decorated the walls of Delmonico's great dining-room, these heads were multiplied with marvelous effect. So that, when Mark Twain rose to speak, hundreds of reproductions of himself looked back at him from the surrounding tables, the whole suggesting some sprightly scene in "Alice Through the Looking-Glass."

Mark Twain's address that night was a masterly one, with its mingling of fun and pathos, never to be forgotten by those that heard it, nor will the picturesque appearance of the speaker ever fade from the mental vision of those that saw him, presiding over the distinguished company of authors and numberless reproductions of himself.

On this occasion Mark Twain was given a scrapbook in which Colonel Harvey, the ever-thoughtful host of the evening, had arranged to have collected a signed communication in prose, or verse, from each invited guest. This gift was highly appreciated by the recipient, and in response he sent to every contributor the following note:

To you, and to all my known and unknown friends who have lightened the weight of my seventieth birthday with kind words and good wishes, I offer my most grateful thanks, and beg leave to sign myself,

Your and their obliged friend,

MARK TWAIN

NEW YORK, Dec. 6, 1905

This communication was done in facsimile of his writing, and each copy was personally signed by him.

My last glimpse of the humorist was when I took leave of him, a study in white hair, white mustache, and cool white flannels, upon the day when Thomas Bailey Aldrich's old home in Portsmouth was opened for the inspection of his friends. Special cars carried the literary guests to "Rivermouth," where they were present at the appropriate exercises held in honor of the creator of the most popular "Bad Boy" in fiction.

The day proved a terribly hot one, each car was like an oven, and the guests mopped their brows and purchased palm-leaf fans. As I walked through the gate to take the train, Mr. Clemens joined me, and we found a seat close to the door, where, if we swallowed cinders, we could get something of a breeze as well. Seated beside me, he let fall various droll sayings which did much to make the trip endurable; he was to be the principal speaker of the occasion, and I fancied that his onerous task of addressing a critical audience on so hot a day was weighing on his mind. I can recall but one of the remarks which he let fall in reference to Aldrich's early home. He said, in his slow way: "Do you know, folks are always asking where my birthplace is, whereas I never had one."

The day, despite its torrid temperature, proved truly memorable. Aldrich's many friends viewed his old home with intense interest, filled as it is with quaint original furnishings and with innumerable associations. The garret, the kitchen, the lovely garden, and the little brick house built to contain in safety the autograph treasures, all were explored with much enthusiasm. Then the guests adjourned to the Rockingham Hotel for luncheon, and at its conclusion the literary exercises were held in an adjacent hall.

Had there been any pervasive atmosphere of gloom such as some of Aldrich's friends were inclined to look for, it must have vanished when Mark Twain stepped to the center of the platform, arrayed in his white flannels. He had come to be gay, and glad, and he refused to reflect one mournful thought. He was jocose and merry, and all his reminiscences of Aldrich were set forth in such a vein as he might have indulged in had the subject been seated beside him on the platform. I can remember his reiterating forcibly: "This is n't Aldrich's funeral!"— as if it were his one wish to show how truly alive Aldrich was at that moment.

And yet, despite his merry jesting, I felt assured

that there was no man present belonging to that circle
of old friends who was at heart more sad at the realization that the subject of this discourse had left the
group where there was none to fill his place. Under
Mark Twain's jocose exterior ran a deep under-
current of melancholy and pessimism, which he
seldom expressed, but which occasionally peers out
between lighter-vein passages. Undoubtedly his
intense consciousness of the sorrows and tragedies
of life did much toward producing the motive-power
which drove him on to fulfill to the last, though sad
at heart himself, his mission of spreading peals of
merry laughter throughout the world

CHAPTER XI

LETTERS FROM "UNCLE REMUS"

JOEL CHANDLER HARRIS might have echoed Mark Twain's assertion that he "never had a birthplace," for its exact location still remains a matter of conjecture; three different localities in Eatonton, Georgia, are said to claim the honor, and Eugene Field amused himself by furnishing *another* birthplace for his friend, in a fantastic sketch; so that this literary favorite of the South may upon the whole be said to possess *four* birthplaces instead of the conventional *one*.

Field, who was greatly admired by Harris, gave to the press a humorous account of his friend's early life, stating that Harris was "on the verge of sailing for Africa, to revisit the little town of Joel, where he was born of missionary parents"; he added that this writer had "lost a leg at the Battle of Lookout Mountain," and recalled other edifying incidents. Harris was at first much amused, and entered into the spirit of the fun, but later, when Field went on to publish tales of the "enormous wealth that he had amassed by his pen," he began to be a bit annoyed, especially as he was flooded with begging-letters, asking him to subscribe to countless causes and impecunious persons. And when an unknown individual wrote, urging him to share the expense of putting up a tombstone for a relative, the limit of his patience was reached.

The thing that will promises to create the
most trouble, so far as I am concerned, is the
introduction, which must be in some measure a study of or an essay on comparative
folk-lore: and I know no more about it all than
the man in the moon.

But we will work through somehow; but
just now let's try and keep cool.
                                    Yours:
                                    Joel C Harris

Jas R Osgood & Co.

Mark Twain early became a stanch admirer of "Uncle Remus," and he first brought together the Southern humorist and his Boston publishers. Upon the famous trip taken during the preparation of the "Life on the Mississippi," when James R. Osgood accompanied its author upon this journey, the three met at New Orleans. Already Twain had suggested that he, Cable, and Harris should conduct a series of joint readings; a project that the latter at first regarded favorably, but which his natural shyness caused him subsequently to decline. The meeting at New Orleans is described in the "Life on the Mississippi," in the chapter entitled, "'Uncle Remus' and Mr. Cable," and the acquaintance with Osgood, which Twain strove to further, resulted, as he hoped it would, in an arrangement which eventually brought about the publication in Boston of the greater part of Harris's books. The earliest of these Boston publications was issued in 1883, some half-dozen years after "Uncle Remus" had first charmed his readers in the sheets of the "Atlanta Constitution," and when one volume of the "Remus" sketches had already appeared in book form. In March of this year the author wrote to his Boston publisher:

"You may begin to make your arrangements for the 'Uncle Remus' book, 'Nights with Uncle Remus.' It will contain seventy stories. Eighteen sketches are already done, and these can go into the hands of the artist on the first of May, and by the first of June I want to have twenty more complete, and the others right along. The introduction will cost me the most trouble and will be about twenty pages, but I'll defer that to the last. The other book sells steadily, about three thousand a year. Now then write me your views and intentions and desires. If half the book is in type by the middle of August you can hit Christmas with it."

The first week in June finds the author the victim of various worries which are the portion of the editor, as well as of the good citizen. He writes as usual from the editorial office of the "Atlanta Constitution":

"Your uncle has been bedeviled by a variety of causes that can scarcely find time to repeat themselves more than once before the millennium. One of our editorial writers has been laid up, and I have been compelled to do his work and my own, too; I have been performing on a jury; the 'Century' has worried me with an objection to the coast dialect, but the objection has been overcome; and last and not least I have been pestered about the order in which the stories shall come — whether they shall fall in divisions of groups, or just run miscellaneously along like dry peas (or beans) out of a tin tube. I want to fix it all so that there shall be as few changes to make after the matter is in type as possible. I shall begin to send copy as soon as I can dispose of some of my own suggestions and things, and by the time you begin to dine with the British dudes I hope we will have at least half the book in type and in the hands of the artists; but I trust you are not figuring to get it out before November. This will give you time to advertise it thoroughly as a holiday book and take advantage of the thousand and one tricks unknown to, but highly appreciated by, your esteemed correspondent.

"The title will be

NIGHTS WITH UNCLE REMUS
Myths and Legends
of
The Old Plantation
by
JOEL CHANDLER HARRIS
Author of " Uncle Remus, His Songs and His Sayings "

Harris's reference in the above letter to being "worried" about the "coast dialect" recalls the fact that his entrance into the folk-lore field was productive of unlooked-for results; from what he supposed was a simple recital of the tales to which he had listened, he found himself launched into the field of folk-lore experts, and he wrote in this connection:

"To be frank, I did not know much about folk-lore, and I did n't think that anybody else did. Imagine my surprise when I began to receive letters from learned philologists and folk-lore students from England and India, asking all sorts of questions, and calling upon me to explain how certain stories told in the rice-fields of India and on the cotton-fields of Georgia were identical, or similar, or at least akin. They wanted to know why the negro makes Brer Rabbit so cunning and masterful."

These letters came from royal institutes, from scholars and travelers, and Harris could only reply: "All that I know — all that we Southerners know about it — is that every old plantation mammy in the South is full of these stories. One thing is certain, the negroes did not get them from the whites."

It may be of interest to note that the head of the English department of the United States Naval Academy announced that variations of the "Tar-Baby Story" were found among the North American Indians, the tribes of Brazil, the natives of Cape Colony, the Bushmen of the Congo, and also among the Hottentots.

In explaining the psychology of the negro's choice of Brer Rabbit for a hero, the author says: "It needs no scientific investigation to show why he selects the weakest and most harmless of all animals, and brings him out victor in contests with the bear, the wolf, and the fox. It is not *virtue* that triumphs, but *helplessness;* it is not *malice*, but mischievousness. Undoubtedly, the case of the weakest of the animals appeals to the humble slave *raconteur* conscious of his own helpless position."

Harris took great interest in the illustration of his books, and carried on long discussions with Church, and others, regarding the depicting of his animals and their characteristics, for he felt that much of the success of his work depended upon happy illustration. So strongly was he impressed with this belief that he wrote to Church in regard to taking up the work: "I trust that you will not enter upon it as a task, merely, or allow yourself to be hurried. Just such another opportunity of catching that incongruity of animal expression that is just enough human to be humorous — just such another opportunity of interpreting the roaring comedy of animal

N.Y. Nov
83

Dear Mr. Pickner

I am delighted with the
Uncle Remus you so kindly
sent me. I hope it will
prove a big success

Rep. F.J. Church

58.8.13.

life — will never occur again while the world stands; and if you can succeed here as you have elsewhere (and no other artist has ever succeeded) in catching and expressing the humor that lies between what is perfectly decorous in appearance and what is wildly extravagant in suggestion, your illustrations will be something more than memorable."

When the "Nights with Uncle Remus" appeared in 1883, it contained illustrations by both Beard and Church, and while the latter had cleverly embodied the spirit of the author's creations, it was evident that Beard had really far exceeded him in the accomplishment of just that subtle delineation that was desired; and the latter's illustrations will continue to impress the reader as the happiest of inspirations. Harris was greatly pleased with them, and his pleasure was only surpassed by his final delight at the Frost illustrations, executed some years later.

In discussing the publication of this volume which was to appear in England, its author writes in 1883, touching upon the forthcoming pictures and showing by his references to Beard his satisfaction in that illustrator's work:

"I am delighted with the type and size of page as shown in the London sheets. I will forward you by express to-day or to-morrow the eighteen stories which are to precede the Trubner sheets in the book. Pray let the one entitled 'A Dream Story' (XVII) fall into Beard's hands. If he deals with it at all enthusiastically, his illustration will make a delightful frontispiece, for in that sketch lies the motive, the undertone of the book.

"I'm not particular about the frontispiece; in fact
I think a frontispiece is rather out of date, but I want
Beard to get hold of XVII. If I do not greatly mis-
understand him, he can deal with it sympathetically.
I have been greatly worried of late by a great many
little things, and my work has been interrupted, but
I see my way clear now, and I think there will be
little delay in the future."

Long before he had any idea of attempting the
negro legends, Harris had cherished the hope of
writing a novel of Georgia life, but it was not until
1878 that he produced as a serial in the "Atlanta
Constitution" "The Romance of Rockville." During
the publication of this serial, the "Uncle Remus"
stories were begun, and for the next three years
absorbed his attention; then he returned to his first
project and the result was the forwarding of "Mingo"
to his Boston publisher, where his suggestion for this
book met with prompt approval. He says of its
preparation, a month after his previous letter:

"I'm almost ashamed to write; but the truth is I
have n't done anything outside of newspaper work
for some time. I have what the doctors call fatty
degeneration of the mind. I sat for a photograph
Saturday and will send you one in a day or two.

"Why in the name of goodness don't you get out
cheap editions of my books? Perhaps you could gull
the public that way!"

Ten days later he forwards some copy, protesting:

"This delay is unforeseen and unexpected and
frets me a great deal more than it does you. The
truth is, one of our writing editors is a New York

man, and is eternally on the verge of hay-fever, or
some other disease, and is always breaking out un-
expectedly. He has been gone now three weeks, and
I have been having the devil's own time. Just as
soon as he returns I am going to take a month off and
devote myself entirely to 'Remus' and Boston. Two
weeks of such work as I propose to put in will clear
up the stories; and the editor is due here this week. I
think I shall come to Boston to write the introduction, so as to take advantage of the folk-lore collection in the Harvard Library. But you may prepare
yourself to think very ill of me when you see me,
because I am not going to subject myself to the
embarrassment of seeing people. I am going to
Boston, and I will have the introduction done before
you know it, and I'm not going to bore you at all. I
saw this in the 'Tribune' about the author of 'But
Yet a Woman': 'Being a modest man, Mr. Hardy,
as soon as he discovered he was about to achieve
fame, determined to master the German language,
and for this purpose rushed off to Germany, where
he now is!'

"I quote from memory; but is this the correct
thing? I want to get into the drift, don't you know?
And that is the reason I ask. If it should ever be my
good fortune to achieve fame, where am I to go? If
I have my own way about it, I shall go to England
and study the English language.

"I enclose a note from David Douglas, which the
firm must answer. I have already written him stating
that his flattering proposition has quite taken away
my breath and all that sort of thing, and that I have

two more sketches to add, and when will he want them, etc. Just write and say his letter has been referred to the firm; that the sketches in question will be issued by you in book form in the spring with the addition of some others now in preparation; that 'Teague Poteet' is to be revised and added to; that 'Mingo' is to be recast; and will Mr. D. D. refrain from bothering about these things until he hears further from the distinguished firm, the pride of Boston, and pray ask the beneficent D. D. what terms he proposes to pay the equally distinguished and notorious author; and say to him that if he has any doubt whatever as to native American pride and honesty, he can test them by sending the money in advance. In short, I hereby authorize the firm to swindle the Scotchman in my behalf."

In "Mingo and Other Sketches," which appeared in book form in 1884, the second story was entitled "At Teague Poteet's; a Story of the Hog Mountain Range." This had been first published in the "Century," and it had originated in a suggestion made to the author during the progress of the trial of two United States deputy marshals for killing an old man whose only crime was that of having a private still for "moonshine." During this period a discussion occurred in the office of the "Atlanta Constitution," as to the use of proper-names for the titles of stories. Harris's companion opened a copy of the Georgia State Directory, and as his eye fell on the name "Teague Poteet," he declared that if the other would put that name to a story dealing with the moonshiner's trial, it would attract widespread attention. From this beginning the story grew, and proved one of its author's favorites; it was later forwarded to Boston for inclusion in the volume of sketches, regarding the value of which he always spoke slightingly, being invariably disposed to under-rate his own work.

Somewhat cheered by the prospect of the return to his editorial staff of the missing New Yorker, Harris writes in August, in his usual deprecatory vein:

"I enclose some more copy. . . . The counting-room has heard from our absent editor and tele-phones me that he is to return 'this week.' If so, I shall devote my whole time to the book, beginning with next week. This means that I ought to average two sketches a day until the whole seventy or seventy-five are completed.

"I hear you are going to charge $3 for the book. This won't do. The public may stand $2 for the trash, but I doubt it, unless you make the cover devilish interesting and romantic, so to speak.

"Send a proof of Beard's largest drawing, where the Rabbit is sitting in his piazza talking to the other animals, to Church and ask him to do something (not in that line, but) in that vein. That hits it exactly. Can't you save me Beard's and Church's original drawings? I should like to have them to hang up at home."

In October, Mr. Harris writes, after his return from the long-planned trip to Boston, regarding the title for his book:

"I can think of nothing better than 'Mingo and

Other Sketches' for the volume which we are to advertise as 'in preparation,' but I will rack my brain until the 1st of November, if that will be time enough to get in an ad. in one of the front pages of 'Nights with Uncle Remus'. . . .

"The drawing of Miss Meadows and Brother Rabbit is charming. By all means make it the frontispiece. It will be more appropriate there than anywhere else.

"My visit to Boston was one of unalloyed pleasure. I enjoyed myself thoroughly. I regret that I could not nerve myself to the point of seeing more of Mr. Howells; I regret, indeed, that I could not have seen more of all of you, and of Boston itself; but what I did filled me with delight."

Harris hated all formal functions and could not be persuaded to be present at complimentary receptions or banquets. He repeatedly refused lucrative offers to go upon the platform, and when a second proposal came to him from Major Pond, offering him $10,000, if he would consent to read with James Whitcomb Riley and Mark Twain, he remarked to a friend: "I would not put on a dress-suit every night in the winter for $10,000, much less go on a stage and make a fool of myself." Yet his desire to escape notoriety and formal functions did not denote an unsocial nature, for he was one who thoroughly enjoyed being in the midst of the social doings of his intimates.

In considering the different methods of work pursued by busy men-of-letters, it will be noted that the majority seek quiet and seclusion, and are invariably trying to escape from the distractions of a household. This was not the case with Joel Chandler Harris, who delighted to keep in constant touch with the family activities. When the sales of "Uncle Remus" had brought him in enough money to enable him to undertake some improvements on his house, more rooms were added, and a study was built for him above the front-hall, but this sanctum remained untenanted by the author, who could not feel comfortable so far away from the life of the family; he therefore continued to write in his bedroom, or near the sitting-room fire, where a certain rocking-chair was his favorite seat. Every detail about the home was of interest to him, and in the midst of his work, he would get up from his writing-table and stroll into the sitting-room to listen to the chatter of the children, while his interest in a new hat or gown for his wife was as keen as her own.

After struggling to complete his work on "Mingo," he writes: "I forward by express to Cambridge to-day the last story. It has given me a good deal of trouble. I have written what is equal to a hundred pages of matter in order to get it to suit me, and even now you will find it crude and amateurish. I'm disgusted with myself, and I've no doubt you are disgusted with me. I'm very unhappy about it, and sincerely trust you have been put to no serious disadvantage by my lack of art. I am convinced that what I send is trash, and I'm in that condition that the very thought of it is offensive to me. My regards to all — if they are not mad."

Four days later, he continues the same strain: "I telegraphed you Friday in regard to the concluding sketch. The form of it worried me greatly, the difficulty being that I had three different combinations of the same incident to choose from. It is not often that such desperate fecundity overtakes a man. What do you think of 'Blue Dave'? And tell me what you think about the last? I'm nervous about the things. What is to be the date of publication?"

The author's anxiety concerning "Blue Dave" was evidently dispelled by a letter from his publisher commending this work. And in replying to this, he makes a noteworthy change in the ending of the story; he writes:

"Your letter does me good, for I have been in a terrible mental stew about 'Blue Dave' and 'A Piece of Land.' If you like 'B. D.', I think you will like 'A. P. of L.', though I'm not sure. I'm afraid it's awkward and crude. Your approval of the death-bed scene reminds me —

"Please have Dave's last words to his old mistress changed thus:

"'Tain't po' Dave, Mistiss! De good Lord done tuck holt er de lines.'

"Have this put in place of: 'Dat I is, Mistiss! Dat I is.'

"If it is necessary to go to the expense of breaking the page to make this correction, charge it to me."

A glance at the last page of this story will easily convince the reader how essential this change was to the beauty of the conclusion. The last lines tell how, when the old mistress came to die, she thought she was taking a journey, driven in her carriage by her faithful negro:

" 'The carriage goes smoothly along here,' she said. Then, after a little pause, she asked, 'Is David driving?' and the weeping negro cried out from a corner of the room,—

" ' 'Tain't po' Dave, Mistiss! De good Lord done tuck holt er de lines.'

"And so, dreaming as a little child would dream, the old lady slipped from life into the beatitudes, if the smiles of the dead mean anything."

An ending as moving as "little Paul's" departure with the "river flowing by."

When at last "Mingo" was issued, its author viewed this literary offspring with keen satisfaction and responded on receipt of it with some droll comments on the cover:

"The books came to hand after I had mailed my last letter. Of course I like them. A book 's a book, you know. There 's a funny streak somewhere in my disposition, and for that reason I like the cocoanut and palmetto-trees on the cover. The man that designed the cover put those trees in because Georgia is a 'Southern' State, and a Southern State must necessarily be in the very bowels of the tropics. The truth is that Georgia is no farther south, so far as climate and vegetation are concerned, than Massachusetts, New Hampshire, and Maine. Nevertheless, the design is very neat, and, to my mind, whatever is neat is appropriate. I'll mail you some songs during the week. I'll also have a photograph taken and mail you one, provided it is for your own private use, and not for engraving purposes. Who is Charles Egbert Craddock? He is a good one."

Mr. Harris's query about Charles Egbert Craddock makes it evident that this writer had deceived many of her own craftsmen in the South as to her sex, as well as her publishers in the North.

In mailing "Mingo" to a friend the author wrote: "I took the liberty of mailing you a few days ago a copy of 'Mingo.' I have no right to attack you in this manner, but you are not defenseless; you are not bound to read it. Indeed it is not a book for young men. It is intended to please the aged and the half-wits of our time, those who are suffering for want of sleep. Under the circumstances you can hardly be prepared to believe me when I assure you, I am,

"Faithfully yours
"JOEL CHANDLER HARRIS"

The fifteenth anniversary of the appearance of "Uncle Remus" was commemorated by D. Appleton & Company's publication of a beautiful edition with illustrations by A. B. Frost, whose pictures so delighted the author that he wrote in the dedication: "The book was mine, but now you have made it yours, both sap and pith. Take it, therefore, dear Frost."

The last two years of Harris's life were devoted to the promoting of the "Uncle Remus Magazine," which he founded, and in the value of which he had great faith. The success which it achieved was a vital interest to him, and during his last illness he discussed its ideals, and expressed his hope that it would continue to stand for what was clean and wholesome, and would advance the spirit of freedom toward all sections.

He said: "If this illness takes me off and they try to start any monument business, don't let them do it. A statue will stand out in the rain and the cold, or, dust-covered and useless and disfiguring, will soon be forgotten except by the sparrows in nesting-time. If what little I have done is found worthy of commendation, tell the people of the South to let the magazine succeed, to stand back of it with their subscriptions — and if it is not too much trouble to Mr. Pritchard, run a little line somewhere: 'Founded by Joel Chandler Harris'."

After the passing of "Uncle Remus," it was decided that his home should be preserved as a permanent memorial, and it was purchased by the Uncle Remus Memorial Association, which, with the help of colleges, and school-children who loved the writer, raised the funds necessary. A formal transfer of the place occurred in 1913, three years after the author's death, and now the visitor may see his bedroom and living-room containing his favorite chair, writing-table, and many relics donated by his family, just as he left them. Other rooms are devoted to the public weal for library or kindergarten occupation, and the grounds are equipped as playgrounds for the children, whose happiness was so close to his heart.

On the boulder of Georgia granite that marks the grave of this widely beloved writer, who passed away in 1908 at fifty-nine years of age, are recorded his own words from his dedication of one of the "Remus" volumes:

"I seem to see before me the smiling faces of thousands of children — some young and fresh and some wearing the friendly marks of age, but all children at heart, and not an unfriendly face among them. And while I am trying hard to speak the right word, I seem to hear a voice lifted above the rest, saying: 'You have made some of us happy.' And so I feel my heart fluttering and my lips trembling and I have to bow silently, and turn away and hurry into that obscurity that fits me best."

CHAPTER XII
WILLIAM DEAN HOWELLS

AMONG the most welcome of literary guests was Mr. Howells, always a prime favorite with children and young people. The designation "gentle" was one which instantly presented itself as applicable to him, for he was truly gentle in all social and family relationships, and his devotion to his children was readily extended to the children of his friends.

As I look back on various pleasant summers, when we were neighbors by the ocean or at the mountains, I see always the smiling, genial visage of Mr. Howells, as he accompanied the young folks to sports and entertainments or walked about with them, keenly enjoying and sharing all youthful enthusiasms. Never impatient or irritable, invariably serene and gracious, I seem to see him on one particular occasion, when we attended a sheet-and-pillow-case party, held in one of the halls at Bethlehem, N. H., for the amusement of the summer visitors. All had been urged to come in costume (presumably easily obtained), and the disguise was to be later dispensed with. As is the custom at many such affairs, most of the guests decided to *look on* instead of *taking part*. The onlookers assembled in goodly numbers; they filled the seats about the hall and overflowed them, being prepared to enjoy the fun of seeing others figure on the floor. They waited patiently for the procession of animated sheets and pillow-cases, which were to make triumphal entry, and then impatiently, as the time slipped away and none appeared; finally through the doorway came a small and insignificant group of some ten or a dozen stragglers arrayed in cotton coverings! They walked in with an abashed air which penetrated even their protecting sheets, a foolish little group which after the long waiting furnished but slight amusement for the assembled guests who, ere long, withdrew in deep disgust. Some were indignant, others bored, but how thoroughly Mr. Howells enjoyed the party! As I watched his keen relish of the affair, I was convinced that some day this especial episode would figure upon one of his delightful pages. Whether it did or not, I never knew.

I think that it was at this mountain resort that Winifred Howells spent her last summer; she was then very ill, and her father was in constant attendance, and he grasped every joyous or bright suggestion and every bit of fun that he might take it back to cheer her. Her great sad eyes seemed always fixed on the next world rather than this, and it was most pathetic to see how the anxious father maintained his cheery smile and hopeful mien. Her death was a terrible blow to him, as she was a girl of great beauty of character and much poetic promise.

It would seem that Mr. Howells's enormous accomplishment in the field of letters, together with his adherence to the high standard that he set for himself, might have entitled him to a freedom from household duties and responsibilities, yet from the earliest days he cheerfully and happily shouldered more than his share of the domestic burdens. No matter what the demands of his work might be, he had always time to devote himself, first to his invalid daughter, and then to Mrs. Howells, who for many years was also an invalid demanding constant thought and care.

In his "Recollections" Mr. Howells has described his first journey to Boston, when as a young writer he sought the Old Corner Bookstore as his literary Mecca. There, upon his entry into the office, he found a welcome awaiting him, and he received from the senior partner twenty-five dollars in gold for a poem of his about to appear in the "Atlantic Monthly." The association thus begun continued for many years and Howells later occupied the editorial chair of the "Atlantic Monthly." His earliest novels bore the imprint of the Boston publishing-house, and his friendship with William D. Ticknor was ere long extended to members of the next generation, who published many of his works; and eventually reached the third generation, including one minor literary worker who cannot too warmly express her appreciation of his kind words of advice and helpful encouragement. He was particularly friendly to the young aspirant in the field of letters, and never was too weary with his own concerns to say a cheery word or offer some constructive criticism. His attitude of kindly hospitality toward fellow-craftsmen made him a constant source of stimulus and pleasure to the visiting author with a limited acquaintance.

Sometimes his kindly efforts were productive of

amusing consequences, and two especial instances
now come to mind, connected with the visit of
Edmund Gosse to Boston. During the stay of this
distinguished Englishman, Howells arranged to take
him to call on various members of the literary profession, Whittier and Norton being among the number. The trip to Danvers to see the former was
fraught with many trials; the snow was deep and the
"depot" conveyances unsatisfactory. They waded
through high drifts to reach the door, and then were
held up, first, by an aggressive watch-dog, and then
by a suspicious maid-of-all work, who was loath to
admit them to Whittier's presence; the whole experience Gosse later described, in one of his pictures of
American social life, as unlike anything that his own
country had to offer. The visit to Charles Eliot
Norton was still less satisfactory from the guide's
point of view, who had felt sure that Norton's great
familiarity with London would prove a source of
pleasure to them all. This hope was destined not to
be fulfilled, however, for hardly had the conversation
opened before Norton began to speak about the great
deterioration which he felt was then taking place in
London society; after citing some most conclusive
instances, he put forth as a climax: "and there is Alma
Tadema, who has married one of the daughters of
Epps, the Cocoa man!" Howells, who had been listening with increasing trepidation, conscious that Gosse
had also married one of Epps's daughters,[1] found it too
late to interpose, and Norton went on unconsciously:

[1] These two charming women had been nicknamed from their
father's famous advertisement.

"I really do not know which one he married, 'Grateful' or 'Comforting'!" Then the bomb was exploded, and before Howells could quickly change the subject, Gosse had replied: "He married 'Grateful'! I married 'Comforting' myself!" Soon after this the call came to a forced conclusion and Howells, having experienced the usual reward of virtue, led his guest back to Boston.

In turning over various letters written by Mr. Howells to my father during the publication of certain books, I dwell with especial interest upon the data belonging to the volume which its author invariably referred to by the initials "S. L."; for from the first its publisher prophesied that "Silas Lapham" would prove his most famous creation. It is worth while to note the different reception accorded this Boston novel from that which greeted James's "Bostonians." The latter undoubtedly presented clever pictures of Boston life, and some distinctive portraits, but in "Silas Lapham" its author created a vivid personality, who has taken his place among the "real folks" in American fiction. As I unfold a yellow proof-sheet, tucked in with some old letters, out falls a page from "Harper's Magazine," in which this story had appeared serially prior to its publication in book form. Oddly enough, the page is that which presents the climax of the book, the burning of Silas Lapham's new house. At the top of the magazine page is the author's description of the scene as his imagination pictured it, when he wrote: "The sky had reddened above them, and turning the corner at the Public Garden, they saw the black mass of people obstruct-

ing *the white perspective* of the *snowy* street." Upon
the page in question, "*the white perspective*" was
queried by my father, who had amended the line to
read, "obstructing the *perspective* of the *brightly
lighted* street." And the accompanying proof-sheet
bearing the altered rendering proved that the author
had accepted the emendation.

Upon this yellowing page Howells's clever char-
acterization of Silas and his wife is rendered in a few
masterly strokes, which picture the demolition of the
ambitious social project of the hero, and the relief of
his wife as news of it is brought her; together with her
fear that her husband may be suspected of setting
fire to the edifice.

" 'Oh, Silas,' she faltered, 'they'll think you set it
on fire to get the insurance!'

"Lapham was staring at a paper which he held in
his hand. 'I had a builder's risk on it, but it expired
last week. It's a dead loss.'

" 'Oh, thank the merciful Lord!' cried his wife.

" 'Merciful!' said Lapham. 'Well, it's a queer way
of showing it.'

"He went to bed, and fell into the deep sleep which
sometimes follows a great moral shock."

When the book containing Mildred Howells's
early sketches from famous European pictures, entitled "A Little Girl Among the Old Masters," was
published, the father's delight in the clever productions of his daughter quite outweighed any enthusiasm for his own works. The drawings made by a
child only ten years old were truly remarkable, and
Howells had written the running text descriptive of

the young artist's various impressions, the whole forming a unique volume, to which he refers in the following brief note, penned in response to a communication from his publisher praising his child's achievement:

My dear Mr. Ticknor:

It was very kind of you to write me about the little book, and your words went straight from one father's heart to another's.

Yours ever
W. D. Howells

After the return of the Howells family from Europe, the father wrote with satisfaction of their settling down once more under a roof of their own, adding: "And the little girl feels again the unwonted charm of the kitchen, where a cook, very much to her mind, allows her unlimited pie-crust dough, and permits her to share in the high work of stoning raisins. These privileges distract her from the pursuit of Art . . . and she offers her tarts and fruit-cake to the family appreciation with apparently the same inspired delight that she felt in their praise of her Saints and Madonnas."

The excessive modesty of Howells made him shun all public entertainments where he was asked to be the guest-of-honor. Following the banquet given by the Harpers for Henry M. Alden, some such recognition was proposed for Howells's seventieth birthday, which occurred shortly after Alden's, but he firmly refused any such demonstration, and it was not until his seventy-fifth anniversary that he at last acceded to the demands of his New York publishers. Yet at the Alden banquet, he could not escape sharing the honors of the evening, where he was seated at the head table, over which presided the host, Colonel Harvey. On either side of Harvey sat Alden and Aldrich, who were sharing a twin-birthday, and who had previously stood side by side in the receiving group. Howells was seated next to the guest-of-honor, and just beyond were Richard Watson Gilder and Edmund Clarence Stedman, two writers soon destined to say farewell to their associates. Of the group at this table no one remains to-day (barring the host) but the then President of Princeton University, Woodrow Wilson, for the advancement of whose future Harvey was at that time using his far-reaching influence.

Howells's seventy-fifth birthday was celebrated upon March 2, 1912, when four hundred men and women distinguished in the field of letters gathered at Sherry's, once more as the guests of the house of Harper. And on this occasion one of the notable features of the evening was the impersonation of Silas Lapham by James Barnes. After Howells had concluded his graceful speech of response, and before the applause had died away, the lights were lowered and there appeared an odd figure, tall, red-bearded, with close-fitting, strapped trousers, and old-fashioned cutaway coat. Then followed Silas Lapham's appreciation of his creator, rendered in amusing verse by Mr. Barnes. A few of the opening and closing lines may fittingly be quoted here:

"I, Silas Lapham, rise to greet you now
On this your birthday and to make my bow
To all your friends and mine assembled here.
To do you honor.   Let me state it clear
You made me live, you wrought me with your pen,
So from your pages I step forth again.

.   .   .   .

"You're older than I be—or was: You mark
Threescore and fifteen years, I'm told. But hark,
We'll live together! So 't is not farewell
To you, good friend of ours; we've quite a spell
To live and to be read. We have no ages,
And so I step once more back to your pages."

In his address of the evening, Howells quoted
Hawthorne's statement that there was "nothing like
recognition to make a man modest." He touched
upon the privilege which he had enjoyed of knowing
many of the bright stars in the earlier literary firma-
ment, and then followed a tribute to the inspiring
work which he felt the living authors were to-day
accomplishing; he called upon all American writers
to remember the debt that our literature owed to
France, whose schools of letters, no less than whose
art, had shed light upon us, for from that French
master and Continental inspiration American fiction
had derived its real vitality.

He closed with a feeling tribute to Mark Twain, in
which he pronounced him: "One humorist who when
he died might well have given us the sense of Shakespearian loss, though we were not yet aware of a
Shakespearian gain," and asserting: "But the soul
of Mark Twain, which divined and uttered the inmost and most immanent American mood, has passed

again so lastingly into the American consciousness that it will remain the inspiration of that high or higher average in humor, which once again is the distinctively American thing. . . . If I had been witness of no other surprising things of American growth in my fifty years of observation, I should think it glory enough to have lived in the same time and in the same land with the man whose name must always embody American humor to human remembrance."

In his famous appreciation of Tolstoy, Howells sounds the keynote of his own life when he says: "Life has no meaning and no happiness except as it is spent for others. It was a life of unselfish devotion and a search for truth, with the desire to tell it in the best form that his genius could devise." And in the same connection, he concludes: "I find nowhere in his work those base and cruel lies, which cheat us into the belief that wrong may sometimes be right, through passion, or genius, or heroism. . . . There was everywhere the grand and noble truth that had looked me in the face all my life, and that I knew I must confront when I came to die. But there was something more than this, infinitely more. There was that love, which is before even the truth, and which, if there is a last day, must appear the Divine Justice."

To the high standard of such thoughts Howells the writer adjusted his literary work, and Howells the man adjusted his daily life.

CHAPTER XIII

TWO MASCULINE PSEUDONYMS

THE coming to Boston of Miss Mary N. Murfree, soon after the publication of her book "Where the Battle was Fought," and some time after she had become well known as a contributor to the "Atlantic Monthly," created quite a stir in literary circles.

Up to the time of her arrival, she had been successfully concealed behind her *nom-de-plume* "Charles Egbert Craddock," and even her publishers had been convinced that it was a man with whom they had been in correspondence. Miss Murfree's large, upright, and very bold handwriting had been responsible for this misapprehension. In answer to her first letter from her publishers, she had signed herself simply "M. N. Murfree," and from that time her communications came addressed to "Mr. M. N. Murfree," and no one knew that the "M" stood for "Mary" until upon a certain day a sweet-faced, gentle little woman walked into the office where she was known only by her work, and announced: "I am Charles Egbert Craddock!"

Soon after Miss Murfree's coming, Mr. Howells decided to give her a reception in order to introduce her to Literary Boston, guarding the secret of her sex by sending out cards in honor of "Charles Egbert Craddock," and thus ensuring a genuine surprise-party. As the result of proper secrecy the occasion proved a most amusing one. Those that had known the writer from her work came with the expectation of meeting a pleasant gentleman from Tennessee, and much fun was experienced as the surprise was sprung upon each succeeding guest. Toward the close of the afternoon came Lawrence Barrett, who in response to the card sent him, dropped in without having the least idea concerning the identity of the guest of the afternoon. He was waylaid by Mr. Howells before reaching his hostess, and he anxiously inquired: "Who is 'Charles Egbert Craddock'? I never heard of him."

At this his host informed him hastily that Craddock was the author of several delightful volumes: "Where the Battle was Fought," "In the Tennessee Mountains," and other works. Then he explained that this was a surprise-party; Craddock was not a man, but an agreeable woman, Miss Mary Murfree.

Barrett immediately grasped the situation, and with a smile that seemed to say, "Now watch me do the trick," advanced with much enthusiasm, exclaiming: "Is it possible that this is Charles Egbert Craddock, the author of 'Where the Battle was Fought,' and that delightful story 'In the Tennessee Mountains'!"

It was a tribute to Barrett's art when, at the end of the exciting afternoon, Mrs. Howells sank wearily into a chair, and, after commenting upon the general astonishment displayed, said to her husband: "I think, dear, that Lawrence Barrett was more surprised than anybody else!"

And the host of that afternoon wrote of his editorial association with Miss Murfree:

"I do not remember any man who feigned himself a woman, but now and then a woman likes to masquerade as a man, though the disguise never deceived the editor, even when it deceived the reader, except in the very signal instance of Miss Mary N. Murfree, whom, till I met her face to face, I never suspected for any but Charles Egbert Craddock. The severely simple, the robust, the athletic hand which she wrote would have sufficed to carry conviction of her manhood against any doubt. But I had no doubts. I believe I took the first story she sent, and for three or four years I addressed my letters of acceptance, or criticism, to Charles Egbert Craddock, Murfreesboro, Tennessee, without the slightest misgiving. Then she came to Boston, and Aldrich, who succeeded me, and who had already suffered the disillusion awaiting me, asked me to dinner. He had asked Dr. Holmes, and . . . I wish I could recall word for word the exquisite terms in which he turned his discomfiture into triumph in that most delicately feminine presence. The proof of identity, if any were needed, came from the rich, full pipe of a voice in which she answered our words and gasps of amaze. In literary history I fancy there has been no such perfect masquerade."

Another truly feminine woman with a masculine pseudonym was Henri Gréville, Madame Alice Durand, who, with her husband, Professor Émile Durand of Paris, awakened a flutter of interest in literary circles. At the time of her visit to America, Henri Gréville's novel, entitled "Dosia," had just appeared; this with "Dosia's Daughter," "Cleopatra," and several others, earned for their author a wide audience in this country to which she journeyed with the expectation of making a successful lecture tour, an expectation doomed to disappointment.

Her novels dealt principally with Russian subjects, as their creator had been educated in Russia, where she had lived for some years prior to her marriage. She conversed fluently in English, but Professor Durand had mastered but a few words of our tongue.

The arrival of this agreeable couple took place just at Thanksgiving time, and they expressed much interest in our celebration of that festival, and in other New England customs which were explained to them. In view of their enthusiasm in this direction, my mother was moved to invite them to share with us a genuine Thanksgiving dinner, of the traditional New England type; a type which recent years have modified into the setting forth of a repast of reasonable proportions. The question, "Why, in the name of Pilgrim Thankfulness, turkey should be accompanied by chicken-pie, and chicken-pie be followed by every other kind of pie conceivable, and supplemented by ice-cream and plum-pudding?" has never been satisfactorily answered. But time, thank Heaven, has gradually reduced the wealth of pies, and lessened the dyspepsia of the day following the feast.

As I recall the Thanksgiving in question, a vision of chicken-pie rises before me, in company with many other triumphs in the field of pie, which were considered as much a necessary part of a Thanksgiving dinner as the traditional turkey, which was selected with especial care on this occasion, in order that our guests from France should partake of as fine and plump a bird as Boston could produce.

This turkey proved, however, a bird of much ill-omen, perchance because it was possessed of a too-tempting exterior; at all events, while it awaited its triumphal entry into the mouths of France, a sad fate overtook it. By some great carelessness the place where this prize bird was for a brief time suspended in the cellar was stealthily invaded by a hungry cat, who, without waiting for Thanksgiving ceremonies, demolished a large part of the turkey before the cook learned of the tragedy.

This sad discovery did not take place until the night before the feast. And then ensued a veritable *mauvais quart d'heure!* We were to show the two distinguished Parisians a real New England turkey dinner, and now the *pièce de résistance* had failed to resist the onslaught of a thieving cat! The shops were closed, or on the point of closing, and all desirable turkeys in a suburban town were long since sold. There was a solemn conclave in which the cook played a pathetic part; then followed a decisive raid upon each one of the surrounding shops where turkeys still remained unsold. And finally, a long, lank, skinny bird, last of his barnyard race, was found to fill the place of the plump predecessor that had appeased the cruel cat. Our guests knew not the turkey story, but we, who were familiar with Thanksgiving turkeys, looked askance at the substitute, which failed to uphold the honor of New England.

How well our guests enjoyed this ample midday

meal we never knew, but they consumed their share of the traditional repast with seeming satisfaction, and were particularly interested in the varieties of pie which were set forth for their enlightenment and for the glory of the Pilgrims. There certainly were mince and apple, cranberry and squash, to choose from, or to combine; a wealth of opportunity in the pie line — which was a bit confusing to our guests, who did not know how many kinds of pie Thanksgiving etiquette demanded the acceptance of.

Professor Durand, who spoke but a few words of broken English, seemed to regard the dinner as an exceptional educational opportunity. He sipped his cider with cheerful expediency, smiled when superfluous chicken-pie followed the lanky turkey, partook of the innumerable vegetables with relish, and in the end, his fancy settled itself upon the humble, and previously untried, squash-pie. He liked this kind of pie, and what was more he liked the name of it. Indeed, the word, "squatch," as he would pronounce it, seemed to possess a kind of fascination for him. "Squatch-pie," he kept repeating with a glad smile; and again: "Some of the squatch-pie, if you please."

Two phrases that he had mastered were "if you please" and "thank you," only his use of the terms threw the maid-in-waiting into a state of dire confusion. She was accustomed to serving persons who, when they wanted something, said, "Thank you"; whereas the Frenchman bowed and murmured "Thank you" each time that he wished to decline a dish. In response to his "thank you" the maid continued to hold the dish for his acceptance, learning at last through numerous delays that in France, "thank you" meant "no, thanks."

In the course of the intervening years, all items connected with this display of our New England customs for the enlightenment of France have vanished, but I still see before me the picture of the scared visage of the cook as she exclaimed: "Oh, mum, the cat has eat the turkey!" And I recall the polite Frenchman's accent as he remarked: "Some of the squatch-pie, if you please."

The tragedy of this Thanksgiving bird was matched by that which overtook a Christmas turkey which, shortly after Dickens's return to England from his final American tour, was sent him as a token of affection by his devoted friend George Dolby. A splendid bird was chosen and packed with other delicacies of the season, all calculated to reach the Dickens family just in time for their annual celebration, which was a most important one with them. Dickens was notified that the bird was on its way and watched expectantly for its arrival as scheduled by his friend, but nothing came.

Dickens then sent a frantic message asking, "Where is the turkey!" — a message that filled Dolby with consternation. He rushed to the shop, railway, and express company, meanwhile seeing pitiful visions of the Dickens family deprived on Christmas Day of this most necessary bird. Vainly he sought to trace the missing gift which seemed to have completely vanished from the world. His efforts for a time proved fruitless, and in consequence the Dickens household was forced to omit the most important portion of their Christmas repast. But finally the mystery was solved, and it was found that in the car which carried Dolby's Christmas offering a fire had occurred, almost completely demolishing the contents. The turkey was reported as cooked quite beyond recognition, but it was rumored that parts of it were not beyond reclaiming by certain hungry urchins, and Dickens, when he heard the story, expressed his satisfaction that, after all, the turkey was enjoyed by those whose appetites undoubtedly surpassed his own.

Dickens's Christmas turkey suffered from a premature cooking, while our Thanksgiving bird suffered from a premature eating; but in New England a grateful cat had one prodigious Pilgrim feast, and in Old England some hungry bystanders partook with satisfaction of that which should have graced the board of the great novelist; which proves that tragedy is seldom without its comedy effects.

Henri Gréville, whose social career in Boston was so successful as completely to mislead her regarding the probable attitude of other American cities, started upon a lecture tour from which she expected substantial monetary returns, only to suffer intense disappointment. While personally agreeable, she had not either the reputation or qualifications to make her a success upon the platform. Her subsequent letters to her publisher, setting forth her surprise and indignation, were frequent and depressing. Yet they were truly characteristic, as picturing the writer's point of view, in her amusing English. And one or two of these communications may be worth printing, as a warning against the false impression, often promulgated, that any foreigner can make a fortune by mounting the American lecture platform.

Madame Gréville wrote of her venture:

"It is high time that I should succeed. My last lecture here has been a very great success as a lecture, but it brought me the *ridiculous* amount of $16, 23 cents. It is no use working so hard for earning that. I will see how the Philadelphia lectures succeed: if they do not, I think I had better go home. It is useless to spend, by living here uncomfortably, *twice* the amount needed to make us live so well in Paris. Decidedly I must come to the conclusion, people here do not care for me. It is unfortunate, but as nobody can help it I must act in consequence. I will not go before lecturing in two or three places where people seem to care for me."

The Philadelphia lectures having proved disappointing, she writes a month later:

"My lectures in Philadelphia have been so far from a success that I came hardly even with my expenses. . . . It is somewhat mortifying to see that so few people care hearing me for money, when they rush upon me with invitations and demands for autographs for nothing. So I think I had better give the autographs, decline the invitations, and keep my lectures for Europe where they are considered as a favor. We shall go home in a few weeks, but not before we have gone to Washington and Niagara."

The close of the disappointing lecture tour found Madame Gréville exceedingly depressed over the result of her American stay, which she felt she could only do justice to in a volume containing her impressions of the United States. Especially had New York fallen from grace, and she wrote regarding it:

"We are sailing for France on the 5th of May. . . . You will have my next novel in a few weeks. . . . About my book on America, I must entreat you to understand me fully. My long stay in New York has brought me such contact with society that I have seen more of its faults than I should have wished for myself. *Things* are great and respectable; *people* have seemed to me very different from things, though I must say that there are very many good and pure exceptions. I would be very sad if the expression of my thought were to hurt you; still I have suffered personally so much from *people* in New York that I cannot judge them with unrestricted benevolence. If I said *all* that has happened to me, my book would be, by simple statement of facts, the most cruel satire; I will not do that: Some New Yorkers, some Philadelphians, *all* Bostonians and Washingtonians have been so kind and warm-hearted to us, that for their sake, I must not say *all* that I have suffered from their fellow-citizens.

"But my book cannot praise only; that would be a lie. There must be some, I will not say blame, for I do not intend to bear judgments; some *restrictions* on facts that have struck me as not being the ideal of perfection, which New Yorkers think they have obtained in every possible thing, moral, material, general, and individual. That book will be read by all, and blamed by almost every one. From what I have seen of New Yorkers, they cannot allow the slightest shade in admiration; you must find everything charming and unrivaled, from their ragged pavement to their blizzard; else they grow oppressive and sometimes very unpolite; I speak of the very best society. I know what I am bringing upon myself if I print that the blizzard is hateful, and that New York ought to be paved anew. They print that themselves in their newspapers, but they will never allow me to hint, even very delicately, to the possibility of that being true, *because I am a foreigner*.

"What I wanted to come to is this: I suppose that you intend to print that book. . . . But I must beg you to have the translator respect scrupulously the text. Not one word must be changed, even if my opinions look harsh, even if they look unjust. It is my opinion, and it must be respected. I hope that my opinions will not bring anything unpleasant upon you. . . .

"You must not think for that that it will be a general abuse of the United States. That is far from my mind. I have found very much to admire, and shall be happy to state it. Only I know there are many people in this country who can suffer no contradiction, which are not even satisfied by silence, but *must* extort from you unlimited praise; those will hate me. I only hope that they will not hate you.

"I should be very sorry if you thought that I am dissatisfied on account of my personal disappointment and that it sours my temper. No. It is certainly unpleasant to think that I have impaired my income for a whole year, and that I have lived very badly in hotels, for *thrice* what I would have spent for living very well at home. I go home with absolutely *empty hands*, and must borrow on my income for the next eight months; that will inflict upon us a very narrow life, a life of every possible privation, from a proper number of servants to dresses and carriages, but that side of the question is merely material. It is a fact, and there is no struggling with facts, that my health has been seriously injured, and that I look ten years older than when I came; that is a fact also, and I submit to it. But all that has no real effect on my judgment on this country. I never allow myself to be influenced by personal motives when I express general opinions, and you will see it.

"We intend to come again to America in two or three years, but it will be on a different plan. We shall bring a great deal of money, and I will not lecture *for anything*, except for charity to our French immigrants. Lecturing has brought upon me such humiliations that I never had imagined could happen, from the lady who offered me ten dollars for coming and lecturing in Germantown, from New York where I was residing, to another who said she would take one course ticket for my last lectures, but that I ought to come and visit her. I will not lecture in the United States next time, and provided I have plenty of money to spend, and no help to need, I am sure that things will go very pleasantly."

After such an experience it is not surprising that this delightful couple did not return to this country, nor is there any record of the receipt of Henri Gréville's manuscript containing her impressions of

America. Her Boston publisher gently and tactfully refrained from offering her any encouragement in this direction, although this work might have proved her most entertaining production.

CHAPTER XIV

JOHN TOWNSEND TROWBRIDGE

ALWAYS smiling and with a merry twinkle in his pleasant blue eyes, I recall Mr. Trowbridge as he stood in the pathway of his Arlington home, where I saw him for the last time, saying: "Come in, come in, I'm glad to see you!" As we walked up the path, he pointed to a ladder placed against the side of the house on which he had been mounted when we arrived, investigating something pertaining to vines or clapboards. When we reproved him for venturing so high above the garden level, he guiltily acknowledged that he had slyly slipped from the family supervision. He was still young when he passed on at eighty-eight years of age, being at that time almost the last survivor of his notable literary circle.

Some writers are admired, others esteemed and envied, but Mr. Trowbridge was truly loved, because, in return, his heart was brimful of love for all his fellow-men. He also loved nature, animals, and simple country life; he knew boys and understood how to appeal to them; and his unrivaled "Jack Hazard" series has never lost its hold upon the growing youth. The home which he acquired in Arlington in 1865, he lived in up to the time of his death, fifty years later, always retaining his enthusiasm for its surroundings, the woods near by, the flowers, and the beautiful lake behind his house where he delighted to sail a boat.

Almost ten years before his coming to his Arlington home, Trowbridge had been the youngest of the group of writers, whose contributions to the opening number of the "Atlantic Monthly" had made that magazine's "début" famous in the world of letters; and of this group he proved to be the last survivor.

When, at the close of the Civil War, the publishers of the "Atlantic" decided to issue a periodical for boys and girls, Trowbridge was asked to become one of its editorial staff. There was considerable discussion as to the title for this magazine, and Dr. Holmes, who had named the former periodical, suggested "The Atlantic Lighter"; but after some consideration "Our Young Folks" was finally selected. And this juvenile monthly achieved immediate popularity, boasting a list of eminent contributors, including Mrs. Stowe, Miss Alcott, Whittier, Miss Phelps, Lowell, Longfellow, and E. E. Hale, as well as Charles Dickens, who furnished a four-part serial. Aldrich's "Story of a Bad Boy" was numbered among other famous contributions to this magazine, which was eventually sold to the house of Scribner and merged in the "Saint Nicholas."

"Our Young Folks" contained many of Trowbridge's best works, including his poem of "Darius Green," "The Vagabonds," and numerous special articles; his name figured upon its cover in company with that of Lucy Larcom and of Gail Hamilton; the latter retained her association with the magazine until she fell out with its publishers over some copyright question, which led her to attack them in an unwise production entitled "The Battle of the Books."

In addition to Aldrich's "Bad Boy" certain other famous juveniles will continue to be associated with "Our Young Folks"; such as Mayne Reid's "Afloat in the Forest," Carleton's "Winning His Way," Mrs. Whitney's "We Girls," and Mrs. Diaz's "William Henry Letters." Not long after Trowbridge had become managing editor, he consulted the publishers as to whom he should invite to furnish the serial for the coming year, as it was late in the season and none had been arranged for. Following his query, one of the firm responded: "Why don't you speak for yourself, John?" Trowbridge inquired if he really meant it, and when the answer came in the affirmative, he at once turned his attention to the production of "Jack Hazard," drawing his background from his own early surroundings in the village by the Erie Canal, introducing a vicious little driver and a noble Newfoundland dog. This story as it progressed awakened such a response from youthful readers that the publishers declared that the boy and dog must continue their career, and so the various sequels followed.

During the days of the editing of "Our Young Folks" the publishers occupied the building at 124 Tremont Street. There Trowbridge had his room up two flights of stairs; Fields, who was then editor of the "Atlantic," had his private room below, where Howells assisted him; and just adjoining was a large reading-room in the corner of which Aldrich conducted "Every Saturday"; while near by in the position of cashier was Edwin D. Mead. In this building was a lunch-room where a table was served at which the publishers and editors could meet to discuss various matters, and the prevailing family-feeling was something which in after years all looked back upon with pleasure. Especially did Trowbridge like to recall those early memories, and after my father's death he sat down to record the story of their long association, endeavoring to picture for the benefit of the next generation the beginning of a warm friendship. This opened when he first encountered the young officer just returned from the Civil War, who had come to take his place with the old firm. On meeting him in the office Trowbridge called out to his elder brother, Howard, that he did not know that such a good-looking member of the family existed, at which Howard pretended to attack him with a roll of proof-sheets, and called out to the cashier to "stop his pay." From the time of this first meeting, Trowbridge traced the stages of his friendly intercourse which extended over fifty years, ending with a last glimpse of my father seated at his desk and reading with intense interest the other's autobiography, entitled "My Own Story," which he enthusiastically commended. How many writers at eighty-six years of age have either the heart or the energy to furnish in a letter of condolence, a painstaking description of a half-century's association?

While the editorial work on "Our Young Folks" was in progress, an episode occurred that showed the editor was capable of heroism outside of that tabulated upon a printed page. Upon a winter's day during this period, a helpless crowd stood on the shores of Mystic Lake watching a drowning boy, who had fallen through the ice. Trowbridge coming upon the scene, at once tore two fragments of board from a fence, and in spite of warning shouts, shot out across the treacherous ice, and although partly submerged himself, dragged in the half-drowned youth, receiving afterwards a silver medal from the Massachusetts Humane Society. When the recipient of the medal referred to its bestowal, he used to delight in recalling the comment of a neighboring farmer, who had asserted that the boy so bravely rescued was "the worst melon-thief in the vicinity" and that his rescuer "might as well have let him drown." A few years after this episode, Trowbridge wrote a story suggested by the incident, entitled "The Silver Medal."

On the occasion of the banquet given to celebrate Whittier's seventieth birthday, Trowbridge was one of those asked to contribute to the evening's pro-gramme. He willingly complied, and wrote his poem entitled "The Story of a Barefoot Boy" founded upon an incident in Whittier's boyhood. This pro-duction he failed to read upon the night in question as the guest-of-honor withdrew before Trowbridge's contribution had been reached, and the latter decided to reserve his verses for publication later. The story in the poem was gleaned from the Quaker poet's younger brother, who had told it much as it is told in the poem; it was the tale of two small Quaker boys in their bedroom under the roof, who acted upon the suggestion that by lifting each other in turn they could rise to the ceiling, and perchance much farther if they were out of doors. They first tried the experi-

ment standing upon their bed, as described by the
author, who, in his conclusion, points out that despite
the boys' seeming ill-success, their plan was not a
failure:

> "Kind Nature smiled on that wise child,
> Nor could her love deny him
> The large fulfillment of his plan,
> Since he who lifts a fellow-man
> In turn is lifted by him."

Trowbridge's poem "At Sea" was a great favorite
with Whittier, and a year or so before his death he
took down the volume containing it and read it aloud
to those present, remarking at the end that "it was
the best work of the writer," and that "nothing
better of its kind was ever written by anybody."

In glancing over various pages of manuscript in
Trowbridge's graceful and distinctive writing, I find
his protest at the ease with which the fickle public
forgets the service rendered by the soldiers, embodied
in a poem, entitled "The Song of the Poor-House
Veterans" (doubtless contained in his collected
works). In reading it one is convinced that the same
constant reminder, "lest we forget," that is to-day
needed, was equally necessary after the Civil War.
In this "Song" the poet has contrasted the wild
acclamations that greeted the men "when first they
came home from the war," with the attitude of the
public a few years later, when those same men were
physically unable to make a decent living, and were
transported "over the hill to the Poor-House." In
Trowbridge's early work he espoused the abolitionists' cause, and his pen continued its public service

throughout his life, ever exerting its eloquence in behalf of truth and righteousness.

During his latest years this writer spent several winters in the South, where he frequently enjoyed the companionship of John Burroughs. Together they walked and talked of mutual literary interests, and upon one occasion they were photographed standing side by side serenely in the sunlight; two straight, vigorous figures of inspiring old age. The erect carriage was especially characteristic of Trowbridge, who always held his head and shoulders as if he were about to respond to the order "forward march." And in connection with this trait, he took much pleasure in recalling an encounter with a very black old negro woman while he was in the South. This "mammy" seemed to regard him with such especial favor that it awakened his curiosity, which continued unappeased until one day, when the old woman approached him and said: "Mr. Trowbridge, I done gotter tell you — I admire you a heap, sah, 'cause you reminds me of my dear dead husband — you walk so proud!"

When a few years before the death of Julia Ward Howe, a complimentary banquet was given in her honor and that of her friend, Thomas Wentworth Higginson, by the Boston Authors' Club, it devolved upon me to secure a collection of brief lines of remembrance from the invited guests. In answer to this request the following stanzas were composed by Trowbridge, which were subsequently inscribed on the evening's menu. He wrote of Mrs. Howe:

"She sang the Battle Hymn that rings
Down the long corridors of Time:
Her lifelong human service sings
Of Peace an anthem more sublime."

And of Colonel Higginson:

"His voice and pen have wrought
A fadeless name for him,
Of high and noble thought
The shining synonym."

CHAPTER XV

EDMUND CLARENCE STEDMAN

My earliest acquaintance with literary New York was gained under the hospitable roof of Edmund Clarence Stedman, known for years as the "banker-poet," a designation which he greatly disliked.

Stedman's home was a center of literary interests and activities, and few distinguished visitors passed through New York without enjoying his generous hospitality. It was a liberal education to sit at Stedman's table and listen to his enlightening descriptions of various men-of-letters and their work. His ideals of literary attainment were of the highest, and he had no patience for slipshod work, or the catering to commercial interest at the expense of the best literary production. He was unsparing in the standard he set for himself, and he demanded the same of others.

The Stedmans' Sunday evenings at home were of exceptional brilliancy, assembling as they did many eminent workers in the artistic and literary professions; the drawing-room was generally filled to overflowing, and the latest imported lion was apt to be the central figure. Refreshments were passed about informally, and as the evening advanced and many took their leave, a small, choice circle invariably gathered in Stedman's study, where, dominated by his magnetic personality, many important literary projects were discussed. Here, so my host asserted, Clyde Fitch drew inspiration for his first success, "Beau Brummel."

Fitch was then struggling to attain a foothold in the field of letters, and having known him previously in Boston, I had suggested that he attend one of my host's Sunday evenings. Knowing his marked peculiarity in dress, I rather dreaded his arrival, feeling assured that he would be startlingly arrayed; and I was not mistaken. He came wearing with evening dress a flowing tie and jewelry in great profusion. His personal appearance made more of an impression upon my host than did his intellectual endowment, and for days afterwards I was favored with sly remarks about my "friend with the necktie and rings."

Upon the night in question, Fitch with his great fund of enthusiasm entered heartily into the spirit of the evening, and he formed one of the intimate circle that later sat over the fire in the cozy study. Here Stedman, as was his wont, launched certain themes that interested him, and in the course of his remarks outlined the plot for a "Beau Brummel" play.

Whether this gave to Fitch the first suggestion of his future production or not, I cannot tell, but Stedman always claimed that on the evening when he "first saw the necktie," the rising dramatist acquired his interest in "Beau Brummel."

Before meeting Clyde Fitch, I had for some time known his mother, who was then living in Boston; a woman of exceptional beauty, who to my school-girl vision seemed always attired in blue velvet touched off with rare old lace, and with her exquisitely arranged white hair surmounted by hats with picturesquely drooping plumes. When I visited her apartment, she entertained me with stories of her son's dramatic and literary attainments, and showed me what he had done to beautify her room; tables, cushions, and lampshades all testifying to his ingenious touch. And upon one occasion, as I sat in a chair that he had decorated, I was allowed the privilege of reading his humorous description of all that he had suffered while tutoring two children at the close of his college days. The story of this episode, which was to his sensitive organization a nerveracking experience, was written to edify his mother, and illustrated by his clever water-color sketches. It had marvelous covers designed by its producer, which were so veritably enchanting as almost to obscure the brilliancy of that which lay between; these were made all of sealing-wax applied with Vedderesque effect, the net result defying all commonplace description. The story contained therein set forth the misery of a tutor's life, too great to be endured by Fitch, who soon relinquished it, having summed up his feelings in the following epitaph, of which he said:

"And on my marble mausoleum let there be carved no autographs of Lily Langtry, Henry Ward Beecher, or Clara Urquhart Potter, but only this simple epitaph:

'Here lies the body of William Clyde,
Who tutored two pupils until he died,
A tutor's life to this youth was not suited,
And gladly he skipped when the Death Angel tooted'."

The memory of the decorated chair and book is

supplemented by various others, one of which recalls
an afternoon in my own home when Fitch was sadly
grieved because he overturned his cup of tea; a
trifling happening, which would have been almost
unnoted by the average guest, but which he took
deeply to heart, so truly did he pride himself upon
performing gracefully and deftly all small social
requirements.

Another recollection of Clyde Fitch is in connection
with his studio at Fifty-third Street, where he gave
readings and presided over dainty little teas, and
where the walls were plentifully draped with fish-net
and decorated with pictures of stage favorites. These
days of strict economy and simple entertainments
contrasted vividly with those which followed a few
years later, when his house was a veritable museum,
and his guests dined in state off a gauzy lace table-
cloth protected by a sheet of glass.

As I recall the figures that filled the drawing-room
at Stedman's home upon those Sunday evenings so
long ago, many are dim and shadowy in my mind,
but some remain as clearly outlined as when I saw
them first. Among these were Mr. and Mrs. Richard
Watson Gilder, whose charming Friday evenings
were also centers of literary interest; Mr. and Mrs.
Stoddard; and Mrs. Sargent, who at that time was
carrying on her social evenings in New York, which
had succeeded her notable gatherings in Boston;
Frank Stockton and dear old Christopher Cranch
were sometimes present, and Thomas A. Janvier
(Ivory Black), a dashing figure, adored by all the
ladies; Maud Wilder Goodwin, Clinton Scollard,

W. D. Howells, Moncure D. Conway, Hamilton Mabie, Laurence Hutton, Henry Harland, Edwin Markham, and many more were frequent guests. There was invariably some brief and impromptu literary feature, some entertaining bit of prose, or a few poems read, but no set entertainment was provided, and no confining camp-stools set about.

One other literary personage whose home had been for years a literary rendezvous was Mrs. Anna C. L. Botta. And I was taken to meet the interesting old lady who had presided over so many groups of gifted and famous persons. In seeing her it was hard to realize that this little lady's memories stretched back to the childhood of literary New York; that when she was Anna C. Lynch she knew Edgar Allan Poe well, in the days when he was struggling to earn a living; and that it was in her drawing-room that he first launched "The Raven" upon an appreciative circle.

Stedman, besides being the friend, adviser, and confidant of a circle of writers older than himself, was called the "Father Confessor" of the younger poets; hundreds of their confidential letters were sympathetically answered by him, and his words of advice and cheer smoothed the path and sustained the courage of many young literary aspirants. He gave freely of himself and greatly exhausted his nervous energy in so doing. A characteristic instance of his kindness may be quoted. One Thanksgiving Day, when he and his guests were about to sit down to dinner, he received a note saying that a young writer's wife and children were in dire want. With his own hands he

packed a basket of food, dispatching it with a check
to the needy family before he would sit down to his
own table.

From the memories which cluster around Stedman's home in New York one turns to those which
are associated with his picturesque summer home at
New Castle, New Hampshire, where he spent many
of his happiest hours, and where it was a delight to
visit. "Kelp Rock," with its stone-tower and its
magnificent sea view, was a veritable poet's Utopia,
and in his study there Stedman produced some of his
finest poems.

From "Kelp Rock" he wrote to my father: "I am
staying a little with 'mine own' in our country home,
which looks now as if we had lived in it these hundred
years. To-day there is a wild so'easter on, which
makes the little fireplace in my turret quite attractive. So here I am writing a few letters. Were you
here you should have a good pipe, the spare rocking-
chair, and look through the windows to sea or harbor
as you chose."

Escaping thither from the pandemonium of Wall
Street Stedman, for a time at least, could throw off
the financial shackles. In his stone tower, he planned
a future in which he could relinquish financial problems and devote his remaining years to literary
labors. At fifty a man may well look forward to
twenty years of fruitful activities, and after years of
drudgery Stedman had secured for himself a comfortable living, and had reached a point where he might
retire from the turmoil of Wall Street. But such
happy dreams proved fleeting, for even as he gazed

on the bright vision from his poet's tower, the "sea-change" came. A sudden financial blow, dealt by his eldest son, who had plunged into some wild business scheme unknown to his father, swept everything away and the long struggle was begun again; a struggle which meant years of strenuous toil. The burden of indebtedness which he then took upon his shoulders was triumphantly discharged at the end of twenty years, and then his burden of life was also laid aside.

After the crash he promptly gave up his charming New York home, and a little later "Kelp Rock," and with it many cherished dreams. Whatever Edmund Clarence Stedman accomplished in the field of letters, although no doubt a monumental work, was to him but a meager showing compared with that which he had planned to do. What others called success, he mourned as failure. Yet whatever mourning may have gone on in the depths of a soul possessed of such ideals and literary aspirations, there was no external sign of depression, save on rare occasions. With a cheery exterior and ever-ready sympathy, Stedman went on his way, adhering to his determination to be gay and to be game.

Regarding the publication of "The Poets of America," he wrote my father in characteristic vein:

"Your note received, with all its encouraging words about my new volume. I hope people will be interested in it; if not, the best and most significant portion of my luckless life, for a few years past, is quite thrown away. For my part it is a perpetual mystery to me *who buys new books*. Of course I expect the public libraries to buy them. Such a work as mine ought to be in every town library, and I am told there are thousands of public libraries in the United States. How do publishers ever reach them scattered as they are? I *know* there is hard work, information, interest and (I trust) good writing in the 'Poets of America,' but are books sure to sell on their merits? That is a mystery to me always.

"Your edition of Howells's poems came last night and is exquisite. I at once wrote W. D. H. expressing my pleasure at seeing his poems in this form. The average newspaper critic, like the public, is an ass. Because Howells had become so notable through his exquisite prose, the press would not recognize the charm and naturalness of his poems. If H. had kept on as a poet, with the same unflinching industry, he would have reached a high mark. But, as I say in the P. of A., he has on the whole done better for our prestige by leading a school of novelists or reaching the head of it, as America already had made a recent march in poetry. I think his poems, in this new form, will do better on this trial."

To the many tempting invitations that came to Stedman from his circle of literary friends in Boston to be present at their various gatherings, he persistently said "no" during those strenuous years in which he toiled to retrieve his fortune.

In October, 1886, he wrote, while away on a brief outing, in answer to an invitation to the dinner given for Lowell:

"Your repeated invitation plainly comes from the heart. If I lived in Boston, nothing could keep me

away from the Lowell-Holmes combination. It will
be an historic, almost dramatic occasion. But I have
lingered here too long. Once in New York, I cannot
and must not be upset by any notable and pleasurable distractions. A spell has rested upon me for
some years; my status will be irretrievable if I don't
pledge all my thoughts and time, the coming season,
to retrieving it. My debts must be paid."

Stedman's life was always lived at a high tension
and daily tuned to concert-pitch, and one can only
wonder that the highly organized, delicate machine
ran on beyond the limit of threescore years and ten.
The atmosphere of the Stedman household was stimulating and often inspiring, but never tranquil. Important guests were always upon the point of arrival
or departure, financial problems were always pend-
ing, and Stedman was always working up to the limit
of his strength and then taking on one thing more.

His attitude toward the great city, of which he was
the "Poet Laureate," on many notable occasions is
summarized in a letter to his publisher, headed "The
Metropolis," in which he wrote:

"No Bostonian ever can comprehend one thing —
the fact that New York does not belong to, or represent, the people who happen at any one time to
occupy its dwellings, but the *whole country*. Every
American who passes one day and night here is as
much of a 'New Yorker' as I am. I have fewer local
acquaintances than I had ten years ago. This island
is simply the meeting-place, the *to be* beautiful and
attractive and cloistered Solomon's Temple for all
our new world Judæa. The city belongs to *all* Ameri-

cans, and it is the duty of all to contribute to and enrich its shrines and monuments."

This "duty" was admirably performed by New York's "Poet Laureate," nor was his sphere of public-spirited activities limited by the boundaries of his city, or his nation. He was identified with the interests of art, letters and humanity the world over. At the time of his death he was making extensive plans for the National Institute of Arts and Letters, in the Presidency of which he succeeded Mr. Warner and Mr. Howells. The Presidency of the American Copyright League was another office which he filled with his accustomed zeal, succeeding there his distinguished predecessor, James Russell Lowell. The Century Association, the New York Authors' Club, the New England Society, and a long list of other notable organizations have benefited by his guiding hand.

Wherever literary interests were at stake or literary ideals threatened, there the voice and pen of Stedman spoke decisively and eloquently. His literary integrity was proof against alluring offers and tempting monetary baits. He often wanted money, but never was the need so great as to cause him to produce a poem or undertake a special article in which he could not embody his best work or highest poetic inspiration.

One of my latest memories of Stedman presents a characteristic incident which occurred a year or two before his death, when he was living at Bronx Park, where I had been for a brief visit. I was returning to New York by the same train that he took in the morning, and was instructed by his family not to allow him to talk during the trip. He had been having trouble with his voice and had been charged to guard it for some important meeting at which he was scheduled to preside, and consequently I was advised to slip away into a separate car so that he might not be tempted to exert himself. I was ready to carry out this plan discreetly, reënforced in my determination by my host's exclamation: "I'm sorry I can't talk to you on the way up to town; my voice is in bad shape."

I begged him not to think of such a thing, and as the train drew up, hastened into a rear car, seated myself, and was contentedly gazing out of the window, when hurrying toward me down the aisle I saw my host approaching with an air of evident annoyance, as if I had been trying to escape him without reason. He took his place beside me and proceeded to converse entertainingly upon all kinds of subjects until the train reached Forty-Second Street. Then he rose, saying reproachfully: "I should n't have used my voice at all! Now I shall pay for it all the rest of the day." And I was left repentant for a sin that I had tried faithfully not to commit.

Stedman's final visit to our home, and his last coming to Boston, was at the time of Thomas Bailey Aldrich's funeral, where he acted as an honorary pall-bearer. I accompanied him to the church, and on the way his alert vision took in every object that came within its range. He had not been in Boston for some years and not a street, building, or landmark escaped his notice. On our return from what was a triumphal service, Stedman declared that to his

"The Undiscovered Country"

Could we but know
The land that ends our dark, uncertain travel,
Where lie those happier hills and waters low, —
Ah, if beyond the spirit's inmost cavil
Aught of that Country could we surely know,
Who would not go?

Might we but hear
The hovering angels' high imagined chorus,
Or catch, betimes, with wakeful eyes and clear,
One radiant vista of the realm before us, —
With one rapt moment given to see and hear,
Ah, who would fear?

Were we quite sure
To find the peerless, friend who left us lonely,
Or there, by some celestial stream as pure,
To gaze in eyes that here were lovelit only, —
This weary mortal coil, were we quite sure,
Who would endure?

"

1865
1907

Edmund Clarence Stedman

thinking Aldrich's existence had been one of "absolute success." Then he enumerated all that life had brought to his friend; health, popularity, a loving family circle, genuine artistic accomplishment, and generous recognition of its value, coupled with freedom from financial worries. He asserted that this life stood out above all he had known as happy and successful from start to finish.

It was during this final visit that I asked him, with some trepidation, if he would copy for me his "Undiscovered Country," which was a favorite of mine. I knew that latterly he had resented the too frequent quotation of this early poem, feeling that he had produced finer things which had received less attention. Indeed, some time before this he had decisively refused its use in an anthology, declaring that it had been reprinted far too often, and he was perfectly astonished that I, who knew his work, should not have chosen something else. Yet, upon his return to New York, he sent me a beautifully penned copy, in his artistic writing, which was so truly a poet's hand. I think that in his heart this poem was so dear to him that he hated to have it bandied from lip to lip by those that had but superficial knowledge of his work.

It was written in 1865, immediately after the passing away of Mrs. Stedman's younger sister, Abby Woodworth, whose last illness occurred at the former's house in New York. Before her death, the young girl said good-bye to her little nephews, and told them, smiling, of the beautiful "Home" to which she was going. After her spirit had passed, and the other watchers had gone to take a rest, Stedman sat down in the library and wrote the first stanza of "The Undiscovered Country," which he read with trembling voice to his sister-in-law, Ella:

"Could we but know
The land that ends our dark, uncertain travel,
    Where lie those happier hills and meadows low,—
Ah, if beyond the spirit's inmost cavil,
    Aught of that country could we surely know,
    Who would not go?"

Then the two discussed the possibilities of the future life, which had seemed so real to the dying girl, and after that, Stedman went to his desk and completed the poem. In later years it was set to music by Dudley Buck, and its author delighted to hear it sung. At his request it was sung at the funeral of his wife, and of his elder son. When at the end of January, 1908, Stedman passed away, it was my privilege to attend the impressive services held at the Church of the Messiah in New York. There a concourse of distinguished persons gathered to listen to the tributes paid by the poet's warm friends, Dr. Robert Collyer and Dr. Henry van Dyke; and at the close of the service "The Undiscovered Country" was exquisitely rendered.

CHAPTER XVI

A LAST GLIMPSE OF THE STODDARDS

SEATED beside the little fireside in their old-fashioned sitting-room, where they had spent so many happy hours in their home on Fifteenth Street, I saw the Stoddards for the last time. Age and infirmities had overtaken this gifted couple, each of whom had played a vital part in the literary and social life of a generation that had passed on.

They were still keenly interested in the activities and movements taking place in the busy world outside, but they were no longer a part of the new life; they had become helpless onlookers waiting the summons to depart from a field in which they had broken so many lances.

As I sat down beside them I found them eager to hear the latest literary news, especially that from New England, the birthplace of both, which had in past years held so many of their friends. Then Mrs. Stoddard spoke of her own books, and said with a blending of fun and sadness: "What do you suppose my royalties amounted to last year? A dollar and a half!"

They were a truly pathetic pair as they sat in the twilight, warming themselves by the small grate and soberly recalling writers and incidents of earlier times. Watching them one could but remember Stoddard's own thoughts about old age, embodied in his poem "The Flight of Youth," written long years before, in which the opening stanza reads:

> "There are gains for all our hopes,
> There are balms for all our pain;
> But when youth, the dream, departs,
> It takes something from our hearts,
> And it never comes again."

At the time when I last saw them, there was, however, a "balm for all their pain" in the person of their son Lorimer, a lovable and brilliant fellow, who had already made a name for himself in the world of letters, and who was looked upon as one of the coming dramatists of his time. To talk of "Lorry" was to banish all regrets and disappointments and to forget the flight of time; he was the joyous, active present; the hope of their declining days, and their enthusiasm centered in his achievements.

I had first met him years before when he had been a frequent visitor at Stedman's home in company with his parents, who were then still a part of New York's literary life and able to enjoy its social functions. During those early days Lorimer's work was read and eagerly discussed by all their friends, and it continued to be the all-absorbing interest of his parents, who little dreamed that he was destined to lay down his pen so soon. Yet, when he passed away, leaving them all alone by the slow-dying embers, they faced the loss heroically.

"Baffled, not beaten," were the words of Stoddard, himself almost completely blind, to a friend who came to see him after Lorimer's death. And this was the keynote of the mood in which he awaited death, after the passing of his wife.

The small brick house on East Fifteenth Street, which was the Stoddard home from about 1870 until Mr. Stoddard, the last survivor, passed away in 1903, was filled with literary treasures. In the study upon the second floor, Stoddard was nearly always to be found at work at his desk, with Thackeray's portrait and verses on the wall above him; strong lights and powerful glasses aided his failing eyesight, in his last years, and books were heaped about him on the floor. Books lined the walls, and there were many rare editions, autograph copies, and all manner of precious memorabilia of famous writers, which Stoddard finally presented to the New York Authors' Club. He possessed many priceless manuscripts and letters of Hawthorne, Poe, Petrarch, Tennyson, and Browning, and he delighted to recount some story which the manuscripts or letters might serve to illustrate.

Especially of Bayard Taylor and Poe was Stoddard wont to speak, explaining that any severe criticisms of the latter which had come from his pen were never the result of any personal animus arising from a youthful encounter with the erratic genius. Despite Stoddard's assurance to the contrary, one was inclined to fancy that it was difficult for him to forget, even if he forgave, Poe's treatment of him when as a young contributor he had sent a poem to the paper Poe was editing. The poem was so good that it was promptly accepted, and then upon further examination Poe found it so remarkable that he decided it was a translation from the French. Stoddard was so informed, and when he came to assure the editor that his work was wholly original, he happened to find him in a moment of extreme excitement, the result being that Poe flatly declared the young man was telling him a falsehood, and rudely ejected him from the editorial sanctum, threatening to help him down the stairs. While Stoddard afterwards reflected philosophically, that Poe's belief that he had stolen the work of some French master was an undoubted compliment, the fact remained that Stoddard's *amour propre* was sadly bruised by the encounter.

Bayard Taylor had been one of Stoddard's closest friends, and held a place of peculiar intimacy in his life and memory, though he had been one of the earliest to leave that literary circle that had gathered at the Century Club for so many years. One after another of that group had gradually passed on, until few of Stoddard's contemporaries remained. And, when, in 1897, the New York Authors' Club honored him by an appreciation, the Century Club shared in the testimonial, which was pronounced the most memorable literary occasion that had taken place in New York since the celebration of Bryant's birthday. Stoddard was overwhelmed by this ovation, feeling that such a tribute was the crowning honor of his life; and in return, he made the Authors' Club a gift of his rare manuscripts and autograph treasures. Less than a year before his death, the club received this notable collection, which he had helped to arrange, and which with the assistance of his remarkable memory had been catalogued and classified.

On that last afternoon spent in the little sitting-room with Mr. and Mrs. Stoddard, I can remember telling them by way of entertainment all that I had been doing, remarking at the end that I had just been shopping for some neckties to take home as tokens to my brothers. Then Mrs. Stoddard promptly expressed a wish to see the ties, and when they were displayed, she became enthusiastic about the style and pattern, which I believe was something in green and blue, with stripes running diagonally across. As she held up one of the ties, she offered the suggestion that something of the sort would look well on her husband.

I eagerly inquired if she meant that Mr. Stoddard could be induced to wear one of these ties?

"Of course he could!" she exclaimed with delight, and I insisted that it would be a privilege to present one to him. The tie was smilingly accepted, and I went on my way without giving the trifling matter a second thought, until a few days later, the story of the tie came fluttering back to me in this wise:

In the course of a conversation regarding some meeting at the Players' Club, a friend chanced to remark: "And I saw Lorry Stoddard there in a resplendent tie!" A sudden thought caused me to ask: "What was the pattern?" And when it was described, I comprehended the whole amusing episode. Dear Mrs. Stoddard's playful suggestion that the tie would well become her husband was only motherly camouflage. She had no idea of wasting the new tie upon her aged helpmate by the fireside. At the first glance, she had thought only of her youthful idol. So "Lorry" wore the tie; but "Lorry" never knew I knew he wore it, and it is likely that he never knew I bought it.

CHAPTER XVII

WILLIAM WINTER

A TRULY picturesque figure, and a lovable though eccentric personality; such was the impression which one received when William Winter dawned upon the vision, with a tangle of white hair that drooped like a fringe over his eyebrows. His form rises before me as I used to see him when he would drop in after the theater at the house of a friend at Staten Island, or at Stedman's home in New York, and discourse authoritatively upon dramatic topics. His early New England associations made him ever turn with interest to the doings in Boston, and his friendship for Longfellow and others of the old "Atlantic" circle was very warm and true.

One of the sorrows of his life was the loss of his son Arthur, a remarkable boy of fourteen years who was killed in a coasting accident, from which tragedy the father never fully recovered. When I first knew him, some years had elapsed following the loss of the boy but one could not fail to perceive how deeply the bereavement had affected his life.

In looking over a collection of Winter's letters dealing with several of his publications, and penned in his extraordinary hand, which at a little distance reminds one of Chinese characters, a number of interesting communications present themselves. Most touching are those written in reference to his found-

ing of the "Arthur Winter Memorial Library" in the
Staten Island Academy, where his son had been a
student. The enlargement of this collection of books
brought him some measure of solace, and his friends
gladly contributed to this project, concerning which
he writes in 1886:

"I observe your inquiry about the Memorial
Library. Any book that you might be pleased to
send would be gratefully received, as a gift to my
dear boy, dead and gone, but never dead to me!"

And on receipt of some books a fortnight later, he
says in response:

"The packet of books so kindly sent by your house
for the Library that I have founded in commemora-
tion of my son has been received. I thank you for
your generous goodness. The selection of books that
you have made impresses me as particularly felici-
tous. The works relative to painting and sculpture
are especially welcome. I cannot find the right words
to use in writing about this lamentable and most
afflicting theme. There is always the danger of my
saying too much, if I say anything. God grant that
you may never know the horror and bitterness of
calamity that has been poured out upon me. Death
as it came to this home, came with all its cruelty, and
all its terrors, and the blow has almost paralyzed my
mind. I live on from day to day and I try to do my
duty as well as I can; but for me the play is over.
I have founded the library in order to keep alive,
for yet a little while, the memory of the noble and
brave and loving and beautiful creature, who once
was my companion, my joy, my hope; and also be-

cause in giving these books I seem to be doing something to make him know my constant love. It will do good to others, likewise, and the whole of his life was passed in doing good. He was a natural benefactor, and he imparted happiness to all who came near him. Your gift is deeply appreciated by me. I can say no more."

After a trip abroad, Winter produced "English Rambles" and "Shakespeare's England," which were among his earliest books. Following his return he wrote:

"I have just arrived home, after a most varied and busy tour, through parts of England, France, and Germany. I have seen many beautiful and impressive sights, but so rapidly that they have bewildered me. . . .

"The homeward voyage began on August 5th, so after all this travel I am here again inside of eight weeks, and shall at once resume my interrupted labors. In London I had some delightful walks with Hutton, and found him even better and dearer than ever, one of the best good fellows that ever lived. I have improved the time night and day, visited old churches, wandering in the streets and in the fields, musing at the tombs of great men, looking at pictures and statues and theatrical performances, and trying (without success) to think it all over.

"I have scarcely slept at all. The social duties were numerous and onerous, and I lost about two days by illness. . . . At Stuttgart I met Miss Blanche Willis Howard, and I was most impressed with her poise of character and elegance of manner. She seems, however, to be chafing against the bars of a cage, in the narrow, restricted life of that conventional, pompous, and stupid capital. We had a pleasant talk of literary activities, and I think that she was amazed at my heterodox opinions. I have met many old acquaintances and several new ones, Irving, Clarke, Bancroft, Hutton, and others. Booth and I were often together. Bond came on the scene, and of course was a genial and welcome companion. . . . Miss Edwina Booth is very much better in health, in fact quite recovered. Hutton has got an excellent idea for a book, and is already hard at it."

Winter's books on England were followed by sketches of Booth, Jefferson, and others in the dramatic world, as well as by the publication of some volumes of verse. He was a great admirer of the work of Fitz James O'Brien, and in 1881 he edited his works, bringing out the first volume of this writer's stories ever published. This book was dedicated to "The Army of the Potomac, under whose flag he fought, and for whose cause he died."

Fitz James O'Brien was but thirty-four at the time of his death, and his writings were scattered far and wide, so that when eighteen years after his departure, Winter, almost the last survivor among his old associates, undertook to gather together his writings, it was no easy task. When it was completed, the volume was issued with an accompanying sketch of the author by Winter.

O'Brien's gruesome tale entitled: "What was it?" was written at odd moments in the lodgings of his friend Aldrich, with whose destiny this writer's was strangely linked. When the Civil War broke out, a chance occurrence placed O'Brien in Aldrich's place, a place in which the former received his mortal wound. It is stated that Aldrich and O'Brien applied at almost the same time for a position on General Lander's staff, and that the application of Aldrich, an old friend of Lander's, was received a few days before that of O'Brien. General Lander sent a telegram to Aldrich at Portsmouth offering him a staff appointment with the rank of Lieutenant. In the meantime Aldrich had left Portsmouth and the telegram remained there unopened. Thereupon, the General, receiving no answer to his dispatch, gave the post to O'Brien, who figured in several brilliant military exploits before receiving his fatal wound on February 26, 1862. On that date O'Brien took part in a skirmish with the enemy in which his cavalry force of thirty-five was pitted against over two hundred Confederate troops, but came off unharmed, except for O'Brien, whose encounter with a Confederate Colonel was practically a duel. At twenty paces, they fired with great deliberation three shots. O'Brien was hit by his opponent's second shot, and the last one fired by him killed the opposing Colonel Ashley. O'Brien suffered for several weeks, then lock-jaw set in, and on April 5th he passed away at Cumberland, Virginia. He was brought back to New York and buried with military honors in Greenwood Cemetery.

In writing to his publishers during the preparation of O'Brien's book, Winter said of him: "He certainly was one of the most brilliantly creative men of genius that have lived within the last fifty years. His early

death in the service of the United States, in our war
for the Union, is another claim to remembrance."

William Winter was born at Gloucester, Massachusetts, which was also the home town of Edwin Percy
Whipple; he was a graduate of the Harvard Law
School, and when he was twenty-three years old
began his literary career in New York; in 1865 he
became dramatic critic for the "New York Tribune,"
a position which he held for over thirty years, and
where he battled valiantly for the upholding and up-
lifting of the American stage.

Soon after his association with the "Tribune" had
been severed, a complimentary luncheon was given
him by his literary friends, and this occasion, which
it was my good fortune to attend, was one of great
happiness for him. He was at that time the recipient
of many touching tributes from a host of fellow-
craftsmen, and when he rose to thank them he was
too deeply moved to speak; tears were in his eyes and
he could only murmur his heartfelt gratitude and sink
into his seat. His last years were productive of much
literary accomplishment, and many volumes of his
collected works were published during his latter days.
He produced many lovely lyrics, and among these,
perhaps the one most widely quoted is that which
closes with the lines:

> "Friends have fallen, youth is gone,
>   Fields are brown and skies are wan;
>
> "One name I shall not forget,
>   Gentle name of Violet."

CHAPTER XVIII

EUGENE FIELD'S FIRST BOOK

ONE evening long ago I sat up very late awaiting the arrival of Eugene Field, who, owing to a sudden change of plan, failed to appear. Upon the following day I chanced to meet him at my father's office, in Boston, and told him of the hours of sleep which I had sacrificed on his behalf. For this he expressed much regret, and after my departure, he called for sheets of paper and bottles of ink (one kind of ink never being sufficient to satisfy his variegated taste in this direction), and in his most exquisite writing did penance, by copying for me one of his loveliest poems entitled "Ye Lyttel Boy." This he dispatched as compensation for my lost sleep, and never were wakeful hours more generously paid for. I later learned that this especial poem, which was one of the writer's favorites, was also one which he had quite persistently refused to copy, even when urged to do so by one of his best friends; so I possess my treasure in grateful memory of the winning and wayward author whose first book bore the imprint of my father's firm.

An author's attitude toward his first book is singularly like that of a parent toward his first child; it may have many superior successors, who are both bigger and more beautiful, but there is never another "first."

Eugene Field's little volume entitled "Culture's

The Chicago Dante.

Dear Mr. Ticknor — I send today the last batch of the clippings and among them you will find two handsome engravings which I have executed for your special (private) edification. The portrait of myself I made from a photograph taken in 1880; I look more like Dante now than I did then. In this packet I inclose one little story which should be put with the other stories I sent you. I had forgotten all about it and found it in the old files. In this lot of stuff you will find a criticism of the Wagner opera, "Die Walküre," when it appeared it made quite a stir among folk here. But I am heartily sick of this whole scheme. Sincerely Yours,

Eugene Field.

May the 22nd, 1887.

Garland" was his first literary baby. He loved it, coddled it, discoursed about it, and dreamed dreams of its future. What mattered it, that a few years later he came to deplore its faults, and sounded an emphatic note for its recall; he had already bestowed upon it that first enthusiasm which never comes but once in the experience of any writer.

In consequence of a suggestion from Edmund Clarence Stedman, who ever watched the rising poets, my father wrote to Field in 1887 asking for a collection of his poems, and expressing keen interest in his work. To this Field replied in the following communication, declining to discuss any poetic proposition, but calling attention to his sketches and short stories which he wished to exploit:

DEAR MR. TICKNOR:

I hardly know what I ought to say in answer to your courteous letter of the 23rd ultimo. I am just enough of a Yankee to be a long time making up my mind when once in doubt. However, it is but fair that you should know what bothers me. I am not troubled about my verse, for I made up my mind long ago that my verse never did and never would amount to a ———. Let us drop the painful subject of verse. I have written about forty short stories (or shall I call them sketches?) in the last two years. I really have a good opinion of them, and this opinion has been encouraged by the favor with which these tales have been received by readers, for you must know that nearly all the stories have appeared in print. I would like to see these tales in book form. I

believe they would sell. Of their merit I have no
doubt, but whether they would strike you as market-
able — why, that is the question. I have spent much
time on them, and if you were to indicate a desire to
publish them I would want to rewrite them over again
— for, just as a mother is anxious to have her little
children appear decently and properly, so do I want
these children of mine to go out into the world
apparelled as neatly as my intellectual purse can
afford. . . .

I send you a schedule which may assist you in
making up your mind as to whether you care about
reading my tales. . . .

Very truly yours,
Eugene Field

Accompanying this letter was Field's diagram of
the forty stories, executed in truly decorative form,
consisting of four columns penned in different-
colored inks; the first, in blue, contained the names
of the stories; the second, in red, the number of words
in each; the third, in green, offered the sub-titles of
the tales; while the fourth, in blue again, defined the
motive of each story, as "pathetic," "gay," "lively,"
and so on.

The result of this letter was the forwarding of a
large collection of stories and clippings, from which
the publisher eventually selected enough material
to make up a humorous little volume, characteristic
of the author's wit, including both brief sketches and
verse; this little book to be the forerunner of more
serious work to come.

With the final batch of copy, which the author apparently felt did not contain his most representative work, he sent the following letter, decorated in his inimitable penmanship with a caricature of himself as the "Chicago Dante," wearing a wreath of sausages about his head:

"I send to-day the last batch of clippings, and amongst them you will find two handsome engravings, which I have executed for your special (private) edification. The portrait of myself I made from a photograph taken in 1880; I look more like Dante now than I did then. . . .

"I am heartily sick of this whole scheme. Why not print the genteel stories and let this flubdub remain undiscovered until I am in heaven with Mr. Stedman and you? Then your grandson (Eugene Field Ticknor) can announce the discovery of genuine old Field manuscripts, the critics will dispute, the public will go wild, fifty editions of the great work will be struck off, the demand will increase in volume and ferocity, etc. Ought we not to make this sacrifice for posterity?"

Field, having learned of Stedman's interest in his work, at once forwarded the suggestion to his publisher that Stedman should be invited to write a preface for his book. This suggestion struck Stedman as truly incongruous, and he declined in such decisive terms that the publisher was forced to soften the refusal considerably before imparting the substance to Field. The latter was keenly disappointed, and continued to refer to the matter in various amusing references to Stedman's point of view, which, however, concealed some little chagrin.

In the meantime his friendly relations with his publisher had strengthened into a warm friendship, which Field expressed in his own original fashion, sending numerous tokens of his regard in the form of beautifully decorative ballads, and pen-and-ink drawings executed with exquisite nicety. From the first he was absolutely indifferent to the monetary side of the transaction as is evident in the following statement:

"So far as the business part of our joint book is concerned, I feel no interest at all. I do not look upon my heaven-given talents with the sordid eyes of the average Chicago *littérateur*. If Mr. Stedman and you think that from the mass of erudition I have wafted Bostonward you can expiscate enough desirable matter for a tome — why, I am going to let you have your own way, and I'm not going to worry about the business part of the scheme. I hope you will let me know when the book is likely to appear, as I shall be hunting a cyclone hole about that time. Perhaps you may remember what that humorous old Aristophanes once said to Critobolus, his Athenian publisher:

[Here Field inserted four humorous lines in semi-Greek and English text, which, when deciphered, read:]

> "It's fun for Ticknor and for Stedman;
> But if that book appears out West
> It's ten to one that I'm a dead man
> Before the next spring robins nest.

"I am strongly of the impression that you ought to inveigle Mr. Stedman into writing an introduction to that book. I have a positive conviction that his apology for the affair would be the most humorous thing between the covers. . . . I suspect that his regard for me is simply the cold, mercenary, sordid passion which the crocodile conceives for a succulent yellow dog; I have discovered that he does not mention me among his Victorious Poets."

As Stedman remained inflexible, it was suggested that Julian Hawthorne should be asked to furnish the Preface, and in regard to this, Field wrote under the heading, "Cool Chicago, June 18, 1887": "I have dispatched a letter to Hawthorne upon the subject of the preface. It was not at all Christianly of Mr. Stedman to inveigle me into this circus and then leave me at the mercy of the multitude. I would not treat him likewise. If he were to ask me to write a preface for any of his books, I would do it, and it would be the boss preface in English literature, too. The plea that he has n't time to devote to it is a feeble one; if I can write an able preface for his book in fifteen minutes, he ought to be able to write a fairly good one for mine in half an hour.

"By the way, do you know this man Fiske, who has written a book on fairy mythology? The work is dedicated to 'my dear friend Howells?' I would like you to get from him a list of the books he consulted in his compilation of the work. I see that he refers to the 'Grettis saga' and I fancy he means Grettir saga. If Fiske is not a moss-back — that is to say if he is one of us who are now on earth — I should like to write to him for some information; I am deeply interested in fairy mythology and I have never yet been able to find a satisfactory work upon the subject.

Grimm, Clouston, Thorpe, and Fiske I have, but none fills the bill.

"I am just now having a beautiful time over the Percy Folio. Why don't some of your opulent publishers form a pool and hire me to travel over the country, getting together old manuscript verse? There are thousands of fine old poems, songs, etc., locked up in the private libraries of your New England villages.

"And the rich old Southerners must have written a power of good verse that has never seen printer's ink. Daniel Webster wrote verse, of course; Rufus Choate, too, and Washington Irving, and John C. Calhoun, and Charles Sumner, and—why, if we could only get a whack at the musty papers which the heirs of your great intellects have committed to the depths of old trunks and cedar chests."

(At the head of this letter was drawn in red-and-black ink a thermometer which registers 110. The letter is written in green ink.)

Following a communication penned in imitation Greek lettering Field remarks:

"You may have some difficulty in reading my Greek, but I think it is best to let you know, every now and then, that you are dealing with a very scholarly person. The trouble with most Eastern publishers is that they imagine that Western *littérateurs* can't do anything but weigh and kill hogs. . . .

"Mr. Stedman need not be ashamed to write a preface for me. I'd have him know that a biographical sketch of myself appeared last winter in A. T. Andreas & Co.'s Pictorial Chicago, vol. 3. It would have had my portrait, too, if I'd been willing to pay $50 for the boon. If Mr. Stedman is smart he will make himself solid with the brain and brawn of the West. A lot of us young *littérateurs* will write the obituaries by and by. Or, if he prefers, I will write the preface and sign his name to it. I fancy that I could say more pleasant things of myself than he could."

The matter of the preface having been finally settled, Field wrote:

"Hawthorne writes me that he will undertake the preface, and I think it will be well to send him duplicate proofs, so that he may get some idea of what he is expected to say. . . . When you see Mr. Stedman, you can tell him (unless you think it would entirely crush him) that I have expunged him from the tablets of my memory. I enclose an allegorical tableau. I had an awful time with the arms, but the verdure on Bunker Hill more than requites the beholder."

(Accompanying this letter was a drawing of a man standing beside a pile of books, with Bunker Hill in the background. Under the sketch was written: "Allegorical tableau representing Ticknor and Co. standing on the shore of the blue Atlantic and pointing with pride to 'Culture's Garland,' saying, 'These are our Jewels!' " To the right appears Bunker Hill covered with soft verdure; near its summit is the famous Tree of Liberty. This drawing was done in black, blue, and green inks.)

One of the amusing features connected with the publication of "Culture's Garland" was the collection of humorous advertisements composed by Field and forwarded to the publisher with instructions to have them inserted at the back of the book. This request was complied with; the material being accompanied by an explanatory note to the effect that, "though it was foreign to their custom to accept advertising for their books, they were making an exception to their rule because of the high literary character of the special advertisements inserted."

The following note from Field purporting to come from an advertising firm accompanied his unique "advertisements":

Chicago, June 26, 1887.

DEAR SIR:

I am informed that one of the leading *littérateurs* of this city is about to produce a book under your auspices. Representing as I do the prominent advertising bureau of the West, I desire to contribute one page of advertisements to this work and I am prepared to pay therefor living cash rates. I inclose copy and would like to have the advertisements printed on fly leaf which will face the finis of the book in question.

Yours in the cause of literature

FELIX J. LONESOMEBOTTOM,

for

LONESOMEBOTTOM & CO.

The following is a sample of the advertising material forwarded:

W. H. Devine

(Indorsed by Theodore Thomas)

Wholesale Dealer in Cream, Milk, etc.,

Chicago, Ill.

Parties, Clubs, Societies and Festivals furnished with suppers or lunches at living rates. Has provided Refreshments for the Thomas Concerts for three seasons.

Devine's Pink Lemonade

A Noble Beverage, which cheers but does not intoxicate. Whets the appetite for Classic Music, and will remove grease spots from the finest fabric.

Field was a faithful student of Chaucer and delighted to produce imitations and paraphrases of his style, and he was never so happy as when making some friend a present of one of these exquisitely illuminated "Old English Ballads."

The following note accompanied one of these poems entitled "Ye divell & ye miller hys wiffe," and the succeeding one brought with it a second ballad entitled "Madge; ye hoyden"; the latter was executed on parchment, done in many-colored inks and decorated with characteristic marginal notes:

DEAR MR. TICKNOR:

I hope you will not print the old ballad in "that book." I have a lot of verse which you may want to put between covers after a while. I have just finished another "Proper" ballad entitled "Ye divell & ye miller hys wiffe." Dr. Bill Poole, our public librarian, is examining it just now to determine whether it is genuine or not. I think I shall have to get up a folio (like Percy's) of old Chicago ballads. I am having the parchment "coffed" at McClurg & Co.'s and shall begin copying at once. Running

parchment through coffee will (I am told) add about
200 years to the age of a poem. Hot? Well, I
should—

Hastily   FIELD

Accompanying the second ballad Field wrote:

"I have come upon quite a literary curiosity and
I will send it to you. It is an old English ballad entitled "Madge; ye hoyden." It was discovered by
an eminent Chicago archæologist and excavator in a
hair trunk in the cellar of a frame house at the north-
west corner of Indiana and Rush Streets, this city.
For many years it has been believed by our best
literati that there used to be genuine old English
balladists in Chicago before the fire; the ballad just
discovered and restored (by Prof. J. Pharaoh Botts-
ford) clinches the story. The Chicago literary club
(by a vote of 37 to 4) has decided that this is a *bona
fide* old ballad belonging to the seventeenth century
A. D. Dr. W. F. Poole, the distinguished authority
on Salem witches, says the ballad is spurious, but
none of the rest of our *littérateurs* go much on what
Poole says. I would like to have Mr. Stedman see
this relic, and Mr. Aldrich, too. But it is yours to do
with as you like."

It was evident soon after the publication of "Culture's Garland" that the little book was not likely
to prove a financial success; and the following communication voices the author's characteristic indifference to royalties. (The first page of this letter
was written in red ink, the second in green, and the
third in blue.)

"In the prospect of reaping a golden harvest in the field of literature, I have bought a large supply of colored inks. I am now prepared to spread ophthalmia all over the continent. The book looks better than it reads. We should have had a bit of tissue paper over the frontispiece — the kind that is put over fine engravings. Again, the frontispiece should have had under it the words 'By himself.' But I am very well pleased.

"At McClurg's the impression is that the book will have a good sale. I don't care a picayune, so long as you get your money back. At the same time I shall keep a black list of my friends who do not buy at least one copy, cloth and net. I would really like to have you get out a book of my stories. Just now I have in hand a fairy story for which Theodore Thomas has arranged the music, and for which Modjeska is making the illustrations. Is n't that a clever scheme?

"I have been elected secretary of the Chicago François Villon Society for the publication of Old English local ballads and such other literature as may be out of print. We have a barrel of money and heaps of sand. At the last meeting of the society I was instructed to write to Prof. Lowell, Dr. Holmes, and other famous Eastern *littérateurs*, asking them to put us on to some rare old poems (smutty preferred) that would be likely to satisfy the craving of Chicago culture. In the matter of going East just now, I find that I have been overtaken by the bitter pill of adversity. The baseball club has gone East without me and is being walloped at every point. I can't visit

Boston until next winter. Then I shall stop at the hotel Von Doam and you must eat with me until I go broke. Then I shall skate home by way of the Lakes. Now let me thank you, Mr. Ticknor, for the kindly services you have done me in the affair of this book. I feel very grateful to you, and I have a good memory."

The final letter in this correspondence relative to the production of "Culture's Garland" was written in November, 1887. In it Field expressed his warm affection for his publisher in whom he had discovered many qualities which appealed strongly to his own temperament. His partiality for the other's society alone, when he came to Boston, was frequently exhibited; he would appear at the Tremont Street office, with the remark: "I have come to Boston to see you, and I won't see anybody else!"

Then he would call for pens and little bottles of colored ink, and seating himself near his friend's desk would while away hours in pursuit of his favorite pastime, the production of quaint bits of verse illumined with various scrolls and many-colored capitals.

Vainly would Ticknor try to make plans for introducing Field to club functions, or assemblages of Boston's literati; he refused absolutely to be lionized or entertained, save in his own whimsical manner.

Eugene Field's first book failed to achieve success. The literary critics, East, as well as West, whose views and pretensions Field had often lampooned so freely, made the most of their innings, and the little book, whose author had not then won the response that was soon to be his portion, had but few purchasers. Field's delight at the appearance of his first book was transformed into a desire to banish it wholly from the book world; and some time after its appearance he exercised his ingenuity in endeavoring to destroy all available copies of the "literary baby" which had given him such joy; thus in the end ensuring the permanent value of the remaining copies of the small edition of "Culture's Garland."

In the final communication concerning this book at time of publication, he said:

"You need not feel any sorrow in any report that you may have to make, for from the very beginning I have known that the book could not meet with a large sale. It will continue to sell for some time here in Chicago, but it is rather too delicate satire to satisfy the average palate. It is fair to presume that any book which pleases Mr. Stedman, Mr. Stoddard, and men of that class would not be to the taste of people who subsist on boiled cabbage and ham rinds. I really *do not care a damn* whether I ever get a penny from 'Culture's Garland'; but I do want *you* to come out square at least. I should hate to think that you lost money on my maiden effort. I am not a millionaire, and, on the other hand, I am not a pauper. I have just enough horse sense to know that there is no wealth in books. If ever I am rich, 't will be either by inheritance, by fire, or by felony. I was telling McClurg's people the other day that I did n't care a rush whether 'Culture's Garland' brought me a cent or not, and they expressed the conviction that I was 'a ——— of an author.' This is an opinion of myself which I've had for a long time.

"I am tickled to death to hear that you are going to bring out Opie Read's story. Here's a man who is all gold — crude, but gold! I think it likely that I shall be in Boston in February. But I don't want any Pap! [Referring to the Papyrus Club.] No, I want a nice, quiet visit with you. I do not want to meet anybody else. All I go to Boston for is to see you and Bunker Hill and the Corner Bookstore. I am hard at work on my folio of Old English Chicago ballads. Here's the last verse of 'Ye Texas Steere':

> So let us singe, long live ye kynge,
>   Long live ye queene, her grace;
>   Long live ye Jack and all ye packe
>   From ten spott down to ace.

"Now don't worry about me! You just let me do the worrying; then we'll both be happy. God bless ye!"

An amusing sequel to Stedman's refusal to write a preface for Field's first book occurred on the occasion of Stedman's visit to Chicago to lecture before the Twentieth Century Club. This gave Field a long-looked-for opportunity, and he made the most of it by announcing the visitor's coming in a way to fill the latter with consternation.

Two weeks before Stedman's arrival, Field's column in the "Daily News" contained an impressive announcement of the lecture and its scholarly importance, closing with the words: "Twenty years have elapsed, we understand, since Mr. Stedman last visited Chicago. He will find amazing changes, all in the nature of improvements. He will be delighted with the beauty of our city and with the appreciation, the intelligence, and the culture of our society. But what should and will please him most will be the cordiality of that reception which Chicago will give him, and the enthusiasm with which she will entertain this charming prince of American letters, this eminent poet, this mighty good fellow!"

This preliminary welcome was followed a few days later by an announcement that was eagerly copied by the New York papers, and which filled Mr. Stedman with a desire to be anywhere but in Chicago upon the coming 29th of April, 1891. The second notice was given with all the careful precision with which a veritable programme of a public procession would have been issued, and after the statement that the "Robert Browning Benevolent and Patriotical Association of Cook County" would give Stedman a complimentary banquet, an outline of the make-up of the procession was printed, stating that the parade which was to meet Stedman at the railway station would be as follows:

Twenty police officers afoot.
The grand marshal, horseback, accompanied
by ten male members of
the Twentieth Century Club on horseback.
Mr. Stedman in a landau drawn by four horses,
two black and two white.
The Twentieth Century Club in carriages.
A brass-band afoot.
The Robert Browning Club in Frank Parmelee's 'buses.
The Homer Clubs afoot, preceded by a
fife-and-drum corps
and a real Greek philosopher
attired in a tunic.
Another brass band.

A beautiful young woman playing the guitar, sym-
bolizing Apollo and his lute in a car drawn by
nine milk-white stallions, impersonating
the muses.
Two Hundred Chicago poets afoot.
The Chicago Literary Club in carriages.
A splendid gilded chariot bearing Gunther's
Shakespeare autograph and Mr. Ellsworth's first
printed book.
Another brass band.
Magnificent advertising car of Armour and Co.,
illustrating the progress of civilization.
The Fishbladder Brigade and the Blue Island
Avenue Shelley Club.
The fire department.
Another brass band.
Citizens in carriages, afoot and horseback.
Advertising cars and wagons.

Field set forth the line of march as follows:

"It will be an extensive one, taking in the packing-
houses and other notable points. At Mr. Armour's
interesting professional establishment the process of
slaughtering will be illustrated for the delectation of
the honored guest, after which an appropriate poem
will be read by Decatur Jones, President of the Lake
View Elite Club. Then Mr. Armour will entertain a
select few at a champagne luncheon in the scalding-
room.

"In high literary circles it is rumored that the Rev.
F. M. Bristol has got an option on all autographs
that Mr. Stedman will write during his stay in
Chicago. Much excitement has been caused by this,
and there is talk of an indignation meeting in Battery
D, to be addressed by the Rev. Flavius Gunsaulus, the

Rev. Frank W. Brobst, and other eminent speakers."

It was small wonder that Stedman dreaded the approach to Chicago, but as the train rolled into the station he was greatly relieved to find awaiting him only a quiet little group of friends, among whom he quickly recognized Eugene Field, "his sardonic face agrin like a school-boy's."

This was some four years after Stedman's refusal to write the preface for "Culture's Garland," but the "Lakeside poet" had not let slip his opportunity to square accounts with the "Poet Laureate of New York," who, however, did not rest content until he had repaid this compliment. The year after the Chicago joke, Stedman met in New York a young woman journalist who had for five years worked on the same paper with Field. On this occasion she was being chaffed by her friends, who accused her of calling the "Lakeside Poet," "Gene." In response to which accusation she indignantly protested: "He was always a perfect gentleman! I never called him 'Gene'!"

This incident gave Stedman just the material he had been looking for, and he immediately wrote a poem entitled "Katherine and Eugenio," of which the opening stanza read:

> "Five years she sate a-near him
>   Within the type-strewn loft;
> She handed him the paint-pot,
>   She passed him scissors oft;
> They dipped in the same inkstand
>   That crowned their desk between,
> Yet he never called her 'Katie,'
>   And she never called him 'Gene.' "

This was signed, "By one of Gene's victims," and appeared in the "New York Tribune." It was copied all over the country and additional stanzas were contributed by all the "funny men" in the newspaper world. It was months before Field saw the last of the refrain: "She never called him 'Gene'," and the fact that Stedman had played the trick was evident to his friend in Chicago, as he always addressed him as "Eugenio" in his letters.

Field's playful suggestion that Stedman should make himself solid with the brain and brawn of the West, where the obituaries were likely to be written by the "young *littérateurs*," was ironically reversed in his own case, for it was the New York poet who paid tribute to the younger man one month after his death. In December, 1895, Stedman, who had been among the first to call attention to this writer, penned an appreciative tribute to his memory. In this, after praising his literary achievement, he likened Field to Shakespeare's Yorick, whose "motley covered the sweetest nature and tenderest heart."

CHAPTER XIX

HENRY JAMES'S "BOSTONIANS"

As I turn to a file of letters in Henry James's bold and flowing hand, which for the most part contain discussions of practical details with his publishers, or careful instructions and corrections for the printer, one or two interesting communications detach themselves, as characteristic of the writer and his methods, and I place by itself a neatly executed title-page drawn up by him, on which the words are penned:

DAISY MILLER

A COMEDY IN THREE ACTS

by

HENRY JAMES

Boston &c.

A page which recalls both the early success of this popular story, and the fact that its author hoped for a satisfactory stage career for it when it was issued in dramatic form in 1883, five years after its first appearance.

There is no more dramatic page in Henry James's own history (except its last and vivid one) than that which contains the story of his aspirations in the field of drama; which tells of his strenuous work and intense enthusiasm expended in this direction; of his brief elation and confidence in his power to succeed, and his bitter and promptly concealed disappointment when he realized his mistake, and turned away wondering why he had presumed to set foot within this path dedicated to popular appeal. For it has been truly said of him that he would "never condescend to give the public what it wanted." Certain it was that he preferred to address a public that could appreciate his art and come with him into the literary labyrinths of his fancy, holding with confidence his delicate thread of discourse and following the winding passages that led to his often uncertain goal.

From James's letters it is evident that in 1882 he was hoping for the dramatic production of "Daisy Miller" in New York, and failing of this, he made a still further effort to have it produced in London. In the spring of this year he had read it aloud to Mrs. John L. Gardner in Boston, prior to its appearance in book form, playfully suggesting his hopes for its production, but no stage presentation followed its appearance in dramatic form. Despite this, and other kindred disappointments, James still believed that he might become a successful playwright, and the belief was not wholly relinquished until a decade later, when he experienced a dismal failure in London, in 1895. There his play "Guy Domville," was produced at the St. James Theater under the most favorable auspices, and after a short run was withdrawn, having failed to meet with popular approval. Its first night, which James regarded as one of the crucial moments in his career, proved a sad medley of applause from his friends mingled with jeers and cat-calls from the galleries.

Daisy Miller: a Comedy.

in Three Acts.

by

Henry James.

Boston.
1c

After this final relinquishment of his dramatic hopes, he wrote back to America in February, 1895: "This poor little play seems already, thank God, ancient history, though I have lived through in its company the horridest four weeks of my life." And after declaring that one must produce a play in order to understand that such a terrible ordeal is only endurable in view of a great success, he concludes: "To-night the thing will have lived the whole of its 31 performances and will be taken off."

From the autograph reminder of James's theatrical disappointments, I turn to a communication which seems to be especially significant in view of the fact that it deals with his one novel of Boston, and also because it presents an example of his method of out-lining a prospective work, as it has been stated that he left behind little data of this kind.

In this letter the writer sketches the plot for the much-debated story of "The Bostonians," and also of "Lady Barberina," produced at about the same time, proving by his concise synopsis that he could, if required, speak in terms direct and simple. The letter was written in April, 1883, shortly before he sailed back to England, where, after this visit, he remained for twenty years before again returning to America.

The story of "The Bostonians" was at this time just beginning to take form in his mind, yet in this outline of the plot one can perceive the author's eagerness to express his disapproval of the woman who relinquishes her home ties for the platform, and who is ready to sacrifice a fireside, which he believes the most sacred thing in the world, for a "cause" which may not prove worth the price.

He wrote:

"I take a few moments before going out of town to say a few words about the novel I spoke of to you to-day. (Proposal 1.)

"The scene of the story is laid in Boston and its neighborhood; it relates an episode connected with the so called 'woman's movement.' The characters who figure in it are for the most part persons of the radical and reforming class, who are especially interested in the emancipation of woman, giving her the suffrage, relieving her from bondage, co-educating her with men, etc. They regard this as the great question of the day, the most urgent and sacred reform. The heroine is a very clever and gifted young woman, associated by birth and circumstance with a circle immersed in these ideas and in every sort of new agitation, a daughter of old abolitionists, transcendentalists, spiritualists, etc. She herself takes an interest in the cause. But she is an object of still greater interest to her family, or friends, who have discovered in her a remarkable natural talent for public speaking, by which they believe her capable of moving large audiences and rendering great aid in the liberation of her sex. They cherish her as a kind of apostle and redeemer. She is very pleasing to look upon and her gift for speaking is a kind of inspiration. She has a dear and intimate friend, another young woman who, in issuing from a totally different social circle (a rich, conservative, exclusive family), has thrown herself into these questions with intense ardor, and has conceived a passionate admiration for our young girl, over whom, by the force of a completely different character, she has acquired a great influence. She has money of her own, but no talent for appearing in public; and she has a dream that her friend and she together (one by the use of her money and the other by her eloquence) may, working side by side, really revolutionize the condition of woman. She regards this as a noble and inspiring task, a mission to which everything else should be sacrificed, and she counts implicitly on her friend. The latter, however, makes the acquaintance of a young man who falls in love with her and in whom she also becomes much interested, but who, being of a hard-headed and conservative disposition, is resolutely opposed to female suffrage and all similar innovations. The more he sees of the heroine, the more he loves her and the more determined he is to get her out of the clutches of her reforming friends, whom he utterly abominates. He asks her to marry him, and does not conceal from her that if she does, she must entirely give up her 'mission.' She feels that she loves him, but that the sacrifice of her sacred mission would be terrible, and that the disappointment inflicted on her family, and especially on the rich young woman, would be worse. Her lover is a distant relative of the rich young woman, who, in an evil hour, by accident and before she was acquainted with his opinion (he had been spending ten years in the West), has introduced him. She appeals to her friend to stand firm, and appeals in the name of their intimate friendship and of all the hopes that are centered on the young girl's head. The tale relates the struggle that takes place in the mind of the latter. The struggle ends (after various vicissitudes) with her letting everything go, breaking forever with her friend, in a terrible final interview, and giving herself up to her lover. There are to be several other characters, whom I have not mentioned — reforming and radical types — and as many little pictures as I can introduce of the woman's rights agitation. I propose that the story shall be of the length of 150 pages of the 'Atlantic'; and I desire to receive $4500 for it. (This means that I shall definitely make it of the length of what I called six 'parts.' I first spoke of five, that is 125 pages of the 'Atlantic.') As regards the period at which I should be able to give it (or the greater part of it) to the printers, I am afraid that November first is the earliest date. The reason of this is partly that I wish to write something else first; and this other production I shall also make the subject of a proposal to you which I here subjoin."

Then follows an outline of a second work, which was completed in accordance with his suggestion:

"I wish to write before beginning the novel above described another 'international episode'; i. e., a story of the same length and character as 'Daisy Miller,' the 'International Episode,' and the 'Siege of London' (the length to be that of two installments of the 'Cornhill' — the form in which those other tales appeared). The name to be 'Lady Barberina.' I have treated (more or less) in these other things the subject of the American girl who marries (or concerning whom it is a question whether she will marry) a

British aristocrat. This one reverses the situation and presents a young male American who conceives the design of marrying a daughter of the aristocracy. He is a New Yorker, a good deal of an Anglomaniac and a 'dude,' and as he has a good deal of money she accepts him and they are united. The first half of the tale takes place in England, and in the second the parties are transported to New York, whither he has brought his bride, and it relates their adventures there, the impressions made and received by the lady, and the catastrophe. I don't know exactly the relation of the 'Atlantic' page to that of the 'Cornhill'; but I call it roughly (about) 50 pages of the 'Atlantic.' I will give you this to do what you choose with (reprint re), for $1000. And that you may conveniently reprint it, I will undertake to furnish you later with two short stories, of the length of the 'Pension Beaurepas' and the 'Point of View,' which could make up a volume with it. I should propose to include in this volume the little story (reprinted some time ago in England) entitled 'Four Meetings,' which I spoke of to you the other day when I said that it might have appeared with the 'Siege of London.' "

These concise and practical suggestions were carried out in the sequence outlined by the writer, and "Lady Barberina," or "Barbarina," as she appeared in later editions, made her bow to the public in the "Century Magazine," in May, 1884; this story covered but two installments, while "The Bostonians" proved a long book and ran for a whole year. Its bulk was afterwards deplored by the author, who wished carefully to revise and condense it, but who failed to do so, though it was always a favorite with him, and he felt that it did not receive the appreciation which he believed it deserved.

In 1884, the year in which he was writing this book, James spent much of the summer at Bournemouth in order to be near his sister Alice, who was sojourning there for her health; and during the following summer he also spent considerable time at that resort, becoming very intimate with Stevenson, who was another invalid sojourning there.

When in February, 1885, "The Bostonians" appeared in the pages of the "Century," it aroused a storm of comment, and those familiar with the figures in Boston's philanthropic circles at once announced that Mr. James had embodied the figure of Miss Peabody in this work and was caricaturing her under the guise of "Miss Birdseye."

In answer to a rather reproachful letter, written him by his brother on the subject, Henry James replied with some asperity that he was perfectly astonished at the accusation, and that not only had he not seen Miss Peabody for twenty years, but he had not the least idea of embodying her, or any other real person in any of his creations. He explained, however, that in elaborating the figure, it had occurred to him that his creation might be identified with the veteran philanthropist, but he saw no reason on that account for not developing his image as he saw it. He concluded with the statement that "Miss Birdseye" was the best figure in the book, and that he thought the book the best fiction he had so far produced. He did acknowledge playfully that he had recalled the fact that Miss Peabody was always losing her spectacles, and that such a small characteristic was too good to be omitted.

Although it provoked much discussion at the outset, this book awakened but slight general interest, and its author was surprised by its lack of popularity, a fate also accorded "The Princess Casamassima," which appeared at about the same time in the "Atlantic Monthly," and he wrote in connection with these two works:

"They have reduced the desire and demand for my productions to zero, as I judge from the fact that though I have for a good while past been writing a number of good short things, I remain irremediably unpublished. I even confess that since 'The Bostonians' I find myself holding the 'critical world' at large, in singular contempt. I go so far as to think that the literary sense is a distinctly waning quality."

Perhaps the answer to the query as to why the latter book failed to win the response looked for by its author may be found in the suggestion that those outside of the "Hub" did not especially care to read about "The Bostonians," and those inside did not relish the picture of their social life which he presented.

When the collected edition of James's works was issued by the house of Scribner, in twenty-four volumes, "The Bostonians" was not included. Infinite time and pains had been spent by the author in editing and revising his works, the prefaces of which must remain invaluable autobiographical contributions, yet James still contemplated adding to the number of volumes issued, and looked forward to revising, after a quarter of a century, his Boston novel.

In one of his last communications to Edmund Gosse, in 1915, he returned to the subject of "The Bostonians," which the other had apparently commended, and regretfully remarked that it was "no success," and that Gilder, of the "Century," had once written him that they "never published anything that appeared so little to interest the readers," but that all the same, he should have liked to have revised it for the collected works. He concluded: "It would have come out a much truer and more curious thing (for it was meant to be curious from the first)," adding: "I should have liked to have written that preface to 'The Bostonians,' which will never be written now."

In looking over various proof corrections forwarded during the production of James's books, it is evident how seriously he considered the correct use of words, or rather their artistic arrangement. Upon a certain page I find him eagerly suggesting two synonyms for a word that he finds has been three times repeated in a very few lines. He ends his note with the assurance that he cannot *bear* the frequent repetition of the same word.

This strong feeling on his part was diametrically opposed to that of Mark Twain in regard to this same subject. He utterly despised the avoidance of repetitions merely because they were repetitions, and if a word served him better or more closely expressed his idea than did some substitute for it, he would use it over and over again on a page, as if defying the reader to produce any other word that as accurately expressed his thought.

In view of James's intense feeling regarding the World War and its destructive forces, one can but wish that he had left one of his wonderful word pictures of Rheims in ruins, to supplement his early description of its cathedral in all its splendor, published in 1884, in his volume entitled "Portraits of Places." A few lines from his description of the cathedral may bear quoting here:

"As, after my arrival, I sat in my window at the inn, gazing up at the great façade, I found something dizzying in the mere climbing and soaring of one's astonished vision; . . . I sat there for a long time watching the great architectural drama. A drama I may call it, for no church front that I have seen is more animated, more richly figured. The density of the sculptures, the immense scale of the images, detract, perhaps, at first, in a certain sense, from the impressiveness of the cathedral of Rheims; the absence of large surfaces, of ascending lines, deceives you as to the elevation of the front, and the dimensions of some of the upper statues bring them unduly near the eye. But little by little you perceive that this great figured and storied screen has a mass proportionate to its detail, and that it is the grandest part of a structure which, as a whole, is one of the noblest works of man's hands."

Had James's vision been able to penetrate the future when he penned these lines he would, indeed, have found the "architectural drama" a moving one. And he could well have supplemented his description of those that had passed through the portals of Rheims Cathedral with a magnificent finale, worthy of his skilled portraiture. He wrote:

"One's literary associations with Rheims are, indeed, very vivid and impressive; they begin with the picture of the steel-clad Maid passing under the deeply sculptured portal, with a banner in her hand which she has no need to lower, and while she stands amid the incense and the chants, the glitter of arms and the glow of colored lights, asking leave of the young king whom she has crowned to turn away and tend her flocks. And after that there is the sense of all the kings of France having traveled down to Rheims in their splendor to be consecrated; the great groups on the front of the church must have looked down on groups almost as stately — groups full of color and movement assembled in the square."

How vividly he might have drawn the picture of the final groups clad in khaki which came at last to champion the "steel-clad Maid," and to espouse the cause which he so longed to have them embrace.

Henry James's last letters [1] reflect the intense feeling which led to his decision to stand with England, and, by so doing, perhaps to help to bring about in his own country the awakening which he hoped would come, but which he did not live to see.

In May, 1915, he wrote: "America, my huge, queer country, is being flouted by Germany in a manner that looks more and more like a malignant

[1] *Letters of Henry James.*

design, and if this should (very soon) truly appear, and that weight of consequent prodigious resentment should be able to do nothing else than throw itself into the scale, then we should be backing you up to some purpose."

For a year he waited, hoping that his "huge country" would throw itself into those scales which were so heavily weighted in the wrong direction, and while suffering acutely, as he watched the heroic struggle of his adopted country, he enlisted all his spiritual force in the deadly conflict, and by innumerable kind acts, strove to do his part in that practical world from which he had always stood so much aloof; he visited the French and Belgium refugees, gave money and delicacies to the wounded soldiers, and opened his house for the reception of those that needed its hospitality; and in July, 1915, he took the step which he felt he must in sincerity take, renouncing his American citizenship and becoming a British subject.

At this time he wrote to his nephew, that, like Martin Luther, he "could no other," declaring that he had testified to his long attachment there, in the only way possible, although he should not have done so had his own country played a different part, and asserting: "Regard my proceeding as a simple act of offering allegiance and devotion, recognition and gratitude (for long years of innumerable relations that have meant so much to me), and it remains perfectly simple."

And thus, in the end, the man-of-letters, the onlooker, became the decisive man-of-action, at a crisis when he felt he must be *of* England as well as *in* England.

In January, 1916, he accepted the Order of Merit from the country whose cause he had espoused, and on February 28th he passed away. Impressive funeral services were held for him in the "Old Church," Chelsea, where another celebrated American, James McNeill Whistler, who also loved England the best, had been paid a like tribute.

CHAPTER XX

THE HOME OF A LONDON PUBLISHER

My first impressions of literary London were gained during my childish days, when I accompanied my father upon a business trip to England, and found myself a member of the interesting household of the founder of the publishing-house of Trübner and Co., of Ludgate Hill.

Nicholas Trübner's early friendship for my grandfather had been extended to the son of his old friend, and as a member of the third generation, I slipped into the home at Upper Hamilton Terrace quite on the footing of a member of the family. In company with Trübner's little daughter, I met many other English children, attended their parties, and had a chance to compare the different methods by which we were being equipped for our "grown-up" existence. My host's daughter dined in her own apartments, but I, being a visitor, was allowed to dine at my host's board, my hostess realizing that it would be a privilege for me to see the guests that came to this truly cosmopolitan household.

A dinner at the Trübner home was without doubt an educational opportunity; and the numerous languages spoken around the publisher's table at times suggested an intellectual Babel; scholars, diplomats, poets, and explorers gathered about the board, over which his accomplished wife, who like her husband, conversed fluently in many languages, presided with tact and grace. The little visitor from Boston listened and tried to understand, securing as many fragments as possible out of the conversational mêlée.

Trübner's wide sympathies made him welcome every new and original contribution to the world of letters, and none will ever know how many struggling scholars owed much of their success to his timely help. He had founded and developed an extensive Oriental publishing-trade, known the world over, and being a great Oriental scholar himself, his home was sought by many leading Oriental scholars from the Far East, and in recognition of his services to literature he was honored with many orders; the one, perhaps, most highly prized being the Order of the "White Elephant," bestowed on him, and also on Edwin Arnold, by the King of Siam, for services rendered to Buddhism in making its tenets known to the Western world.

As I look back upon the evenings spent in this English home, I recall certain figures that vividly impressed my childish imagination. And first of all, the vision of a dark Indian Prince rises before me; he was fearful and wonderful to look upon, but his ebony hue did not in the least interfere with the cordial reception accorded him. Frith, the painter, who had just completed a picture of the Court, much discussed at the time, was another guest; and in those days I had my first glimpse of Du Maurier, heard tales of Bret Harte's life in London, and listened to thrilling stories of Lord Napier's exploits, from members of his family, who were my hostess's relations; she was the daughter of Octave Delapierre, a writer of distinction, formerly Belgian Consul at London, and a niece of "Napier of Magdala," who was at that period Governor of Gibraltar.

Trübner was deeply interested in all American publications, and in the study of the early Indian languages. In 1855 he brought out a "Bibliographical Guide to American Literature," shortly after he had made a visit to my grandfather in this country. He was warmly received by American scholars, and while in New York met Dr. Herman Ludwig, who was preparing a manuscript on "American Aboriginal Languages," and on his return to England Trübner brought out Dr. Ludwig's volume. While this was going through the press, its author died, and the English publisher extended and edited the work; a task which was but one of his many linguistic achievements. "Trübner's American and Oriental Literary Record," which he first began to issue in 1865, became a valuable adjunct to every great library. And it is worth noting that through the doors of his publishing-house in London came the opening of the closed book of India, and almost simultaneously a work dealing with the American aborigines.

Mrs. John Maxwell (Mary E. Braddon) was a frequent visitor at the Trübners', and was much beloved by all the household; she first dawned on my vision as a dashing matron in the splendor of a very décolletée gown, decked with a wealth of jewels; this early memory of her gave place to quite a different one when I saw her again twenty years later.

She was then a sedate, middle-aged woman, kindly and sympathetic and still exceedingly fond of jewelry.

When I returned to London after this long interval, my friend Mrs. Trübner, who had been a widow for some years, had removed from her London home, to "Beveree," Hampton-on-the-Thames, but a few miles from Mrs. Maxwell's place at Richmond. Before this time my hostess had completely lost her eyesight, and one of her great joys was Mrs. Maxwell's weekly visit; the latter came regularly to spend an afternoon and read aloud to her with unfailing devotion. With Mrs. Maxwell at times came her two sons, lively, athletic fellows whose conversation was wholly devoted to stories of the hunting-field, but later I learned that the mother's literary talent had descended to the next generation, and that Captain William B. Maxwell was producing many excellent novels. (He served during the World War in the Royal Fusiliers, and has, in addition to many years of previous military activities, already published some sixteen books.)

During my last visit at Hampton I went with the daughter of my hostess, then an attractive English matron, to a luncheon at Mrs. Maxwell's home, "Litchfield House," at Richmond-on-the-Thames. The house was spacious and the entrance was reached through an arched-over, tessellated walk, which ran from the gate to the front door. Having mistaken the time by half an hour, we arrived early and found the novelist not quite ready to appear; yet she ran down to welcome us attired in a simple dark gown,

and then said she "must go and dress," meanwhile
urging us to make ourselves at home.

We did so, strolling about the library where there
were priceless books and paintings, and gazing out
into the lovely garden at the rear of the house where
a long strip of beautiful green turf led to a Grecian
summer-house that rose like a shrine in the distance.
Ere long our hostess returned ready to meet her
guests, and I looked for the threatened change of
costume, only to find that she had on precisely the
same gown that I had previously seen. I looked
again, and then discovered that she had decked herself with chains and bracelets, pendants and brooches,
which method of ornamentation had doubtless in her
mind filled all requirements; "dressing herself"
meant putting on her jewelry, which was the outward adornment that most appealed to her. At all
events, she was delightful in her chains and brooches,
and no one cared whether her gown was satin or
alpaca. To me it was a privilege to see her in her
lovely home, and if the group of Englishwomen who
that day gathered around her luncheon-table were
rather dull and ponderous, it was a matter of no consequence to me. This fact, however, weighed upon
the spirits of my companion, who made no comment
until we had reached "Beveree," then, in response
to her mother's inquiry, she exclaimed impulsively:
"Mother, it was a very stupid hen-party!"

With memories of Miss Braddon are closely asso-
ciated those of Linda K. Walford, another favorite
English novelist, who produced many volumes.
Mrs. Walford was a fresh-looking, handsome speci-

men of womanhood, with a breezy, Scotch intonation; she was the granddaughter of Sir James Colquhoun, and inherited her gift for writing from her father, John Colquhoun, who was also an author. On meeting her one was impressed with her wholesomeness and poise; she efficiently conducted her large household, brought up seven children, and at the same time accomplished a large amount of literary work; for four years she was the London correspondent for the "New York Critic," and when she passed away, in 1915, she had brought out thirty-six books which had attained wide popularity.

Her husband, Alfred S. Walford, spent much time at "Beveree," and during my stay there kept me posted regarding the various historic spots and literary shrines that should be visited, taking pleasure in personally conducting me to the Old Charter House, with its wealth of associations. I well remember the impressive atmosphere which pervaded the place, as we stepped into the old chapel, once a twelfth-century monastery. We entered through an outer court (where there are tablets to Thackeray and also to Roger Williams, who was a pupil there in 1624), and passed out through a long cloister that skirted one side of the playground, in a corner of which occurred the famous fight that left its trace upon the countenance of Thackeray. As we stood looking out upon the grounds from the Norfolk room, with its carved oak paneling, fine tapestries, and huge fireplace, my guide stated that he represented the fourth generation of his family that had attended school there.

"In this hall," he remarked, "I heard Thackeray say, while pointing out of that window: 'There is the corner of the playground where fights are allowed. That corner is responsible for my broken-nose.' And let me tell you," added Mr. Walford, "my father was the second of the boy who did the damage."

Then we passed on to the quiet inner courtyard dotted with white-haired pensioners, over fifty of whom were at that time living in the peaceful old edifice. The stately old dining-hall, with its splendid carved gallery and black oak paneling, was as it had been for some four hundred years, and pausing there, one could for a time dismiss all belief in the proximity of a whirling twentieth century.

From the historic memories that clustered round the Charter House, it was an interesting transition to turn to a certain modern school quite unique in its way, namely, that at "Kneller Hall," where were drilled all the army band-masters. We drove there at the invitation of Colonel and Mrs. Barrington Foote, who had asked us to come to tea and to hear the band concert upon the lawn. The Colonel, who was the head of the school, did the honors of the place, and after we had listened to the music from the lovely terrace, we were conducted about the historic mansion once the home of Sir Godfrey Kneller. We explored the garden and admired the beautiful surroundings, but far the most interesting feature of the house was the Colonel's study, the walls of which were covered with caricatures of England's famous statesmen and soldiers. These were all signed by the men themselves, and we were told that this was probably the finest collection of its kind in England. "And they are the best portraits of these men that can be found," exclaimed our host, "the best and truest."

How many cups of tea, partaken of in that part of the world were flavored with literary or historic memories! Among these was one enjoyed in the stately rooms of Lord Napier's daughter, Mrs. Gore, at Hampton Court Palace, where the apartments are bestowed only upon the families of distinguished persons, in token of the Crown's appreciation. There are some forty-five apartments allotted by the King to those deserving this special privilege; a truly kingly courtesy which makes the Government provide room in its *palace*, rather than its *poor-house*, for those that have served well the nation.

Lord Napier's service had been extraordinarily brilliant. After a number of military exploits, he had in 1857 arrived in Calcutta when the Indian Mutiny was in full blast, and when, on September 25th, he entered Lucknow with Sir Henry Havelock, it was found that the siege-train bearing the wounded and the supplies had been cut off. Napier volunteered to go to the rescue, and with a hundred Highlanders, a few native troops, and some artillery, reached the rear-guard under sharp fire, removed the wounded into Lucknow, and also the whole supply-train. This was the *first* relief of Lucknow, and in the *second*, he did equally notable service. In 1868 Napier commanded an expedition to Abyssinia, which resulted in complete success, and ended with the storming of Magdala. After a march of 480 miles, and an ascent of

7400 feet, the plateau of Magdala was reached and King Theodore defeated, the latter perishing by his own hand. At this time General Napier was raised to the peerage, as Lord Napier of Magdala, and so widely was his military prowess recognized in England, that when he was interred at St. Paul's, in 1890, it was said that there had been no such demonstration since the funeral of Wellington.

Some years after the publication of Tennyson's "Relief of Lucknow," Lord Napier made the poet a visit, and they discussed the accuracy of the Laureate's description of the affair, Napier declaring that from the poem he would have judged that the writer had been present at the siege. He then gave the poet a detailed account of his thrilling experience in mining a house occupied by the rebels, and of his own hairbreadth escape at that time.

Recollections of her father made Mrs. Gore's tea-party a memorable one; she showed us trophies and silver cups with which he had been presented, and many other mementoes. From the windows of Hampton Court we gazed upon the lovely gardens, the daily resort of thousands of visitors, whose presence in the grounds was viewed with some resentment by the dwellers in the apartments, who found their privacy invaded by the hordes of sight-seers.

To have upon one's card the magic words, "Hampton Court Palace," is a mark of distinction, yet after visiting some of the kingly habitations, I came away more content with simple dwelling-places, having discovered that an apartment in a palace was very much like an apartment elsewhere, only more primitive in its appointments, and unprovided with desirable modern improvements. The rooms were dimly lighted, and an oppressive air of antiquity pervaded them. It was delightful on a sunny day to sit in the deep window-seats and gaze out on the splendid grounds, but when it stormed, or when the twilight deepened, a sense of gloom pervaded everything and seemed to emanate from the massive surroundings; and visitors hurried through the dim cloisters and up the narrow stairways, relieved to reach their destination without encountering historic ghosts. And there were ghosts innumerable! Every inhabitant had some especial ghost-story to tell with feeling and conviction, and tales of the unexplained noises and startling visions made one prone to inquire if such a royal grant were not a "gift-horse" which one should look well in the mouth before accepting.

Among those cups of tea, with which were mingled memories of past romances, was one served on the lawn of the estate at Hampton, close by the river, where once dwelt frail and lovely Nell Gwynne. It was a perfect afternoon in late September, which had been prefaced by a morning spent among the beauties in the gallery at Hampton Court, where I had studied attentively the features of the favorite whose name was the last on the "Merry Monarch's" lips as he murmured, "Don't let poor Nelly starve."

The old estate where "Nelly" dwelt more than two centuries ago (then the home of an agreeable Englishman who was our host) was but a short walk from the palace, and here we sat out on the lawn close to the river, gazing upon the scene that had changed little since it was viewed by "Nell" and her adorers. At one end of the garden which sloped down to the water was a stone bath, shaded by over-hanging branches. A clear spring fed it on one side, and at the other was an outlet through which the overflow trickled down to the river.

The table was spread under the trees, and as we watched the punts that glided past, and sipped our tea, it seemed as if there must dawn on our sight a slowly moving barge, which, having reached the mooring-place, would land at the foot of the garden, and from it we should see the fascinating actress stepping ashore. Perchance the "Merry Monarch" would appear at her side! Indeed, so real the presence of the actress seemed in her own garden that had her ghost sat down to tea with us, it would have appeared but a natural conclusion to that September afternoon. Yet the conclusion was a fitting one, for as we talked of bygone days, our host said smilingly, "I want to show you something."

He motioned to the men who served us, and in a moment a large trunk was brought from the house and placed before us on the lawn.

"It's only fair that a favorite of France should share the honors with a favorite of England," our host declared, lifting the lid and drawing out some exquisite embroideries which he spread out upon the turf. These lovely antique fabrics bespoke a royal origin, and noteworthy among them was a magnificent satin bedspread covered with marvelously embroidered flowers.

"These belonged to Madame de Montespan," our

entertainer said, tossing out from the trunk one silken garment after another. "Is she not a fitting companion for Nell Gwynne? I wish I could have seen the two together!"

This wish we all reëchoed, as we begged for the story of the embroideries. These, we learned, had been brought to England from a château in France, which was the property of our host's family. In this château, Madame de Montespan once lived, and there these fabrics had been for long years packed away. So in the deepening twilight we studied the things that had belonged to the French favorite, as we sat in the garden of Nell Gwynne; and when we took our leave, it was easy to fancy that underneath the trailing vines, in the secluded arbor by the river, the two favorites of kings, on whose caprices once hung the fate of nations, had drawn together in friendly converse, and were awaiting with impatience our exit from a domain on which we had intruded.

The brick seat at the end of the long garden at "Beveree" was a favorite resort upon a summer afternoon, where, alone with my hostess, I passed many delightful hours listening to tales of famous personages. Especially did I enjoy the stories of George Eliot, who dwelt close by the Trübners' former home at St. John's Wood. There Mr. and Mrs. Lewes were familiar figures and much-prized neighbors. When they walked out, they were perhaps the most extraordinary couple that ever promenaded side by side, but the charm of their personalities was more than compensation for their peculiarities of person, gait, and costume. When viewed in their own home, they were the most delightful hosts imaginable.

"The Priory," at 21 North Bank Street, St. John's Wood, was a square, unpretentious house, surrounded by green turf and a fine garden, and shut in by high walls. There on Sunday afternoons Mrs. Lewes was in the habit of receiving her friends from two to six o'clock, and these gatherings brought together painters, musicians, and men-of-letters. My father often described his attendance upon them, as among his most interesting experiences, and he declared that Mrs. Lewes was the most fascinating conversationalist to whom he ever listened. Her voice possessed a musical and sympathetic quality which is rarely vouchsafed to woman; quite without effort she was able to draw the best from every one, and her plainness of feature was wholly forgotten under the spell of her magnetic personality.

When the drawing-room door opened, a first glance revealed her always in the same low armchair beside the fireplace. On entering, the visitor's eye was at once arrested by the massive head. The abundant hair, streaked with gray, was draped with lace, arranged mantilla-fashion, coming to a point at the top of her forehead. If she were engaged in conversation, her body was usually bent forward with an eager, anxious desire to get as close as possible to the person with whom she talked. She had a great dislike of raising her voice, and often became so much absorbed in conversation with one guest as to be almost unconscious of the arrival of others. Early in the afternoon, with only a few visitors present, the talk was

always general, but when the numbers increased,
Mrs. Lewes preferred to sit quietly conversing with
one or two, while her husband flitted from guest to
guest. It was difficult for her to touch lightly upon
many disconnected subjects, as she liked to discuss
things seriously and at length. Mr. Lewes, who was
a brilliant talker, supplied any qualities of general
sociability which were lacking; he was a delightful
raconteur, and always able to bridge over any awkward pauses, and, by his skillful manipulation of
various groups, ensure the social success of these
afternoons, which were often varied by good music
when some fine musician happened to be present.
Among the guests who gathered there were Herbert
Spencer, Huxley, Trollope, Sir Frederick Burton,
Tennyson, and many others known in the literary
world.

In addition to these Sundays at home, Mr. and
Mrs. Lewes at times gave charming little dinners,
never exceeding six covers, and at one of these,
Tennyson, who at that time lived in this vicinity,
entertained the party by reading aloud "Maud."

Mr. Lewes's guardianship over his wife's strength
and time was one of his most admirable achievements; he spared her petty worries, warded off interruptions, and in every way aided her to store up
nervous energy to be devoted to her work. The year
after his death, which occurred in 1878, she left
"The Priory," which had been her home for nearly
fifteen years. Before this time her friends the
Trübners had removed from that neighborhood to
the London home where I first saw them. During my

second visit, my hostess and I drew very near together in the absence of her daughter, whose presence with that of her husband, was required at many social functions. I had loved Mrs. Trübner from childhood and it was truly an inspiration to see with what enthusiasm and sweetness she now lived a shut-in existence illumined by a bright inner light. Once, as we sat in the big library, where were assembled the most valuable of her husband's books, she asked me to take out the priceless volumes, one by one, reading the titles off to her, and then letting her hold them in her hands.

"These books I know so well, and love so dearly," she murmured, as she tenderly touched them. "The young people are so much interested in outside things, they do not care for my husband's treasures."

How long a time we spent with the beloved books I cannot say, but afterwards she expressed a wish to "see" her flowers, and with her I walked over the garden, where she could make her way quite without guidance. There she stooped down and touched her favorites, even as she had done in the library; then we sat down in the brick seat, which commanded such an enchanting view of all the blossoms that she could not see, to talk over what she pronounced "a happy afternoon." Its brightness was suddenly clouded by her realization that her most precious ring was missing from her finger, a magnificent emerald given to her father by the Belgian King. She said it was an heirloom to be handed down to her grandchildren, and I was distressed to think that it had disappeared during an afternoon when I was guiding her movements.   I searched the library without success; and then she told me she feared the ring had slipped from her finger as she caressed the flowers.   I therefore searched among the blossoms, and sank upon my knees before roses and lilies, but all in vain.   It was a gloomy dinner-table across which I later endeavored to direct cheerful conversation, for all the while I could see only the gleam of a reproachful emerald hidden beneath some cruelly secretive plant.

But there was light ahead, and ere I laid me down for a sleepless night to be tormented by the vision of vanished heirlooms, the return of a faithful attendant revealed the fact that the ring had been slipped off and dropped into some small receptacle, where it reposed in safety, far from the dangers of the garden and the fatal proximity of mother earth.

CHAPTER XXI

DU MAURIER, MOSCHELES, AND OTHERS

It was during my youthful visit to London that I had my first glimpse of Du Maurier, and of Hampstead Heath, his abiding-place. The latter dawned upon my sight as I rode, three in a cab, ensconced between my father and a well-known representative of the house of Harper, who was in close touch with the famous contributor to "Punch."

Riding three in a cab in a moist London fog was just then supplementing the process of riding three in a cab in rainy Paris, where I had seen hardly a ray of sunshine. And in the latter place the accompanying *third* person had occupied even more space in the conveyance than did the agreeable Harper representative. In Paris we had been favored with the companionship of one of nature's noblemen, the genial Clarence King, regarded by all his friends as the brightest and gayest comrade in the world. To my immature mind, however, he seemed only a damper on my happiness, for in addition to the space he occupied, he instituted himself a culinary guide, and joyfully conducted us to little restaurants where curious dishes and unique sauces were provided; these dainties, in which he and my father delighted, did not appeal to me, so I refused them with dignity and ate, instead, long rolls of bread, and little dishes of ice-cream, sighing meanwhile for the brilliantly lighted hotel dining-room with its lively surroundings.

In after years, I had a better chance to appreciate the many talents of Clarence King, who had cast not only a shadow, but a heavy substance, between me and my Paris joys; he was said to have known the literary world of his day better than any other man; and he was generous to a remarkable degree, royally entertaining his many friends, even when he could ill-afford it. His attitude toward money was voiced in his response to one who asked him, "Why do you suppose the streets of Heaven are paved with gold?" — to which King instantly replied "To show how little they think of it there."

Not long after we saw him in Paris, he was the purchaser of some Fortuny water-colors; these he soon took to London, where he met Mr. Howells, who was shortly returning to America. King told him of his purchase, and Howells said, "Fortunate man, to own Fortunys." To which his friend responded, "I will give you one." Howells supposed this was a joke, and was filled with astonishment when, shortly after, one of the precious pictures reached him at his lodgings, and he found that its donor would brook no refusal of his gift. While he lived in London, King used to give talks on Sunday afternoons to a class of girls who worked in Crosse and Blackwell's pickle-factory, and finding them ignorant of the joys of grass and flowers, he organized a "happy hen-party" for them, and aided by his aristocratic friends, secured such privileges that he was finally conveyed on a special train to have

211 Tremont Street

Boston,
Aug 6. 1889.

Alfred, Lord Tennyson,
  Dear Sir:
        I venture to
send my cordial Congratulations
to you upon your anniversary
today; and I trust they will
not seem inappropriate, and
will be felt as sincere,
coming from the son of your
original American publisher.
    Believe me, Sincerely and
              Respectfully Yours,
        Benjamin H. Tickner.

afternoon tea on the lawn at Windsor Park; and there the Queen, who had learned of the project, came out of the palace and accepted a cup of tea from a proud member of the company.

King's book, "Mountaineering in the Sierra Nevada," will probably remain his monument, though his contributions to science and his years of work in organizing the United States Geological Survey can never be forgotten. He exposed a great fraud in the Arizona "diamond fields" in 1872, and at its outset stopped a most gigantic swindle.

Friends who went out to dine with King, when he was camping on some high elevation outside of Salt Lake City, told of a table set as daintily as in a refined home, and the adventurous host appearing dressed as immaculately as if he were attending a fashionable lawn-party; this, he assured them, was done to keep him from relapsing into barbarism. During his Western life he had always some faithful body-servant who attended to his personal wants and aided in his geological work; of one of these he liked to tell, whose standard of excellence was attained in a fine country-seat with well-trimmed lawns and good servants' accommodations, including ample facilities for blacking boots and brushing clothes. On one occasion King, attended by this man, made his way to the Grand Cañon in Colorado, and stood for a time, silent upon its brink, overwhelmed by the scene. At last he turned, and, feeling that he must speak, said, "Well, Joe, how does it strike you?" To which the other replied: "It is no place for a gentleman, sir!"

Among King's friends his brilliant sayings and clever paradoxes were a source of continual amusement, and after his death one of them exclaimed, "It is strange that the Creator, when it would have been so easy to make more Kings, should have made only one."

King used to remark philosophically: "I have enough for my necessities. What I wish for now is enough for my eccentricities." By his friends he was looked upon as one who made the success of every dinner he attended, but to me he must ever remain, as I first knew him, the man who spoiled my dinner-parties, and who took up a large share of the seat when we rode three in a cab.

My kind friend from the Harpers' was very slim, and riding in a cab between him and my father was almost comfort. As we approached Du Maurier's home at Hampstead Heath, in the chill February afternoon, this famous spot seemed dreary, bare, and smoky, and I could only wonder why people said that it was worth looking at; therefore, it was with satisfaction that I alighted at an interesting, rambling house covered with ivy. (In this home Du Maurier lived for over thirty years, moving to a house in Oxford Square shortly before his death, which occurred in 1896.)

Upon entering this dwelling we were ushered into the drawing-room where Mrs. Du Maurier was serving tea, assisted by three pretty daughters, and even as a child I was impressed by the likeness of our hostess to the typical, handsome English matron, whom the artist was so fond of picturing, while the daughters, all extremely attractive, tall and willowy, looked as if they had just stepped out of the pages of "Punch."

Du Maurier himself was the embodiment of cordial hospitality, and after we had finished drinking tea, offered to conduct us to his studio. He led the way across a hall and down two or three steps, and I remember that I left the drawing-room with great reluctance, being completely fascinated with staring at the pretty daughters, who, with their tight-fitting jerseys buttoned up the back, were such perfect reproductions of the pictures I had studied at home in the bound volumes of the English periodical.

Two things only stand out in my memory in connection with Du Maurier's studio. The first was the splendid St. Bernard, that like the others of that artistic household had figured so often in black-and-white, and the second was a marvelously lifelike dummy-man arrayed in a dress suit.

The St. Bernard was comfortably stretched on a big divan at one side of the studio, and seemed accustomed to the homage which he received from his master and his master's friends; the latter approaching with a deference which was slightly tinctured by a suggestion that this king of St. Bernards might not always exhibit the best of tempers now that advancing years were well upon him. (I was warned not to touch him, and I think that this much-admired dog lived but a short time after I saw him presiding over his master's studio.)

The dummy-figure, that remained so clearly outlined in my childish memory which retained no recollection of the artist's work, stood with hand extended, close to the doorway through which we entered. So realistic was this gentleman that I was on the point of begging his pardon as I brushed past him, at which the artist told me, laughing, that many of his visitors made that mistake, and oftentimes he had the fun of seeing his guests try to shake hands with his hospitable model. I was firmly convinced that the dummy-man was placed in his position on purpose to fill the unwary with confusion and to afford his owner much amusement.

Many years have elapsed since my first trip to London, but the picture of the Du Maurier family as I saw them has always remained a clear-cut, cameo impression. As permanent as one of his own drawings is my memory of the artist, his home, his stately wife, his fascinating daughters, and his beloved St. Bernard.

Du Maurier's sons Gerald and Guy have figured conspicuously in public life in England; the former as a successful actor, the latter as a writer, dramatist, and soldier, who gave his life in the World War.

Lieutenant-Colonel Guy Du Maurier's play entitled, "An Englishman's Home," which was produced in 1909, caused an immediate sensation in London. It was brought out anonymously under the signature, "A Patriot," and it was not until some time had elapsed that it was known to be the work of Guy Du Maurier, then serving in the army in Africa with the rank of Major.

The play presented an ordinary middle-class family immersed in their own small interests and amusements, and heedless of the graver issues of life, suddenly brought face to face with the reality of an invasion by "a Northern Power," popularly supposed to be Germany.

A realistic bombardment of the "home" was among the mechanical successes of the play, which further pointed the moral it was intended to convey, when the elderly Englishman, who seized his rifle in defense of his property, was led out to be shot by the invaders for daring as a civilian to carry arms. When this play was produced by Gerald Du Maurier, it met with both praise and blame. Some held it to be an impossible exaggeration of anything that was likely to happen, while others welcomed it as a much-needed reminder of national danger. Undoubtedly the play aided the Territorial movement which was then somewhat languishing.

Du Maurier the father, with his pen and pencil, brought home to England many hidden truths, and his son Guy did his part in trying to awaken his country to the realization of its unpreparedness; the latter wrote for England, and also fought for England, and the news of his death in action at the front was brought to his brother Gerald just as he was about to go upon the stage in a London theater. Perhaps the most dramatic thing in the history of this distinguished family was the brief announcement that evening which told the audience quietly that Lieutenant-Colonel Guy Du Maurier had been killed and that his brother Gerald would not appear.

When I returned to London after the lapse of

nearly twenty years, the place and friends that had
known George Du Maurier knew him no more, but I
became acquainted with one of his earliest and closest
friends. At the home of Felix Moscheles, artist,
author, and philanthropist, I listened to many
reminiscences of the friend who had passed on; and as
I listened I turned over the contents of a large portfolio of Du Maurier's early sketches. These were
drawn while he and Moscheles were fellow-students
at the famous Antwerp Academy. Moscheles shared
many of the pranks and escapades which are set
forth in the pages of "Trilby," and it was his early
interest in mesmerism which inspired the motive
for the book, he himself standing as the original
Svengali.

In reading Du Maurier's books it is of interest to
trace the portions of them that are autobiographical.
In "Peter Ibbetson" he tells the story of his happy
childhood in France; in "The Martian" he describes
the second phase of his life, at a Paris school; then
comes the story of his studio days in "Trilby," when
he had passed through agonizing anxiety concerning
the loss of his eyes. During the latter period he was
cheered by a copy of "Punch's Almanac," in which
he studied Leech's drawings, and it was then that he
was fired with the desire to become a humorous
illustrator. In 1860 his association with "Punch"
began with the sending of his first contribution, and
after the death of Leech, Mark Lemon appointed
Du Maurier as his successor, warning him "not to
be too funny." For the next thirty-six years he was
connected with this magazine, during which time one

of his cherished dreams was realized in the illustrating of Thackeray's "Henry Esmond."

In 1896, after his friend's death, Moscheles brought out a volume entitled "In Bohemia with Du Maurier," which he filled with memories of their studio days, and illustrated with sixty-three of Du Maurier's early sketches; these date from the time of their first meeting, when they addressed each other in painful French, until a fellow-student, an American, came up and spoke to one of them in English, at which Du Maurier exclaimed, "What the D——l are you, English?" — and Moscheles answered, "And what the D——l are you?" After which they continued their friendship upon a national basis.

When Du Maurier published "Trilby," he said to his old friend: "You'll see that I have used up all your mesmerism, and a trifle more." And this remark set them to discussing the past and overhauling the early drawings which vividly recalled those days, and it seemed then worth while for Moscheles to put together these drawings and to accompany them with a study of the studio days of the author of "Trilby."

The proofs of Moscheles's work were in the process of final revision when word reached him of the death of his friend, and he wrote sadly in a prefatory note: "Now all is changed, the joyous note of these pages jars upon me. How differently would I attune the story of our student days were I to write it to-day in loving memory of my friend."

Yet it was well that this spontaneous production was quite complete before the shadows fell, for it must have lost its charm and sprightliness had it been penned from a more serious angle. The book, beginning with the episode of their first meeting, extends through their bachelor days and ends when the matrimonial junction has been reached.

Du Maurier's early sketches are thoroughly characteristic, and the descriptive text most entertaining. One sees foreshadowed the future contributor to "Punch" in sketches such as the picture of a pretty girl and a young man gazing into each other's eyes, while she remarks, "I do not see the mote in your eye," and he responds, "Ah, but I see the beams in yours," entitled "A New Adaptation from the New Testament."

I shall not soon forget my first Sunday afternoon at Felix Moscheles's studio into which I was ushered through rambling hallways and rooms filled with artistic treasures, whence I emerged upon a balcony from which a stairway descended into the spacious studio.

My name having been announced by the butler, I made a cautious descent into the room below where the host and hostess were receiving their literary, musical, and artistic friends. I listened to songs by a young prima donna just back from Paris, accompanied by a gifted musician, and then wandered about the studio studying its many curios and pictures. Across the room upon a platform facing the balcony was set an organ and over it the sunlight streamed in through a Tiffany-glass window. Above the organ on either side the artist had converted a huge Japanese cabinet into a series of shelves and cupboards which contained the splendid collection of music bequeathed him by his father, the musician and composer, who was also the especial friend of Felix Mendelssohn, who stood as godfather for his namesake, Felix Moscheles. One corner of Moscheles's studio was devoted to souvenirs of Mendelssohn, whose death-mask hung there, and also a cast of his expressive hand; there was a little sketch of the "Bridge of Sighs" painted by him, and, close by, a lock of his hair, and also of Goethe's.

A glass door at one end of the studio opened into the garden where the guests strolled about, returning by another flight of steps which led up to the dining-room. Here were two noteworthy pictures, the artist's portrait of Mazzini, and opposite, a picture dear to the painter's heart for its association with his friend Robert Browning, who spent many Sunday afternoons here. The latter watched the progress of this picture, which he christened "The Enchantress of the Isle," and when it was completed, wrote some descriptive lines which stand underneath the canvas. This represents a sleeping nymph watched over by two children; the face of one of these youthful guardians is that of a grandchild of Charles Dickens, who is also a grandniece of Mrs. Moscheles; making the picture a composite of interesting memories.

After the other guests had gone, I sat for a while in the deserted studio listening to reminiscences of many famous persons, as Moscheles seated in a great carved chair, picturesque with his flowing white hair and beard, discussed his friends, his memories of America, and his especial hobby, "World Peace," to which he was so passionately attached.

I seem to see him now surrounded by his treasures; the setting sun slanting in through the stained-glass window illumining his white hair, and just across from him his famous sketch of Joseph Israels, who had been prevailed upon by him to sit for a brief space of time, and then had jumped up from his seat and had written across the canvas, "I have endured this for one hour, but refuse to stand it longer."

Moscheles's portrait of Browning hangs in the Armour Institute at Chicago; he also painted a portrait of Grover Cleveland when he came to this country with his friends Irving and Terry. At that time he was intent upon producing the "Life" of the great composer who had been his godfather.

After the death of Mendelssohn in 1847, Moscheles's father took charge of the music-school at Leipzig, which he regarded as a heritage bequeathed him by his friend; this he conducted for twenty-three years, laboring to instruct the rising generation of musicians and to instil into their minds Mendelssohn's artistic principles. After the death of Moscheles, senior, in 1870, his son laid aside the personal correspondence of the two men, feeling that it was too soon to give it to the public, because it contained allusions to many prominent musicians then living. But in 1888 the "Letters of Felix Mendelssohn" were published by my father, with many quaint illustrations from the great musician's pen-work and autograph material; the frontispiece of this book being reproduced from a water-color made by Felix Moscheles in the study of Mendelssohn, a few days after his death. The widow, Cecile Mendelssohn, had locked the door of the study after her husband passed away, and nothing had been moved or touched when she unlocked the sanctuary for the godson who took his place in the room and reverently sketched it, reproducing it in detail just as it had been left by its famous occupant.

It is probable that Moscheles's end was hastened by the terrible awakening to the fact that despite his theories such a conflict as the Great War could convulse the world. He passed away just before Christmas in 1917, so that he did not live to see the cessation of hostilities. He was always surrounded by famous persons and painted many notable portraits, although much of his work was designed to aid some cause, and could be catalogued under the heading, "pictures with a purpose." He was devoted to the spread of Esperanto, and was up to the last president of the London Esperanto Club.

CHAPTER XXII

SOME BITS OF OLD CHELSEA

UPON the day when James McNeill Whistler was buried from the "Old Church," Chelsea, I visited this quaint historic structure, arriving, alas, too late to join in the tribute to the eccentric genius, of whom his countrymen are justly proud.

A most distinguished company had gathered in this famous edifice to pay their respects to the great artist, who had dwelt for years in this locality, hallowed by its associations with men of genius. And those that gazed on the impressive gathering in the "Old Church" realized full well that the author of "The Gentle Art of Making Enemies" had not failed in the art of making many warm friends who mourned him deeply.

Whistler's funeral in the "Old Church" and that of Henry James have added to the interesting associations which cluster about this edifice in which Henry VIII wedded Jane Seymour. Sir Thomas More was early identified with it, and there Charles Kingsley, the elder, preached for many years. Imposing tombs and blazoned tablets testify to the noble dead interred there, and near one window is displayed the smallest tablet ever placed in any church: a tiny metal plate measuring hardly more than three inches by six; a truly modest memorial.

Whistler lived in Lindsay Row, close by the river,

and there produced many of his remarkable pictures of the Thames, as seen from his house and its immediate vicinity. Within this neighborhood dwelt Carlyle, and a warm friendship sprang up between the two. They used to take long walks together, and this association led to the painting of the famous Carlyle portrait which was shown at the first exhibition of the painter's work in 1874. It is amusing to recall that when the Glasgow authorities purchased this picture, they emphasized the fact that they had bought it, not to endorse the painter's art, but because they desired the great Scotchman's portrait. For this statement the canny Glasgowmen were made to pay dearly, for the artist doubled his price on hearing the uncomplimentary assertion.

Carlyle's house is but a few steps from the "Old Church," and at the close of Whistler's funeral services, many notable people, who found themselves for the first time in this neighborhood, turned their steps toward the famous house in Cheyne Row, which still displays its number 5, although the street has long since been renumbered. Upon that day an inundation of literary and artistic folk swept over the threshold of the home of the Carlyles, filling the soul of the conscientious caretaker with consternation, and making her task of opening the door, offering explanations, and taking shillings an arduous one.

It was a pleasure to wander through the house, which had been as nearly as possible restored to its original condition, and which in every room seemed to reflect the characteristics of its former occupants. The well-worn furnishings, tables, chairs, desks, and bookcases filled with books, all spoke of the rugged apostle of bluntness, who swept aside conventions and seized upon the simple substance of things. A glimpse into the little garden, where he so often rested during warm weather, and the rude furnishings of his own bedroom and his dressing-room, where hung the cane he carried for so many years, brought the original occupant before one even more vividly than did his various portraits upon the walls.

Scattered about the house in numerous glass cases were many interesting books and autographs, and many hours might have been spent inspecting letters from celebrated people, medals and testimonials, and priceless bits of manuscript. Here and there one discovered some charming little inscription or playful verse, penned by Carlyle upon a card or slip of paper which once accompanied some gift made to his wife upon a birthday or special anniversary, testifying to much thought and tenderness upon the donor's part.

Perhaps the most touching and at the same time characteristic bit of writing was the letter penned by Carlyle after learning of the destruction of his first volume of "The French Revolution," the manuscript of which he had loaned to his dear friend John Stuart Mill, to read, and which, having been left in that gentleman's library, was used by his maid to kindle the fire.

Nothing could be more exquisitely simple, loyal, and philosophic than this communication, explaining the catastrophe to his publisher. The author stated briefly that through no one's fault, but by a sad accident, the work of many months had been destroyed, that he wished nothing said about the matter, and that he would do his best to have ready, at the end of a few months' time, a volume to take the place of that destroyed. He expressed his realization of the fact that the new volume could never be quite like the first, in which he had embodied an inspiration that could not come again at will, but adding that in the scheme of Divine Providence it was doubtless best that he should suffer this discipline; therefore he begged his publisher would not pity him, but would aid him to go speedily at his task again.

No life-sized portrait of the writer could ever be half so much Thomas Carlyle as this characteristic expression of himself executed by his own pen. The cruel loss of an important work constituted a bond of sympathy between Tennyson and Carlyle, for the former had also lost the earliest manuscript of "Poems, Chiefly Lyrical," which fell out of his great-coat pocket one night when he was returning from a neighboring town, so that he also was forced to labor over a second production. During the eighteen-forties these two writers saw each other frequently and often took long walks together at night, discussing many subjects. Ruskin and Turner and also George Eliot lived in this pleasant neighborhood, the latter having come there after her marriage with Mr. Cross in 1880. There she spent her last days, passing away in less than a year from the date of her coming to make her home in this locality, the very atmosphere of which bespeaks dear associations with the best in art and literature. Yet in order to inhale this atmosphere intelligently, the visitor must have his powers of literary respiration in proper running order, or he may saunter by the various houses sacred to the appreciative without distinguishing them from other buildings in the vicinity. Many prosaic residents of Chelsea would doubtless think a shilling badly wasted upon Thomas Carlyle, and some are as unlearned in sentimental lore regarding their neighborhood as was a man recently accosted by an enthusiastic American woman bent upon viewing all the homes of genius in that espécial quarter. To her exclamation, — "Oh, can you point me out George Eliot's house?" he replied, "No, I can't, mum, for I don't know him, but if you call in at the public-house around the corner, no doubt they'll tell you where to find him."

The aged rector of the "Old Church," who guided us about the building on the day of the funeral service, had been in early years the associate of Kingsley. He loved to show the tattered banners and chained Bibles, and his eyes flashed with merriment as he pointed out a stately tomb to which two American families of the same name laid claim. The representative of each household had seriously interviewed the rector, equipped with proofs sufficient to justify him in carrying off to his own democratic land, if not the tomb itself, at least triumphant assurance of his ownership therein. Only a favored few can carry from Old Chelsea an aristocratic ancestor, but all may find much of unusual charm in this quiet neighborhood, once a center of literary and artistic life.

In taking leave of the "Old Church," I too carried away something belonging to it, which, if I had retained it, might have been productive of serious results. The kind old rector, who had conducted my American companion and myself about the church, was called away, and, after begging us to finish viewing the place, left in my hand a huge and antique key which he instructed me to leave at his home when our tour of inspection was complete.

I still recall the curious sensation that came over me, perhaps something akin to that experienced by Bluebeard's wife when she was given the little key, as I at last found myself quite alone with the gigantic one, my friend having been forced to hasten on. I locked up the dimly lighted church with its romantic memories, and walked away, while deepening shadows solemnly descended, and all at once I seemed to be a part of the historic past instead of an American tourist entrusted with an "Open Sesame" to the twelfth century. The key which had been casually thrust into my hand took on a vast importance. How old it looked, and massive! How many strange stories it would divulge if it could speak! What if I lost it, or stole off with it? Had I remembered rightly the number of the house where the old rector lived? I hastened onward in the dusk and reached the doorway where I was sure I had been told to leave the key; yet it looked so much like the doorways on either side that, as I followed my instructions to slip the key in through the letter-slot, I wondered if I were making a mistake and thereby creating an international misunderstanding. But no news ever reached me to that effect, so I relinquished my anxiety, only retaining my precious memories. And I still wonder if it was but a chance happening that on the day when Whistler, who had escaped from the thrall of his own country, was buried from an English church, it was one of his countrywomen who locked the door of the old edifice and in the twilight carried the great key to its home.

That afternoon of deepening shadows is exquisitely pictured in Whistler's own description of painting in the twilight:

"As the light fades and the shadows deepen, all the petty and exacting details vanish; everything trivial disappears, and I see things as they are, in great, strong masses; the buttons are lost, but the garment remains; the garment is lost, but the sitter remains; the sitter is lost, but the shadow remains. And that, night cannot efface from the painter's imagination."

And the shadow cast by this weird and almost Mephistophelian figure has strengthened into a vivid reality, which shall continue its permanent existence in this man's beautiful creations.

CHAPTER XXIII

MEMORIES OF THE COLERIDGE FAMILY

My first meeting with Ernest Hartley Coleridge, grandson and biographer of the poet, took place under the clock at the British Museum. This rendezvous had already occasioned my London hostess much merriment, when she had been informed of the plan briefly outlined by Mr. Coleridge, in answer to a letter from a mutual friend announcing that I was in town.

Clocks were at that time playing an amusing part in my London experiences, for a dashing captain, who came to call upon me, had sent in a card, upon the back of which was penciled a message intended for some other feminine eye, which read, "Meet me under the clock at Hampton Court at twelve" (whether midnight or noon I never knew), but it was none the less a source of interest to my friends. It is well known that the clock at Hampton Court is an historic wonder that performs ghostly "stunts," and is regarded with fear and awe for its extraordinary behavior; therefore a rendezvous beneath its giant face was more alluring than that suggested by Mr. Coleridge under the more prosaic timepiece at the British Museum.

However, at eleven o'clock, on a warm July morning, I reached the appointed spot, and stood beneath the clock. Almost at the same moment Mr. Coleridge appeared, a sympathetic and agreeable man of middle age, cordial and smiling, who explained that he had selected this place as one where we could meet without mistake. He was working at the Museum daily, intent upon completing the bibliography of Byron which he was then compiling. To him, the meeting beneath the clock presented a prompt and practical method for saving time, and he would have been much astonished had he dreamed of the "chaffing" that I received in consequence of his suggestion.

A third clock, which had just then proved an exciting house companion may well be mentioned here, for never did a clock of my acquaintance create such an unlooked-for stir. This clock was a near neighbor of that at Hampton Court, and had long stood in its position in a big hall in the third story at "Beveree," where a gay week-end party was assembled. Among the guests was a nervous and timid woman, with a tremendous fear of ghosts, who loved to tell in detail all the ghost-stories that she could summon to thrill her hearers. Gathered about the fire, upon the night in question, we had discoursed upon this subject till the small hours; at last, saying "good-night" in a state of high tension, for the *raconteur* had seen ghosts, heard, and felt them, and knew that they were lurking about us, likely to emerge from their hiding-places at any moment.

A couple of hours later, I was awakened by a terrific crash not far from the room occupied by the imaginative guest. It sounded as if a burglar had tumbled in through one of the long windows and had fallen prostrate on the floor after some dreadful scuffle! I

jumped up and opened my door a crack, hearing at
once a general stir about the house. Something
ghostly had happened, or else a burglar was in our
midst. Doors bordering upon the hall outside my
room began to open, and guests in pink and blue
bath-wraps and dressing-gowns appeared. I meanwhile, keeping my hand upon the lock, decided that
I was quite as safe inside as elsewhere, as I could turn
the key if any burglar dashed my way. Through the
crack I could discern lighted candles and hear muffled
voices, and soon my host was seen to cross the hall
waving a golf club, and closely followed by his wife
who carried a coal-shovel, or tongs, I can't remember
which.

My host mounted the stairs, and an investigation
immediately revealed the fact that the tall clock in
the hall overhead had fallen flat upon its face and lay
in a pitiful heap upon the floor. I caught the reassuring cry, "It is only the clock which has fallen
over and smashed," and then I stole back to my bed
without joining the pink and blue robes in the corridor. At breakfast, the affair was discussed with
excitement, as no one could determine what had
made the clock fall from its high estate without the
slightest provocation. It had just happened — and
there was only one anxious and pallid guest who
knew the reason; this was the timid woman, who had
her bags already packed and was leaving by the first
train because of this occurrence. She declared that
as she lay in bed she had heard stealthy steps creep-
ing up the broad stairway near her door; it was one
of those ghosts that constantly pursued her; the

ghost approached the clock, and suddenly! — Well,
we all knew the rest, and if any one doubted, then let
him inspect the broken glass and shattered frame of
the old timepiece. So this clock took its place in my
collection of London memories, to be pleasingly
supplemented by a tiny gold clock hung on a little
chain, given me by my host as a souvenir of the
ghostly evening, though he declared I must have
slept through the affair, or I could not have failed to
have been present at the exciting pink-and-blue
party in the halls.

All this comes back as I recall Mr. Coleridge's
rendezvous at the British Museum, where he proved
a delightful guide. He summoned the head librarian
who did the honors of the place, taking us into various stacks and showing us the especial treasures not
generally displayed. At last we paused in a small
room where, under a glass case, we found a large
collection of books that had belonged to Samuel
Taylor Coleridge.

"These are the books that should be now in my
own library," my guide said sadly. "By some mistake they were placed here instead of being left in my
possession as my grandfather intended"; and he
added, nodding at the librarian, "this gentleman will
tell you that I cannot be left alone here one moment
with these books, to touch them or consult them —
that is indeed the irony of fate!"

After doing the honors of the British Museum, and
seeing that I had whatever privileges there I might
desire while in London, Coleridge's grandson asked
me if I would not like to go with him some day to the

home of the late Lord Coleridge, now in the possession of the latter's widow, where the rest of the priceless Coleridge volumes remained. And consequently, a few days later, we had tea at the stately home.

The late Lord Coleridge, Lord Chief Justice of England (great-nephew of Samuel Taylor Coleridge), had passed away in 1894, and his cousin, Ernest Hartley Coleridge, was then engaged in completing the two volumes of his "Life and Correspondence," which later appeared.

Eleven years before his death, in 1883, Lord Coleridge had visited America, as the guest of the New York Bar Association, and had been the recipient of the highest honors in all parts of this country. He had been especially urged to make this visit by James Russell Lowell, who felt that his coming would help to strengthen the cordial relations between the two countries. It required some little courage on the part of the Chief Justice to embark on this enterprise, as the Irish Brotherhood had just "sentenced him to death" for the part he had taken in the trial of the dynamite conspirators, he having tried and sentenced to penal servitude several of the Fenian dynamiters. It was rumored that Lord Coleridge's life was likely to be forfeited before he had ended his American tour, and in consequence the United States Government detailed Lieutenant John McClellan, U.S.A., to escort him upon his travels.

During his stay Lord Coleridge did his best to strengthen the bonds of friendship between England and the United States, and in October, 1883, he said in the course of his reply to an address by Mr. Evarts:

"It is no rhetorical exaggeration, it is simple truth, to say, that joined together as allies, as friends, or comrades, England and America are absolutely irresistible to the world. I most earnestly hope the present happy state of feeling between us may long continue. Believe me, there is not in the mind of any honest Englishman a trace of jealousy or a shade of greed when he thinks of the magnificence of your future and your present great development."

Lord Coleridge sailed for England in October, 1883, and it was on his homeward passage that he made the acquaintance of his second wife, Amy Augusta Jackson, whose father was in the Bengal Civil Service. She was many years his junior, but the acquaintance resulted in their marriage in August, 1885. Lord Coleridge's first wife, by whom he had four children, died in 1878, and his second marriage, which was not approved of by his children, estranged him from his family, and after his death his widow presided over the family possessions in solitary aloofness. Indeed, I was informed that Ernest Hartley Coleridge, who was then editing the "Life and Letters" of the late Lord Chief Justice, was at that time alone in touch with the occupant of the beautiful London home. He had been allowed constant access to Lord Coleridge's documents and papers, and Lady Coleridge had lent him whatever aid was needful in handling the data.

I watched the keen enthusiasm displayed by my guide for the literary treasures so dear to his heart, as he climbed the library steps and brought them down in order that I might read the varying inscriptions. Apart from those containing Samuel Taylor Coleridge's own annotations and autograph inscriptions were first editions of Charles Lamb, in which he had written his own whimsical thoughts and greetings, and many other priceless books. There were six volumes of Wordsworth annotated throughout, and some of Coleridge's works containing his proof corrections and remarks to the printer; also the "Address at the Apothecary Shop," on Norfolk Street, Strand.

So absorbed were we in studying this "poet's corner" that we reluctantly retreated to the tea-table, where our hostess awaited us a bit impatiently. She seemed so much apart from the literary atmosphere pervading the place, that I could not escape from the impression that even the books felt it, and longed to slip away to some possessor who had a genuine affection for them. As we sat down to tea, my guide still cast lingering glances toward the library steps which he would gladly have climbed many more times. The massive silver service spoke of family associations, as did all the surroundings. Upon the walls were numerous portraits of the late Chief Justice, showing him at almost every stage of his career; some of them the work of the first Lady Coleridge, who was a gifted painter. The earliest of these portraits showed the subject when he was but ten months old.

At last we took leave of our hostess, and as we silently descended the broad stone steps, I felt quite sure that the same thought was in both our minds. I glanced back at the almost deserted home of the late Chief Justice, and as I did so seemed to hear the mournful voices of the imprisoned books murmuring: "We are so lonely. Life here is very dull. We are pining for the companionship of some congenial spirits."

Before taking leave of those memories which cluster about the British Museum, I cannot refrain from recalling one trifling episode which at the time was certainly annoying. I had been entrusted with a literary errand, which I fulfilled at the expense of time, patience, and no doubt literary reputation, if I had any of that product. All are familiar with the cruel infliction of those "trifling" commissions handed one by devoted friends, which sound so simple and easy of performance and are so pitilessly exacting: "just a few pairs of gloves," from one especial place, "certain silk scarfs, from Liberty's," and other "mere nothings," that to the friend at home mean very little, but to the traveler who has given a thoughtless promise mean hours of inconvenience, interference with truly important plans, and finally an added agony with custom-house officials. These little nothings have clouded many happy days for foreign travelers and have frequently stretched the bonds of friendship near to the breaking-point.

Added to little promises in the glove category was one made to an enthusiastic Boston writer who was deep in some interesting researches regarding Benjamin Franklin. His hunt for new and vital data had led him straight to the manuscript material in the British Museum, where he had found there was in existence a truly wonderful and enlightening Franklin letter, which must be given to the world. He was the one to give it; and incidentally, I being on the spot, the one to get it straight from its hiding-place in that remarkable Franklin collection in London.

The time was short, but I determined that I must not let this opportunity escape for giving to the world a document which should no longer lie hidden from the light of man's appreciation. Putting aside other engagements I sought the shades of the Museum and by means of my card, secured by Mr. Coleridge, made my request to one of the librarians who was in charge of the most precious manuscripts.

Benjamin Franklin was either hard to find or very safely guarded in the Holy-of-Holies. I waited patiently; I was presented to still more inaccessible librarians, and was led through long and winding passageways. Finally I was deposited in a small and secluded room far from the habitual readers. Once more I waited for the important letter to be unearthed from its abiding-place, and as I sat there I recalled with amusement an incident recounted by Mr. Coleridge concerning his search for a certain missing line of Byron's which he discovered was to be found in a manuscript in the Drexel Institute, Philadelphia. He promptly wrote to those in charge in order to secure the data, and ere long received word that they regretted their inability to comply with his request; they explained that the manuscript was locked up with other valuable material, and the head-custodian, who had the key in his pocket, had gone away on a vacation, and nothing could be done until his return.

I was beginning to imagine that something of the kind had happened to the Franklin letters, when the door opened and a young man appeared laden with manuscripts and bound volumes. On one hand he carefully deposited the original manuscripts, yellowed with age, and none too easy to decipher, and on the other side he placed numerous volumes of Sparks's "Life of Franklin." The young man looked at me respectfully, as if at a loss to understand my vital interest in Franklin's penmanship, which had no doubt given him some painful research, and then he remarked quietly, "I have also brought you the 'Life of Franklin,' in which the letter you desire to see in manuscript is fully printed. It may be easier for you to read it in that form."

Oh, cruel Boston friend, who had sent me to unearth the manuscript of this especial letter, which he could have referred to any day, in the Boston Public Library! I thanked the kind custodian for his trouble, and read the Franklin letter, but not in the original, after which I said "farewell" to the British Museum.

Long after my return from England, I cherished the hope that sometime Ernest Hartley Coleridge, with his wealth of Coleridge memories and data, might appear on the lecture platform of this country (I know he hoped that he might sometime be a contributor to the "Lowell Lecture" courses), but I presume the opportunity never came to him, and on February 19, 1920, his death was announced in the English papers.

He was the only surviving grandson of the great

poet, and was born in 1846, being the son of the Reverend Derwent Coleridge. It was not until after he was fifty years old that he relinquished his vocation of teaching for the field of letters. He acted as secretary for his cousin, Lord Coleridge, for some time before the latter's death, and in 1895 published the "Letters of Samuel Taylor Coleridge," in two volumes. This work was followed by a volume of selections from his grandfather's notebooks; then, turning from Coleridge to his one-time admirer and patron Byron, he spent seven years in editing and annotating Byron's poetical works. This edition contains an additional stanza to "Don Juan," not before printed. (Doubtless the one which was locked safely in the Drexel Institute manuscript.)

For ten years Ernest Hartley Coleridge worked on the biography of his kinsman, the Lord Chief Justice, which he was completing when I saw him in London. His final production was a two-volume life of Thomas Coutts, which has been commended for its grasp of eighteenth-century political and social history. He was a charming personality, with a tremendous fund of interesting information regarding some of the greatest figures in English letters.

CHAPTER XXIV

JANE AUSTEN'S GRAND-NIECE

THE graceful pen of Anne Thackeray Ritchie has set forth with tender appreciation the portrait of Jane Austen, with whose family she was for years on terms of warmest friendship, and it was at her house that I became acquainted with Mr. Austen Leigh, who asked me if I would not take tea some afternoon with his aunt, the grand-niece of Jane Austen, who possessed many cherished belongings of her famous great-aunt. As the result of this suggestion, I found myself, upon a lovely August afternoon, in one of London's most attractive suburbs, through which we drove until we reached a charming country-house, the home of the Austen Leighs. The house, which was skirted by beautifully trimmed lawns, was backed by the prettiest of English gardens, and as we waited for the appearance of our hostess, I gazed through the long windows of the drawing-room upon a brilliant mass of flowers; paths led down from one terrace to another, to a dark background of fine trees, and a sun-dial in the center of the garden lent a picturesque touch.

The hostess, who was picking flowers, came up the path to greet her visitors with gracious hospitality, approaching with a basket of cut flowers upon her arm, dressed in flowing gray silk, and bringing with her a delicate impression of what her great-aunt might have been.

A tea-table was drawn close to the long glass windows which faced the garden, and as we listened to some delightful reminiscences, the decorative background of trees and flowers seemed like some cleverly painted stage scenery, and the interior a dainty bit of Cranford.

"Over the tea-cups" I heard from those, to whom their great-aunt's memory was both an inspiration and a sacred trust, many brief anecdotes and little personal details of special interest to those who had but known her from her work.

"Will you bring Aunt Jane's desk?" the hostess said to her brother, who had joined the group, and when the cups were emptied, he entered with the precious desk which he placed on a table and opened reverently.

"This is the desk upon which she wrote all of her books," he announced, lifting an inner cover, "and here is her last unfinished manuscript." This he took from the desk, while all admired the fine, beautiful writing, and noted the careful and painstaking corrections. I glanced over a number of the delightful letters contained in the old desk, all to the very last penned with the same beauty and neatness. Most characteristic of the writer was the last letter, which was bright, lively, and cheerful, written during her illness; the lines expressed much gratitude for the good care she was receiving and for her pleasant surroundings, and ended with a joke concerning the deterioration of her handwriting during her illness. Beside this letter was one from her father announcing to the family the seriousness of her malady, and voicing his sorrow at the realization of her approaching end.

I longed to devote many hours to the perusal of the letters in the old writing-desk, most of which were addressed to the writer's nephews and nieces. They were all sweet, kind, and helpful; this one encouraging some member of the family in her efforts to write, that one referring modestly to her own work; and while one read, the intervening years slipped suddenly away, and the voice of the writer, now earnest and again playful, came with direct appeal, and for a few enchanting moments the past and present were indistinguishably mingled. Then the old letters were replaced and half a century ruthlessly thrust itself between the gentle speaker and the attentive listener.

Of this "little mahogany desk," now so dearly treasured by the author's grand-nieces and nephews, she speaks in her correspondence, and in a letter to her sister tells of a narrow escape which it had in the autumn of 1798, when its owner was taking a short journey with her parents; they stopped for a night at the "Bull and George," at Dartford, and Jane wrote from there:

"After we had been here a quarter of an hour, it was discovered that my writing and dressing boxes had been by accident put into a chaise which was just packing off as we came in, and were driven away towards Gravesend on their way to the West Indies. No part of my property could have been such a prize before, for in my writing-desk was all my worldly wealth, seven pounds. . . . Mr. Nottley immediately dispatched a man and horse after the chaise, and in half an hour's time I had the pleasure of being as rich as ever; they were got about two or three miles off."

Had the desk been by accident transported to the West Indies, perchance some one of this writer's novels might never have been published, for at this time she had her three earliest books almost completed; the first, "Pride and Prejudice," had been rejected, and she was doubtful as to its being worthy of a public hearing; it was not published until some fifteen years after this time, when it was very much revised, and its first title changed. It was originally called "First Impressions," and "Sense and Sensibility" was named "Elinor and Mareanne."

As we examined various mementoes, our hostess said: "Everything that Aunt Jane did was done most perfectly," and she produced an elaborately embroidered muslin scarf, an example of her exquisite needlework. Among other mute reminders of Jane Austen, none brought her gentle personality nearer than did a tiny "huswife" prepared for an especial friend about to take a journey. This was a most minute and also ingenious piece of handiwork, containing needles, thread, and various other sewing-furnishings, condensed into the smallest possible radius and executed with the finest stitches.

"You have not seen it all," declared our hostess as she unrolled it, and revealed a small inner pocket cleverly concealed; from this she drew a carefully folded paper on which were written a couple of graceful verses touching upon the tiny gift, the friend's departure, and expressing the writer's love and best wishes.

In response to a query concerning a picture of the novelist, a colored porcelain was brought out; a lovely, sympathetic likeness, which has been reproduced in one or more of the memoirs of Miss Austen.

"It is the only picture we have of her," the grand-niece said, "and was done from a sketch made from life by her sister. And this," she added, "is her ring." And she extended her hand displaying a single large turquoise of perfect coloring, held in the simplest of gold settings, which seemed of all others the ring one must have chosen as absolutely suited to its first owner.

Her brother then took down from the adjacent shelves various volumes of the valuable first editions, displaying his great-aunt's writing upon the yellowing fly-leaves, "Presented by the author," and other brief inscriptions to various members of the family, penned when the volumes made their entry into the world of letters.

Then from the desk in which were stored so many sad and happy memories, he drew a soft brown curl, silken and beautiful, which all regarded silently, for it was something that brought the writer even nearer than did her handiwork; then the old desk was closed, and the past slipped away again as the guests laughed and chatted about contemporaneous matters; yet, when we took leave of our hostess, we carried with us something we never should relinquish, a personal ownership of a collection of enchanting memories.

Born in an epoch of revolution and international

strife, Jane Austen's nimble fancy was content to
play about the quiet scenes with which she was familiar. She realized that she could excel in her own field,
and not in that which was Napoleon's, although she
heard the echoes from his guns, and her own brothers
in the English navy brought home to her the news of
daring exploits upon the seas. Refusing to be
tempted from her own ground, she skillfully depicted
those types which she had been enabled to study
carefully, and knew so well.

She is buried in Winchester Cathedral, where a
beautiful memorial window has been placed by her
American readers; yet better than any view of a
cathedral window, or fitting epitaph, is a brief glimpse
of that which brings the fortunate beholder near to
Jane Austen through her intimate belongings, now
cherished by her family. Their point of view regarding this sacred trust was voiced by my attentive
hostess, who, as she waved me farewell from the
doorway, exclaimed: "Please don't tell any Americans where we live!" — a promise I am trying to
fulfill.

CHAPTER XXV

ANNE THACKERAY RITCHIE

HAD there been nothing else in London worth seeing, a few hours spent in the society of Thackeray's daughter would have amply repaid one for the journey thither. Charming, serene, and gracious, her rare personality impressed itself upon all who approached her, and quite defied description. I felt it as one feels the cheerful sunlight breaking through a London fog, as the drawing-room door opened and she came forward to greet me with that cordiality which radiates from the ideal hostess, and makes each guest feel truly happy and at home while in her presence.

With Lady Ritchie came her daughter Hester, a lovely, slender creature, with a dreamy, poetic face, who looked very unlike her mother. Anne Thackeray Ritchie bore a striking resemblance to her distinguished father; she was tall and well-proportioned, but had not her daughter's regularity of feature. Passing her casually upon the street, one might have pronounced her "plain," yet she was beautiful, possessing as she did that grace and charm which so delight that they exclude all criticism of mere detail.

Lady Ritchie had not long occupied the home in St. George's Square where I first saw her. Thackeray himself had never lived there, and it was with the

house at Kensington that an earlier generation of my
family had learned to identify the novelist's household. Yet, although Thackeray never dwelt in this
charming habitation, his spirit surely permeated the
place, and every nook and corner spoke to the visitor
of him. Perhaps this all-pervasive influence came
from the many things that once were his, perhaps it
came from the strength of the undiminished love and
reverence with which all the household regarded his
memory.

I could distinguish Lady Ritchie's house from the
others in the block, by its great window-boxes of
daisies all in bloom. Throughout the house there was
a mingled atmosphere of sunlight, books, and flowers;
not hothouse flowers, nor books in dressed-up bind-
ings, but simple flowers that seemed to trail a bit of
the green fields in at the windows, and books worn
and well read. Books everywhere, as many in the
dining-room as elsewhere, nestling comfortably in
odd shelves and bookcases of varying shapes and
sizes, as if they were at liberty to wander anywhere,
and might rest where they chose.

I had been asked to an informal luncheon, and
there were two or three intimate friends who had
dropped in as well, including a charming, æsthetic
Mrs. Leigh-Smith, and Mr. Grant, a brother of Lady
Colvin; also a dear old Mr. Marshall, for whom the
late Queen had stood godmother, and who in consequence owned a precious cup given him on his marriage. I found that such a gift was a weighty and
vital circumstance to those concerned, and the fact
that the lady whom Mr. Marshall had married pos-

sessed a similar cup, made the joining of the two royal goblets of almost international importance.

A quick adjustment to the English point of view concerning social values should be acquired at the start by any visiting American who does not wish to have a choice *bon-mot* turn out a serious *faux-pas*. And this is especially desirable when a discussion deals with royalty. In coming from a land where general criticism of the Government's highest official runs rampant, in press and drawing-room, it is hard to remember that in England, while one may have a grievance against the Crown, one is not expected to make the King the subject of a joke. This I learned on the first day of my "grown-up" arrival in London, where I was privileged to see the royal train draw up at Paddington Station, and watch King Edward and Queen Alexandra alight and take their places in the impressive royal carriage in which they drove off followed by Prince George and Princess Mary and various members of the Court. The King, having entered his carriage, lighted a large cigar and puffed it nonchalantly as he drove off beside the Queen, a procedure which filled me with surprise.

That it was best to make no comment on this episode was not brought home to me until that evening, when, at the dinner-table of a member of Parliament, I was responding gaily to queries as to my impressions of London. In a pause which ensued, I ventured to remark upon my glimpse of royalty, concluding that I did n't think "the King exceedingly polite to smoke a big cigar when riding with the Queen."

This seemingly harmless suggestion, which I presumed would meet with a smiling response, provoked a gloomy silence. I glanced around a tableful of sober, unmirthful faces; then, from across the board, a slender, tense young man uttered the following rebuke:

"You know that here in England we do not presume to criticize the manners of the King."

I did not "know" till then, but the knowledge acquired in that moment of ominous silence stood me in good stead during the remainder of my stay; and I grew to respect the splendid loyalty which every Englishman displays for the royal figure who occupies the highest and most honorable position in his land.

The conversation at Lady Ritchie's luncheon-table was most delightful, dealing with interests political, literary, and above all philanthropic, as our hostess was ever heart and soul in enterprises for the betterment of London. Just at that time she was sending communications to the papers to aid in the preservation of Hampstead Heath for the enjoyment of the city's poor; and she was also working to secure the money needed to buy some eighty acres to be laid out in playgrounds. Her friend Mr. Barnett, of Toynbee, another luncheon guest, was a prime mover in the scheme, and all those present were thanking Lady Ritchie for her last letter to the "Times"; a lovely bit of prose, which I later procured, and from which I cannot forbear to quote one graceful paragraph:

"Last night from the brow of Hampstead Heath,

with many others, we watched the sunset lights traveling across the great valleys and the beautiful fields that run towards Harrow and the Chiltern Hills; a worn-out, shabby man lay in the grass gazing at the noble view; a little family, father, mother, and children, sat in a Raphael-like group against a sand-heap watching the exquisite lights and the flow of the beautiful open country turning to dreams. Turner's pine-trees, somewhat the worse for wear, were in the foreground; close at hand stood the old cottage where Blake used to visit his friends. In the valley beyond, the haymakers with their wagons were bringing in their last loads of hay. A noble ridge of woods fringes the other side of the open country, where the birds come and go unmolested under the pastoral rule of the Ecclesiastical Commissioners."

After describing the cruel plan, "all of which means that the very soul of the harassed Heath will be destroyed," she closes with the words: "To bring building speculations into the center of such peaceful beauty, calls to mind the well-known text concerning the money-changers, who should be sent outside and not allowed to encumber the Temple itself."

We lingered long over the simple luncheon, consisting of not more than three courses, while Lady Ritchie told many reminiscent bits about her father, and before leaving the dining-room I was shown numerous souvenirs and pictures. Over the fireplace hung a most exquisite portrait of Thackeray's father, when a young man. I gazed upon it and then at Hester sitting opposite, being at once struck with the extraordinary resemblance of the young girl to her great-grandfather.

Lady Ritchie pointed out to me an engraving which hung in one corner. "Here is another portrait which you must see, she said. It was "The Minuet," by Millais, and as I seemed a trifle puzzled by the statement, my hostess laughingly explained, pointing to a chair in the picture: "This is a portrait of one of our old carved chairs, borrowed for the occasion." She then related several anecdotes regarding the intimate friendship which existed between her father and Millais, and touched upon the latter's habit of borrowing bits of furniture, which shortly reappeared in pictorial guise, but owing to the painter's forgetfulness sometimes failed to return in practical form.

Everywhere, framed upon the walls, there were sketches done by Thackeray, but upstairs, just back of the long drawing-room, was a small study especially dedicated to Thackerayana. My hostess took pains to show me all that was of interest. Here was her father's last drawing, and there various sketches of herself when a child; among other things a large number of playing-cards decorated with those inimitable caricatures which Thackeray loved to draw.

Upon the mantel was a most unique sketch of him, done by Millais, which, while being a clever likeness of the writer, bore also a strange resemblance to Millais himself; for this reason Lady Ritchie wished to call my attention to it. This room contained various portraits of Thackeray; a large drawing of him, which his daughter approved, and a statue, for which she did not care. In one corner was an interesting bust done when he was a boy, from plaster laid directly on his face, which made the reproduction exact.

Wandering back into the drawing-room, we paused before the painting of a quaint-looking old lady. "This," my hostess said, laughing, "is the ancestress who is responsible for William Makepeace Thackeray. She was the mother of seventeen children, the youngest of whom was my great-grandfather." As I stood scrutinizing the pleasant face before me, she added, "The husband of this lady died of joy, a privilege accorded to few of us." I was about to ask if the joy was occasioned by the possession of such a progeny, when she continued: "It had been his life-long ambition to be made a Bishop, and he had waited patiently to realize his heart's desire; at last the honor was conferred upon him, and the pleasurable shock was too much for the good old gentleman."

We strolled about looking at pictures and manuscripts, and noting the immense difference in Thackeray's penmanship in later years from that of his early handwriting.

Lady Ritchie referred with pleasure to the long association that had existed between her family and that of Charles Dickens, whose books had been one of her chief delights in early youth. In her own works she has described her childish joy at attending the Dickens Christmas parties, and has pictured the spirit of gaiety and fun which prevailed because of the magnetic leadership of the host, who threw himself with zest into these entertainments.

In the course of a discussion of various literary

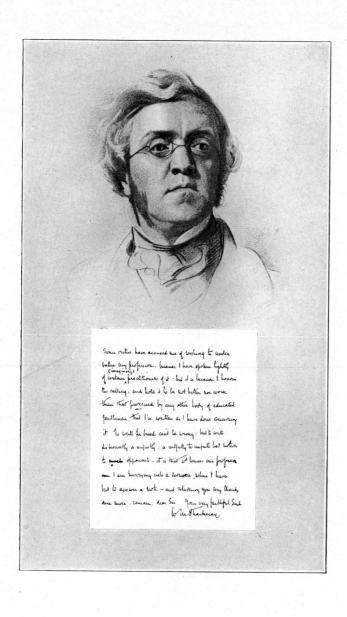

Seven critics have accused me of wishing to under
value my profession, (imaginary) because I have spoken lightly
of certain practitioners of it : but it is because I honour
the calling, and hold it to be not better nor worse
than that pursued by any other body of educated
gentlemen, that I've written as I have done concerning
it. To write for bread can be wrong : but to write
dishonestly & unjustly ; & wilfully to impute bad motives
to opponents - it is that we lower our profession
— I am hurrying into a sermon, when I have
had to answer a note - and returning you my thanks
once more, remain, dear Sir   Your very faithful Servt
                              W M Thackeray

friends, Lady Ritchie spoke of Henry James, regretting his desire to withdraw from all society and to seclude himself; of Barrie's shyness, which made conversation with him so difficult; and of her admiration for Mr. Howells. She deplored the latter's antagonism to her father's work, and remarked, smiling: "I should sometime like to say to him, 'Dear Mr. Howells, I feel sure that when you get to Heaven, you will change your views regarding him.'" A prophecy that may already have been fulfilled.

Only too quickly the time sped away, as it did on the various occasions when I had the pleasure of spending a few hours in that delightful atmosphere, with its charm, culture, and simplicity, where the presiding genius, with her keen sympathies and ready understanding, did so much to strengthen international good-fellowship.

And here it may not be amiss to mention a gifted and gracious American hostess, who for thirty years made her summer home in England, Mrs. Louise Chandler Moulton. This poet's "afternoons" in London, assembled (as did her "afternoons" in Boston, during the winter season) many of the literary fraternity, who mingled in her drawing-room with poets and men-of-letters from far and near. For over a quarter of a century, this tactful hostess afforded her own countrymen this pleasing opportunity to meet their fellow-craftsmen, and many warm friendships between English and American writers originated under her roof.

Having since childhood known Mrs. Moulton in her Boston home, it was of especial interest to see her with her London friends, and on the several occasions when I attended her receptions, I found there many well-known writers. Among those that frequented her afternoons were Hall Caine, Theodore Watts Dunton, Mr. and Mrs. Egerton-Castle, Anthony Hope, Sir Frederick and Lady Pollock, and Mrs. Meynell. Barrie was sometimes to be found there, and also Thomas Hardy. To this group might be added numerous other English writers who frequented Lady Ritchie's drawing-room, where literary pilgrims from America were also truly welcome.

Thackeray's daughter was for years identified with the literary circle at the Isle of Wight, where as a girl she had first gone with her father. From that time she had continued to spend a certain portion of each year at Freshwater, at the western end of the island, which was also the home of Tennyson. That writer's beautiful place "Farringford" was, during his forty years' residence, a Mecca for literary pilgrims; too much so for the comfort of the poet, who resented intrusions into his privacy. As Freshwater became more and more crowded with summer visitors, he built a summer home, "Aldworth," on the mainland, where he spent many happy seasons, and where he died in 1892.

Lady Ritchie was one of the last remaining friends who called him "Alfred," and she was full of entertaining stories about him. Her description of her first impression of "Farringford" gives a charming picture of the place as she saw it when a very young woman:

"For the first time I stayed in the island, and with

the people who are dwelling there, and walked with
Tennyson along High Downs, hearing the surf, listening to his talk, while the gulls came sideways flashing
their white breasts against the edges of the cliffs and
the poet's cloak flapped time to the west wind.

"The house at Farringford itself seemed like a
charmed palace, with green walls without, and speaking walls within! There hung Dante with his solemn
nose and wreath; Italy gleamed through the doorways; friends' faces lined the passages, books filled
the shelves, and a glow of crimson was everywhere;
the oriel drawing-room window was full of green and
golden leaves, of the sound of birds and of the distant
sea."

One of Tennyson's fancies was his preference for
seeing the ears of women covered, as he asserted that
"few of them had especially small and well-shaped
ears." He much preferred hair that fell over a
woman's shoulders, in what he deemed the most becoming manner. Upon one occasion, when Lady
Ritchie and her sister, then young girls, were dining
at "Farringford," this subject was under discussion,
and Tennyson voiced his regret that all women did
not wear their hair flowing, and suggested that all
those present should try the effect at once. To please
him, they complied, and all sat round the table at
dessert-time, with their hair hanging down their
backs. The host's approval was warmly expressed,
and he stated that he could only wish that the Em-
press Eugénie would set such a fashion.

All who were privileged to hear Tennyson read
aloud his poems found the experience a memorable

one. The roll of his great voice was described as sometimes like a chant, sometimes like the swell of an organ; it possessed tones of delicate pathos and of mighty strength and passion, and to hear him interpret his own creations was a delight that the listener never forgot. Lady Ritchie was one of those who, during a period of many years, frequently enjoyed this pleasure.

In view of the discussions one often hears regarding matrimonial happiness, where there is a great difference in years, it may be of interest to note that Lady Ritchie was nearly twenty years her husband's senior, and used to laugh about having held him upon her knee when he was small. Yet the union was an ideal one, which proves there are exceptions to every rule, or else it proves that any man would have been truly happy with such a woman as Anne Thackeray Ritchie. Her husband, Sir Richmond Ritchie, who like his father was prominent in Indian affairs, was knighted in 1907. He was private secretary to Lord George Hamilton, Secretary of State for India from 1895–1903; later was permanent Under-Secretary of State, in the India Office. He died in 1912, six years before his wife.

Lady Ritchie's last days were spent at St. Leonard's Terrace, Chelsea, when she was not at the Isle of Wight. Throughout the World War her spirit of patriotism was as keen as that of any of the younger generation, but she suffered from the strain, and especially from her own experience of German aircraft. In 1918, when Chelsea Hospital was bombed, she had a narrow escape. Her house was facing the hospital and every window-pane in it was shattered. She was sitting in her drawing-room at the time, but was untouched by the flying glass, remaining calm and unruffled while the crashing went on all around her. Yet her friends noted that after this shock she did not regain her accustomed strength, although she allowed nothing to quench her brave and cheery spirit. When America entered the War, she was filled with joy, and she wrote to an old friend in New York[1] that she rejoiced to think that "two old ladies of eighty were fighting shoulder to shoulder," and she proceeded to put up a small American flag beside her own Union Jack, at the door of her summer home.

Not long after that, the friends who had known and loved her learned with sorrow that the beautiful and useful life had ended; a life that had contributed generously to its country's needs and to the delight of its generation. In speaking of this daughter, Thackeray frequently asserted that she was a "far better writer than her father," a verdict which the majority of Thackeray lovers will hesitate to accept, yet many will echo the words of the London critic who exclaimed: "Farewell, dear lady! You were Thackeray's finest work!"

[1] *London Days*, by Arthur Warren.

CHAPTER XXVI

TWO "LAUREATES"

As Tennyson was to his England, so was Whittier to his New England, of which he also has been called the "Laureate." Although they never met, there were, from first to last, numerous links that bound these two together. In outward circumstance, social environment, and personal characteristics, they were exceedingly dissimilar, and yet there was a fundamental likeness that will reveal itself to any one who studies the two men.

This likeness has been impressed upon my mind ever since I began to follow the line of thought suggested by their communications already referred to, in which, after the lapse of half a century, each poet voiced his gratitude for favors rendered in early years. In studying these and other letters, the kinship of these writers becomes more and more evident, and it is interesting to discover, that apart from the similarity of the impression made by each upon his countrymen, they influenced each other, and greatly enjoyed one another's work.

In 1867 a letter written by Bayard Taylor described an evening spent with the English poet, when he had listened to the reading of "Guinevere," at which time a volume of Whittier, in "blue-and-gold," lay on Tennyson's table, and the latter made numberless inquiries about the "Quaker poet," whose

To B. H. Ticknor Esqre   Septbr 6th 1889
        Aldworth
        Haslemere

Dear Sir,

        I thank you most
sincerely for your kind
words on my eightieth birthday.
    It is an especial pleasure
to me to receive them from
the Son of one who gave
so honorable an example
to his countrymen —
forth in the highest sense.
Truly & gratefully yours
                Tennyson.

"Snow-Bound" was then being much discussed in England. And during the last year of his life Tennyson declared to a friend that "My Playmate" was to him a "perfect poem," while he praised Whittier's descriptions of scenery and wild flowers as "ranking with those of Wordsworth."

On the other hand, Tennyson's "In Memoriam" was deeply appreciated by Whittier, who derived much consolation from it in time of loss, and referred to its beauty and power in letters to his friends; especially when discussing the claims of spiritualism did he mention this work as bringing him a higher form of consolation.

In a letter written by Dr. Holmes, during a stay in England, he described a visit to Tennyson, remarking that when he saw the Laureate walking among his trees he was "reminded of Whittier" as he had seen him in his orchard at Danvers: a curious impression, in view of the absolute dissimilarity in the two men's outward semblance.

Both Whittier and Tennyson were enthusiastic admirers of General Gordon, and followed his career with intense interest, Whittier having so freely expressed his sentiments in this direction as to be criticized by John Bright, who charged him with eulogizing a fighter and thereby showing himself an unworthy member of the Society of Friends. In response to this, Whittier replied that "for centuries no grander figure had crossed the disk of our planet" than Gordon.

Tennyson's first meeting with Gordon was in the eighteen-seventies, when the latter was ushered into

the poet's presence while he was at the luncheon-
table, and exclaimed eagerly: "Mr. Tennyson, I want
you to do something for our young soldiers! You
alone are the man to do it. We want training-homes
for them all over England." Plans were then discussed for carrying out such a project, but they failed
to materialize because Gordon was ordered away to
Mauritius. Years later, following the death of the
great soldier, Tennyson took up this work and ini-
tiated the Gordon Homes, in memory of the hero of
the Soudan.

After Gordon's death, Charles C. Reed, of London,
asked Whittier to write an ode to his memory. This
Whittier felt unable to attempt, but in regretting
that ill-health made it impossible for him to do so,
he suggested that if he could only reach the ear of
Tennyson, he would urge him to perform this important task. His suggestion was forwarded to the
Laureate, who later responded with a letter to the
American poet, in which he said that the other's
communication had been sent him, and that he had
written the epitaph for Gordon which had been
placed in Westminster Abbey. He then enclosed the
epitaph which reads:

"Warrior of God, man's friend, not here below,
    But somewhere dead far in the waste Soudan,
  Thou livest in all hearts, for all men know
    This earth hath borne no simpler, nobler man."

On receipt of these lines, Whittier expressed his disappointment that Tennyson had not produced the
ode.

These two "Laureates," who were but a year and

a half apart in age, passed away within one month of each other, Whittier dying on September 7, 1892, and Tennyson on October 6th, of the same year. No other two poets have so truly contributed toward comforting the bereaved. Out of his grief for his beloved Hallam, Tennyson produced "In Memoriam," which has helped to soothe so many sorrowing souls; and Whittier's "Eternal Goodness," written after the death of his sister, eloquently voices his fullness of faith, which is also embodied in "Snow-Bound" written at about the same period.

These two poets, who for more than half a century contributed so much to the delight and inspiration of their day, "crossed the bar" at almost the same time; and permanently linked together must remain their immortal verses, which will continue to fall from the lips of those who offer consolation to the mourners, and who follow Whittier's words:

> "I know not where His islands lift
> Their fronded palms in air,
> I only know I cannot drift
> Beyond His love and care."

— with Tennyson's lines:

> "I hope to see my Pilot face to face,
> When I have crost the bar."

Near the edge of a long white cliff, known as "Tennyson's Down," where for forty years the poet had paused in his daily walks, stands the memorial which was erected by his friends and admirers on both sides of the Atlantic. There, seven hundred feet above the sea, stood for long years a blackened timber beacon, from which in old times signal fires blazed. This beacon, under the supervision of the Lighthouse Board, had served for decades as a mark for navigation, being continually sighted by the ships passing up and down the English Channel.

To-day another beacon, a graceful Celtic cross, in Cornish granite, surmounts the cliff. A splendid and inspiring memorial toward which thousands of lovers of Tennyson's works contributed.

Beneath the beacon-cross which has now fronted the storms for a quarter of a century is an inscription which binds us to our English brothers. It reads:

IN MEMORY
OF ALFRED
LORD TENNYSON
THIS CROSS IS
RAISED AS A BEACON
TO SAILORS BY
THE PEOPLE OF
FRESHWATER AND
OTHER FRIENDS
IN ENGLAND
AND AMERICA

. Tennyson highly prized each link that bound together the English-speaking peoples, and he declared "It is the authors, more than the diplomats, who make the nations love one another."

His beacon-cross guarding the English Channel with outstretched arms bears testimony that the poet's country is a boundless realm, unlimited by any man-made confines; and yet there is no fiery patriot who loves more fervently or aids more valiantly his native land than does the poet. And each of our well-beloved writers leaves behind that which shall stand, as does this beacon, high on the headland, pointing the way.

THE END

INDEX

Abdul Hamid Khan II, and Lew Wallace, 100, 101, 108–11.

Alden, Henry M., 175, 176.

Aldrich, Thomas Bailey, 210, 211; anecdote of, 58; rhymed autograph of, 83; his last poem, 92; public opening of his old home, 149, 150; relations with Fitz James O'Brien, 222.

Arnold, Edwin, 258.

Austen, Jane, her writing-desk, 305, 306; other mementoes, 307–309.

Authors, classified by their clothes, 57.

Bacon, Delia, her book "The Shakespeare Problem," 33, 34.

Barnes, James, impersonates Silas Lapham at Howells's seventy-fifth birthday celebration, 176, 177.

Barrett, Lawrence, 103; and Charles Egbert Craddock, 180.

Beadnell, Maria (Mrs. Louis Winter), the original of "Dora," 21; meeting with Dickens after a quarter of a century, 22, 23.

Beard, Daniel C., illustrates "Uncle Remus," 157, 161.

Beecher, Edward, always in a great hurry, 82.

Beecher, Henry Ward, anecdote of, 81, 82.

Bellamy, Edward, his first book, 112; letters to B. H. Ticknor about "Looking Backward," 113, 114, 116; did not like being boomed, 116; his death, 117; popularity of "Looking Back-ward," 117; believed heartily in nationalization of industry, 117, 118; Howells on, 119, 120.

Benjamin, Park, 49.

Botta, Mrs. Anna C. L., 204.

Braddon, Mary E., 259–61.

Bray, Evelina, a classmate of Whittier's, 85, 86.

Bridge, Sir Frederick, 18.

Browning, Robert, and Felix Moscheles, 283, 284.

Buck, Dudley, 212.

Burroughs, John, 198.

Bynner, Edwin Lasseter, 60; his "Agnes Surriage," 61.

Carlyle, Thomas, portrait painted by Whistler, 287; his house in Cheyne Row, 287, 288; letter about the burning of a manuscript, 288, 289.

Cartland, Gertrude, Whittier's favorite cousin, 88, 89.

Charter House, the, 262, 263.

Chesterton, Gilbert K., 19.

Choate, Rufus, 49.

Church, Frederick S., illustrates "Uncle Remus," 156, 157, 161.

Clemens, Samuel L. *See* Twain, Mark.

Clocks: "some clocks I have known," 293–96.

Coleridge, Ernest Hartley, 293; the author's guide at the British Museum, 296; editor of the Life and Letters of Lord Coleridge, 297, 298, 303; amusing search for a missing line by Byron, 301; his death, 302; his literary work, 303.

Whittier, John Greenleaf, his friendship with Nora Perry, 65; mobbed as an abolitionist, 74; receives a strange paper-weight, 75; loyal and grateful, 75, 79; his early work, 77; letters to his publisher, 78, 79; an early contributor to the "Atlantic Monthly," 79, 80; "Skipper Ireson's Ride," 80, 81; a characteristic autograph, 82; his friendship with Lucy Larcom, 84; color-blind, 84; a great admirer of Dickens, 84, 85; his friendships with women, 85, 86; a literary pilgrimage to the Amesbury home, 87–90; celebration of his seventieth birthday, 90, 91, 196; and Tennyson, two "Laureates," 322-27.

Winter, Arthur, 218, 219.

Winter, Mrs. Louis. *See* Beadnell, Maria.

Winter, William, a picturesque figure, 218; memorial to his son Arthur, 219, 220; a fruitful trip abroad, 220, 221; an admirer of Fitz James O'Brien, 221, 222; his literary career, 223.